A Conceptual Guide to OpenOffice.org 3

Second Edition

R. Gabriel Gurley

A Conceptual Guide to OpenOffice.org 3: Second Edition
Gabriel Gurley
Copyright © 2009 by Gabriel Gurley

For further information, visit the author's website at **http://www.gabrielgurley.com/**. To report errors, please send an email to editor@gabrielgurley.com.

Cover Illustration: A computer-generated illustration of Ocracoke Island, North Carolina. Illustration created by Gabriel Gurley.

Purchasing Information
Individuals who prefer to purchase a paperback copy of this book may do so through the author's website at **http://www.gabrielgurley.com/** and at finer online and independent booksellers worldwide. Educational institutions, bookstores, businesses and organizations interested in placing orders may do so through the Ingram Book Group. Additional information, including Ingram contact information, can be found at **http://www.gabrielgurley.com/**.

Disclaimer
All names and addresses found in this book are fictitious. Any resemblance to real persons, living or dead, situations or environments is purely coincidental.

Created in the United States of America.

ISBN-10: 0-9778991-7-9
ISBN-13: 978-0-9778991-7-3

3 1813 00392 4361

Contents

LESSON

1

Overview and Installation of OpenOffice.org 3

Lesson Objectives

In this lesson, you will learn the following:

1   Become acquainted with some of the new features available in OpenOffice.org 3.0.

2   Learn about the accessibility features available within the OpenOffice.org suite of applications and how to customize them.

3   Learn how to install OpenOffice.org 3.x on Microsoft Windows, Linux and Mac OS X platforms.

4   How to Set OpenOffice.org to Automatically Open Microsoft Office Generated Files.

Overview

The release of OpenOffice.org 3.0 has been one of the most anticipated software packages among open source advocates and corporate information system specialists. OpenOffice.org 3.0 not only has made many advances in terms of features and capabilities over previous versions, but its convenient licensing terms has brought it to the attention of corporate IT departments, small businesses and individuals alike. This book has been created to provide users in academia a hands-on approach to learning the fundamentals of one of the most popular office productivity suites.

Before proceeding with the hands-on exercises related to document creation and formatting, we must first discuss the various features and installation process of OpenOffice.org. Upon completion of this lesson, you will become familiar with the new features found in OpenOffice.org, including accessibility features for users with physical and visual impairments. The system requirements for computers to meet in order to use OpenOffice.org will also be discussed, along with instructions for completing the installation of OpenOffice.org on a Microsoft Windows-based or Linux-based computer workstation.

Lesson Structure

This book was created to give students, faculty and administrators an introduction to OpenOffice.org 3.x and its capabilities as an office productivity suite in an academic and business environment. Individuals, who are learning the fundamentals of using an office productivity suite, or those who have had prior experience with other office applications and wish to become acquainted with OpenOffice.org, will gain much from the hands-on exercises and step-by-step instruction provided in this book.

However, this doesn't mean that individuals who are not pursuing an education would not benefit from this book. This book was not only created to provide hands-on experience with using OpenOffice.org, but has also been designed to teach the fundamental concepts of formatting and editing documents often created by individuals both in an academic and corporate environment. The concepts could not only apply to OpenOffice.org, but to other office productivity suites as well. What makes OpenOffice.org unique to other office productivity suites is that its licensing terms and cross-platform support provides students, educational institutions, individuals and corporate enterprises a full-featured, low cost alternative to performing the fundamental tasks necessary for document creation.

This book comprise ten unique hands-on lessons to assist users to become familiar with the fundamentals of creating various documents with OpenOffice. org 3.x. These lessons walk readers step-by-step through the process of creating a variety of documents using the four core applications within the OpenOffice. org suite: Writer (word processing application), Calc (spreadsheet application), Impress (presentation application) and Base (database application). Each lesson not only provides step-by-step instruction for the creation and formatting of documents, but also provides information regarding additional resources that readers may consult to further their conceptual knowledge related to the tasks discussed within. These lessons include:

- Lesson One – Overview and Installation of OpenOffice.org 3

- Lesson Two – Creating a Resume Using Writer

- Lesson Three – Formatting a Research Paper Using Writer

- Lesson Four – Creating a Brochure Using Writer

- Lesson Five – Creating a Basic Spreadsheet for Calculating Household Expenses Using Calc

- Lesson Six – Creating a Balance Sheet Using Calc

- Lesson Seven – Creating a Cash Flow Statement Using Calc

- Lesson Eight – Creating a Basic Educational Slide Presentation Using Impress

- Lesson Nine – Creating a Bulk Mailing List Using Base and Writer

- Lesson Ten – Analyzing North Atlantic Hurricane Data Using Base

Following the ten lessons, several appendices can be found to provide a quick reference for each of the four core applications within OpenOffice.org 3.x. These quick reference guides are suitable to seek guidance regarding performing specific tasks, or to consult regarding tasks not covered within the hands-on exercises.

New Features Available in OpenOffice.org 3.x

OpenOffice.org 3.x contains many new features over its predecessor. Users of OpenOffice.org 2.x will notice a number of enhancements both in usability and added features. Users who are familiar with other office productivity suites will find that compatibility with other formatted documents to be seamless, while providing the vast majority of tools and features they are accustomed to. Among the new features found in OpenOffice.org 3.x are:

- ***Native Support for the Mac OS X Operating System*** - OpenOffice.org fully supports the native Aqua interface for Mac OS X. This means users of OpenOffice.org on the Macintosh OS X platform no longer have to rely on the X11 environment to operate the office productivity suite.

- ***Support for the Microsoft Office 2007 File Format*** – Beginning with version 3.0, OpenOffice.org supports importing and exporting of files in the Microsoft Office Open XML file format. This includes Word 2007 (.docx), Excel 2007 (.xlsx) and PowerPoint 2007 (.pptx) formats.

- ***Support for Microsoft Visual Basic Macros*** – Calc will support the execution of VBA macros from Excel files.

- ***Start Center*** – When launching OpenOffice.org 3.0, users are presented with the Start Center that allows the selection of an application within the office productivity suite without having to click the File | New menu.

- ***PDF/A-1 Support*** – OpenOffice.org now supports the popular PDF/A format for creating read-only files.

- ***Calc Columns Support*** – the new version of Calc now supports a maximum number of columns of 1024, up from 256 in the previous version.

- ***View Multiple Pages in Writer*** – OpenOffice.org 3.0 allows Writer users to view pages with single-page, two-page side-by-side and book layout options.

- ***Improved Notes*** – The new version of Notes in OpenOffice.org 3.0 provides additional formatting, spell checking and accessibility features while displaying notes within the margins.

- ***Enhanced Grammar Checker Integration*** – With OpenOffice.org version 3.1 and higher, the grammar checker framework has been extended so that extensions like LanguageTool can now be accessed from the Tools | Spelling and Grammar menu option. Note that OpenOffice.org has a grammar checking framework, but a grammar checker extension needs to be downloaded and installed for functionality to exist.

- ***Enhanced Monitor Support for Impress*** – The Impress presentation application supports multiple monitors.

For additional information regarding all the new features available within OpenOffice.org 3.0, obtain the OpenOffice.org 3.0 Feature Guide at the OpenOffice.org website. The web address is **http://marketing.openoffice.org/3.0/featurelistbeta.html**.

About the OpenDocument File Format

The OpenDocument format (ODF) is a vendor-neutral format for exchanging editable office-related documents, including word processing, spreadsheets, and presentation files. Moreover, ODF is an open format, meaning that companies and developers, regardless of whether their software is open source or proprietary, can incorporate the format into their software and view the specifications for further development. This makes the format increasingly attractive for users and software developers alike, as it assures that documents saved in the format can be edited and accessed by many different applications, regardless of whether the application that was used originally in the creation of the document is available in the future.

Beginning with version 2.x.x, OpenOffice.org has provided native support for the XML-based OpenDocument file format and is the default format for creating and saving files within the office productivity suite. This includes the Writer word processing application, the Calc spreadsheet application, the Impress presentation application and the Base database application.

For more information regarding the OpenDocument format, visit the OASIS consortium website at **http://www.oasis-open.org/home/index.php**.

Accessibility Features

OpenOffice.org 3.0 provides a number of features that are available to help individuals that are physically or visually impaired in using the office productivity suite. These features include support for external devices and applications for use by individuals with physical or visual impairments, access to all functions via the keyboard, improved readability of screen contents, zooming of the on-screen user interface for menus, icons and documents and more.

For detailed information regarding accessibility features available within the OpenOffice.org suite of applications, including a list of supported devices and applications, view the documentation available by selecting the Help menu and use the search term *accessibility*. Accessibility features can be customized within OpenOffice.org by clicking the Tools menu and selecting Options from the menu list.

OpenOffice.org 3.0 System Requirements

This training book assumes you have fundamental knowledge of operating your computer and the operating system. The fundamental knowledge you should have before proceeding with this book includes using the mouse and keyboard, launching applications and using standard menus and commands. If you need to review these techniques, see the printed or electronic documentation included with your system or enroll in a basic computer course through your local school, community college or community parks and recreation department.

System Requirements for Installing and Operating OpenOffice.org 3.0 for the Windows operating system include:
- Windows 2000 (Service Pack 4 or higher), Windows XP, Windows 2003
- 128 MB Random Access Memory (RAM)
- 200 MB available hard drive space
- CD-ROM
- Monitor that displays a minimum 256 colors and 800x600 pixels.

System Requirements for Installing and Operating OpenOffice.org 3.0 for the Linux operating system include:
- Linux kernel version 2.2.13 or higher, glibc2 version 2.3.0 or higher
- 128 MB Random Access Memory (RAM)
- 200 MB available hard drive space
- CD-ROM
- Graphic interface environment that displays a minimum 256 colors and 800x600 pixels (Gnome 3.0 or higher required for use of the OpenOffice. org Assistive Technology Tools).

System Requirements for Installing and Operating OpenOffice.org 3.0 for the Macintosh OS X operating system include:
- Intel-based Macintosh
- Mac OS 10.4 or higher
- 128 MB Random Access Memory (RAM)
- 200 MB available hard drive space
- CD-ROM

Installing OpenOffice.org 3.0 for Windows

Before proceeding to the rest of the material covered in this book, your computer must have a copy of OpenOffice.org 3.0 installed on it. Below you will find step-by-step instruction to installing OpenOffice.org 3.0 on a Microsoft Windows-based computer. To utilize all of the features OpenOffice.org has to offer, however, your computer must have Java Runtime Environment (JRE) version 1.5 or higher installed. Fortunately, if you select to perform a Complete Install during the installation process, OpenOffice.org 3.0 will automatically install the JRE for you.

To install OpenOffice.org 3.0 on a Windows-based computer that meets the minimum system requirements, follow these steps:

1 Using a web browser, go to **http://download.openoffice.org/**. When the web page appears, click on the Installation Sets link for OpenOffice. org 3.x.x. Using the popup menus that appear, select the appropriate version of OpenOffice.org for your operating system. After completing the selection, the software will begin downloading. Once the software has completed downloading, find the location where you selected to save the Setup installer file and double-click it to begin the installation process.

2 After double-clicking the installation setup file, a window will appear prompting for the preparation of the installation process. Click the NEXT button to continue the installation.

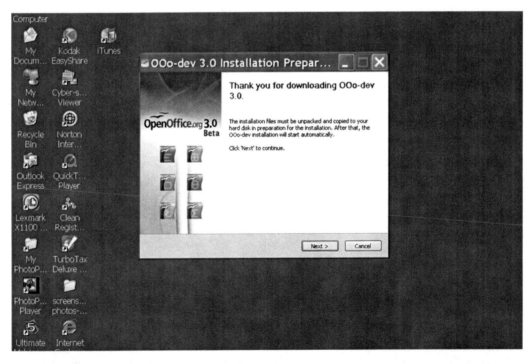

3 After progressing from the welcome window, the installer wizard will ask you to specify a location as to where you would like to unpack the necessary installation files. You may choose whichever location you prefer, but typically the ideal location would be within the Program Files folder located on the main hard drive (C:). Specify the location you wish to unpack the installation files using the BROWSE button provided and click the UNPACK button.

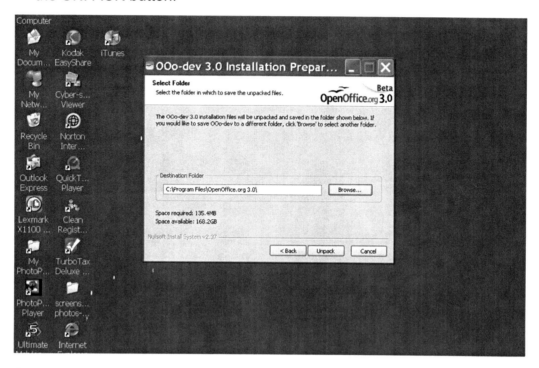

4   After the installation files have completely unpacked, a window will appear to welcome you to the installation program. Click the NEXT button to continue the installation.

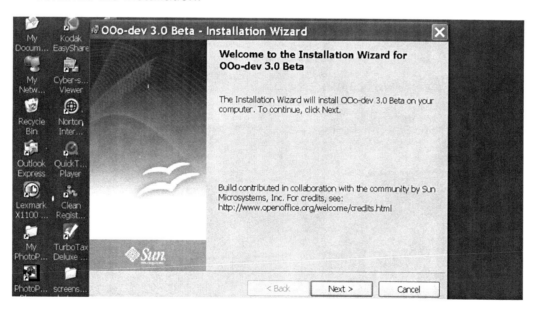

5 The next window will ask whether to perform an installation of OpenOffice. org for use by all users of the computer workstation or for individual use by the installer of the application only. In most circumstances, you would want to select the All Users option by clicking on the appropriate radio button provided. You may also type your contact information related to the installation of the software. If you would like to skip the contact information portion of this step, simply leave the provided text fields blank, click the NEXT button and no information will be entered into them.

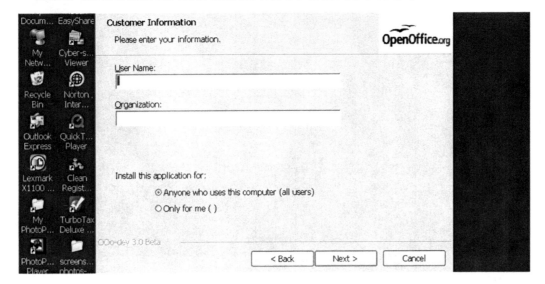

6 In the next step, choose "Complete Installation" to install all of the software features that accompany OpenOffice.org version 3.0 by clicking on the radio button provided. Then click the NEXT button.

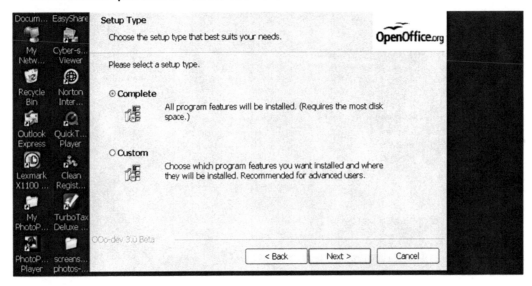

7   In the next step, a window will appear to ask what file types to automatically open with OpenOffice.org. OpenOffice.org will automatically open Microsoft Word, Excel and PowerPoint applications if you wish the application to do so. If you do not own a licensed copy of Microsoft Office, this can be useful. Place a checkmark next to each selection that you wish OpenOffice.org to automatically open on your computer. If you wish Microsoft Office or another application to be the primary application for opening these file types, leave the selections unchecked. Then click the NEXT button.

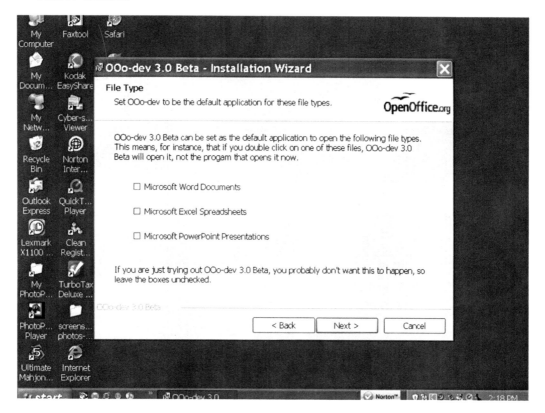

8   The next window will indicate that the installation of OpenOffice.org is ready to begin. To do so, click the INSTALL button. The Installation Wizard will begin the installation process. The installation process is performed in two primary stages. The first stage is the installation of the Java Runtime Environment (JRE), which is necessary to utilize all of the features OpenOffice.org has to offer. The second stage is the installation of the OpenOffice.org program itself. Both stages of the installation should not require any additional interaction by the user.

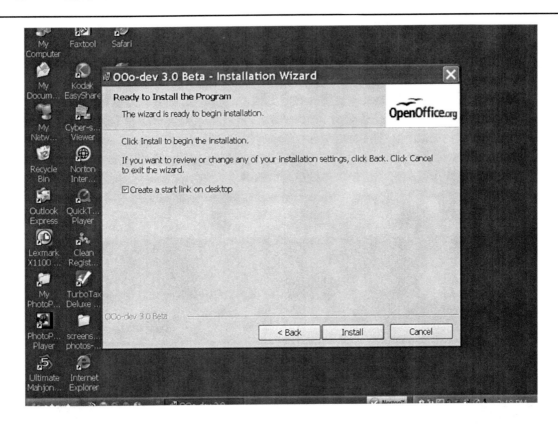

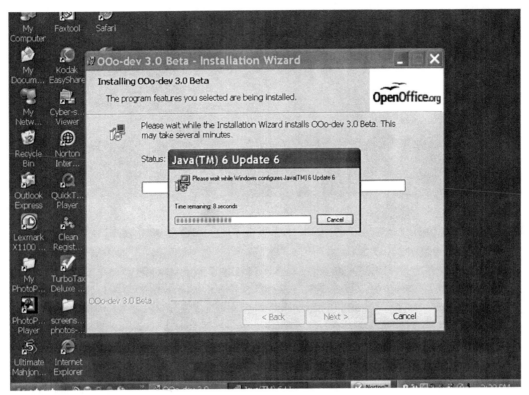

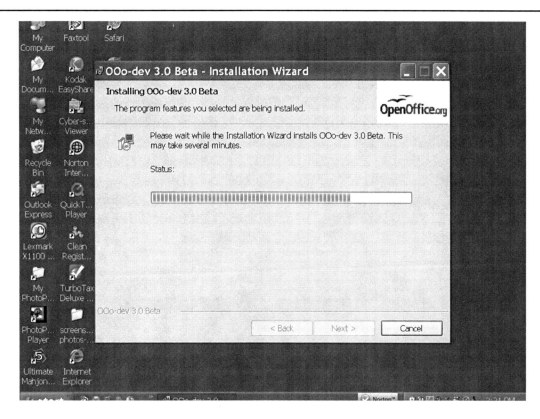

9 When the installation has completed, click the FINISH button.

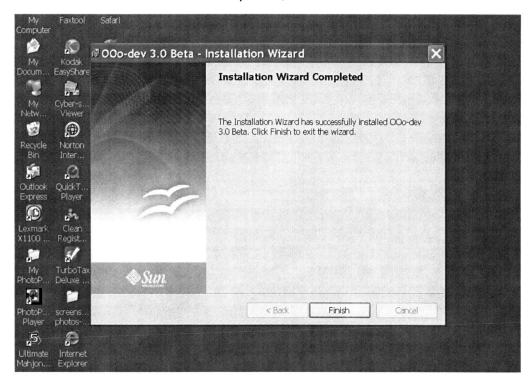

After the installation is complete, you can find the OpenOffice.org suite of applications by clicking on the START button on your desktop, then choose the PROGRAMS option, and then select the OpenOffice.org 3.0 folder for all applications that are included with the software suite. When launching the OpenOffice.org application for the first time, a Registration Wizard will appear and ask you to enter your full name, select an online application update process and register the software. Everything within the Registration Wizard is voluntary. If you do not wish to enable any of these options, simply leave the appropriate text fields blank, select the appropriate radio buttons and checkboxes, and click the NEXT button to advance through the wizard. Once you have completed this wizard, the OpenOffice.org application is ready for use.

Installing OpenOffice.org 3.0 for Linux

Unlike the Microsoft Windows and Apple Macintosh computing platforms, a version of Microsoft Office does not exist for Linux. Therefore, many Linux users have found OpenOffice.org to be a viable substitute for their office productivity needs. Not only can OpenOffice.org produce complex word processing and spreadsheet documents, but it can also open and save documents in the various Microsoft Office formats. Such flexibility allows OpenOffice.org users to share files and communicate ideas with Microsoft Office users.

Because OpenOffice.org is an open source application suite and a favorite among many Linux users, the OpenOffice.org suite is very often included with most Linux operating system distributions. So when the installation of Linux on a computer system is complete, often OpenOffice.org has been installed within the process as well. This makes it convenient for new users of the Linux operating system, as each Linux distribution has its own peculiarities regarding the installation of applications.

Therefore, this book does not contain step-by-step instruction to installing OpenOffice.org on the Linux platform. However, if your computer workstation does not have OpenOffice.org 3.0 already installed, the official OpenOffice.org Setup Guide can provide assistance. The Setup Guide provides step-by-step instructions for RPM-based, Debian-based, Gentoo-based and Slackware-based installations, depending upon which method you need to use for the particular Linux distribution your computer workstation has installed. To download the official OpenOffice.org Setup Guide, see the Additional Resources section at the end of this lesson.

Installing OpenOffice.org 3.0 for Mac OS X

With the introduction of version 3.0, OpenOffice.org fully supports the native Aqua interface for Mac OS X. This means users of OpenOffice.org on the Macintosh OS X platform no longer have to rely on the X11 environment to operate the office productivity suite. To install OpenOffice.org 3.0 on a Macintosh-based computer that meets the minimum system requirements, follow these steps:

1   Using a web browser, go to **http://porting.openoffice.org/mac/index. html**. When the web page appears, click on the appropriate link to download the OpenOffice.org 3.x.x installer for Mac OS X. After completing the selection, the software disk image will begin downloading.

2   Once the software has completed downloading, find the location where you selected to save the disk image (typically the Desktop) and double-click the image to begin the installation process.

3   Once the disk image has opened (mounted), simply drag the OpenOffice. org application icon into your computer's Applications folder. If you are currently logged in as a standard user, the Mac OS X operating system will prompt you to enter your system's Administrator username and password to complete the installation. Once the OpenOffice.org application has completed its copying process into the Applications folder, the installation process is over. You can then launch the OpenOffice.org application, complete its setup wizard and begin using the application.

Installing OpenOffice.org Extensions

OpenOffice.org has already proven to be a powerful, feature-rich, yet flexible office productivity suite. However, with the release of version 3.0, OpenOffice. org is providing even greater flexibility and features through enhancements in its Extensions framework. OpenOffice.org Extensions are simply tools developed by third-party developers that provide additional functionality to the office productivity suite. This may include not only specific functionality, such as the ability to edit a Portable Document Format (PDF) file, but may also include image galleries and document templates as well.

Before selecting and installing extensions, you must first understand the two basic categories of extensions and how you plan to utilize them on your computer workstation. The two categories of extensions include:

- **User Extensions** – User extensions are those that are installed and are only available to the user who initiated the installation process. User extensions are installed within the 'My Extensions' directory folder, and Administrative Write privileges to the OpenOffice.org installation directory is not needed to install and maintain them.

- **Shared Extensions** – Shared extensions are those that are installed for intended use by all users of a computer workstation. Shared extensions are installed within the 'OpenOffice.org Extensions' directory folder, and Administrative Write privileges to the OpenOffice.org installation directory is needed to install and maintain them.

After deciding the appropriate level (user or shared) for the work environment you wish to utilize the extension in, you can then proceed with the installation of an extension. OpenOffice.org provides three easy ways to install an extension. These installation methods include:

- **Open File Method** – You can install an extension by downloading the extension file (*.oxt) from the Internet to your computer, then double-clicking the extension file icon on your computer.

- **Hyperlink Method** – You can also initiate the installation of an extension simply by clicking the hyperlink to an extension found on a webpage. The hyperlink must be linking directly to the extension file (*.oxt) hosted on the web for the installation to be successful.

- **Extension Manager Method** – Within the OpenOffice.org application, you may click the Tools menu and then select the Extensions Manager menu option to perform an installation of an extension. For details regarding how to perform an installation using this method, follow the step-by-step instructions provided next.

Installing Extensions Using the Extension Manager Method

To install extensions using the OpenOffice.org Extensions Manager, whether they are intended for an individual user or for shared use among multiple users, follow the steps below. Extensions of interest may include a gramamr checker for use within Writer for a specific language, a book report template, a document language translator and more.

1   Go to the OpenOffice.org Online Extension Repository at **http://extensions.services.openoffice.org/** and select the extension you wish to install. You may also install an extension from any webpage where a hyperlink is provided with a direct link to a hosted extension file (*.oxt). Once you have selected the extension you wish to install, click the GET IT button located on the repository's Extension product page to initiate the downloading process for the extension. You may also download an extension by clicking your computer's right mouse button on a hyperlink and selecting Download File from the contextual menu that appears. Macintosh users who have a one-button mouse can initiate the same process by holding down the CONTROL button on the keyboard and click their mouse button on a webpage's hyperlink. (HINT: If your operating system provides you with an option for selecting where you wish the file to be downloaded and stored on your computer, select the Desktop for easiest access later in the installation process.)

2   Within the OpenOffice.org application, click on the Tools menu and select the Extensions Manager menu option that appears.

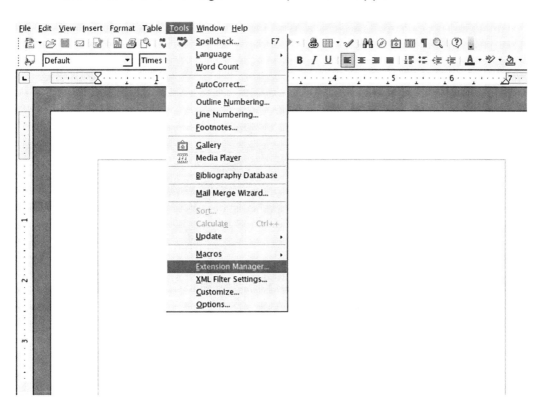

3   When the Extensions Manager window appears, select to perform a User
Extension installation or a Shared Extension installation by single-clicking
the appropriate directory. Remember, you would select the 'OpenOffice.org
Extension' directory to perform a Shared Extension installation and the 'My
Extensions' directory to perform an installation of an extension for use by
only the user who initiates the installation process.

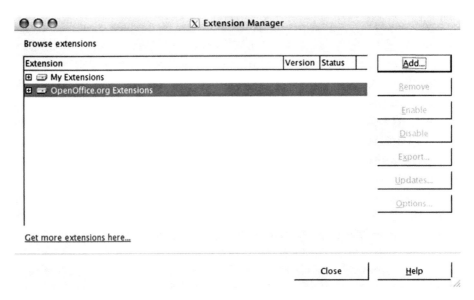

4   Once you have selected the appropriate directory to perform a specific
installation type, click the ADD button located within the Extensions
Manager window.

5   When the Add Extensions window appears, use the file browser navigation
buttons located in the upper-right corner of the window to locate the
extension file (*.oxt) you downloaded. Once you have located the
extension file, single-click it within the window. Then click the OPEN button
to begin the installation.

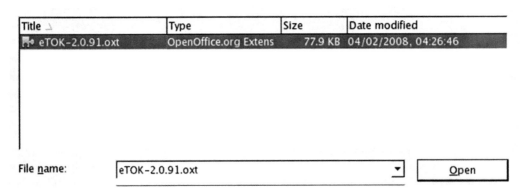

6   When the installation is complete, you should be automatically returned to the Extension Manager window. To double-check to make sure the installation successfully completed, double-click the directory you selected for installation in Step #3. When the directory list collapses, the extension should appear in the directory's content list. If the ENABLE button located on the right side of the window is greyed out, this signifies that the installation is successful and is ready for use.

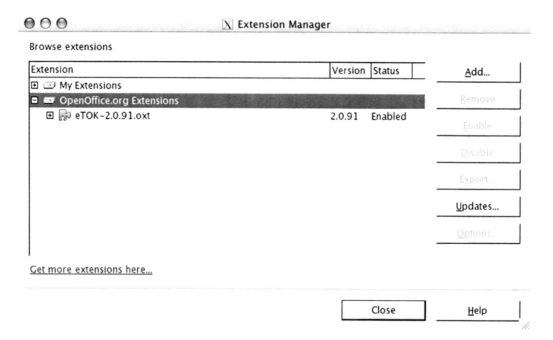

7   In some instances, you may need to shut down the OpenOffice.org application and relaunch it for an extension to become available for use. If you have problems accessing the functionality of an extension that has been installed, perform this operation. You can double-check to see if an extension is enabled at this point simply by returning to the Extension Manager and see if the ENABLE button is greyed out within its window. Many extensions also install a guide within the OpenOffice.org Help menu that can assist you with the use of the extension as well.

Adjusting the Page View

To adjust the view of the document you are working in, click on the View menu and select Zoom from the menu list. You may also select to Zoom by clicking on the magnifying glass icon within the Standard toolbar located just beneath the main application menu.

How to Set OpenOffice.org to Automatically Open Microsoft Office Generated Files Using Windows

If you did not choose during the installation of OpenOffice.org to have the software automatically open Microsoft Office formatted documents, you may select to do so by following these steps:

1   Close all OpenOffice.org applications and return to your desktop.

2   Click on the Windows operating system Start button and select Control Panel from the list that appears. Then choose Add or Remove Programs from the submenu that appears, followed by the OpenOffice.org 3.0 list option, then click Install/Uninstall.

3   In the window that appears, click the NEXT button, select the Modify option and click NEXT until the wizard prompts you to select the file types you wish OpenOffice.org to automatically open for you.

4   Select or deselect the file types you wish OpenOffice.org to automatically open for you. Click NEXT until it prompts you to click Install to complete the setup. Clicking the Install button will make the necessary changes to automatically open the file types you selected. You should not need to have the installation CD inserted into your computer's CD-ROM to complete this process.

INGOTs Certifications

International Grades in Office Technologies (INGOTs) is a platform and application-independent certification created and administered by the Learning Machine, Ltd. in the United Kingdom. INGOTs academies, which are schools and organizations approved to offer training and perform certification assessments, are located throughout the world, including Europe, the United States and the Western Pacific region. INGOTs provide a motivating progression route from complete beginner to professional level expertise in commonly used productivity tools found in the modern workplace, such as word processing, presenting and searching for information.

What makes INGOTs unique compared to other certification programs is that the certification is not dependent upon a user utilizing a specific office productivity suite or operating system. Rather, users are assessed for being awarded a certification based upon successfully demonstrating their ability to perform certain tasks by using the office productivity suite of their choice. Currently, there are four levels of INGOTs certification – Bronze, Silver, Gold and Platinum. For specific information regarding each certification level, including Frequently Asked Questions (FAQs) and Assessment Criteria, download the Assessor Handbook at **http://theingots.org/guides/ handbook-en-2007-02-20.pdf**.

Benefits of INGOTs Certification

INGOTs certifications have many benefits for users, employers and educational institutions. For a student or user, receiving an INGOTs certificate demonstrates to prospective employers that they are proficient at using office productivity applications to perform tasks demanded in today's modern office environment. For employers, an individual holding a specific INGOTs certificate provides a way to determine the skill set of prospective employees utilizing a certificate program developed by an independent third-party. Moreover, educational institutions and training companies can add value to their services by incorporating INGOTs into their office productivity curriculum, as well as helping seek instructors with appropriate credentials.

How to Find an INGOTs Academy

For more information about INGOTs, including locating an academy in your area or for the criteria for an institution to become an academy, visit the INGOTs website at **http://www.theingots.org** or email at the appropriate address located at **http://www.theingots.org/contact**.

Additional Resources

The Official OpenOffice.org Installation Setup Guide (English)
http://documentation.openoffice.org/setup_guide2/2.x/en/SETUP_GUIDE.pdf

Frequently Asked Questions Regarding OpenOffice.org Licensing
http://www.openoffice.org/FAQs/faq-licensing.html

Complete Guide to New Features Within OpenOffice.org 3.0
http://marketing.openoffice.org/3.0/featurelistbeta.html

OASIS Website
http://www.oasis-open.org/home/index.php

Information Regarding OpenDocument via Wikipedia
http://en.wikipedia.org/wiki/OpenDocument

Review Questions

1   What is the maximum number of columns Calc supports in the newest version of OpenOffice.org?

2   What are the enhanced features available in the version of Notes within OpenOffice.org 3.0?

3   What is the purpose of the Start Center in OpenOffice.org?

4   (True or False) Detailed information regarding accessibility features available within OpenOffice.org can be found by selecting the Help menu and use the search term *accessibility*.

5   (True or False) OpenOffice.org has the capability to automatically open Microsoft Office generated files.

LESSON

2

Creating a Resume Using Writer

Lesson Objectives

In this lesson, you will learn the following:

1 The three common types of resumes and their advantages / disadvantages.

2 How to insert and format text within the OpenOffice.org Writer word processing application.

3 Learn how to save an OpenOffice.org document using the most commonly supported file formats.

4 How to check a Writer document for spelling errors.

Overview

At the heart of the OpenOffice.org office productivity suite is a full-featured word processing application called Writer. Writer is a very capable word processing application that has virtually all of the features students, faculty and enterprises need to create even the most complex documents for print or electronic distribution. Included with Writer are features and capabilities unavailable in many of the popular word processor applications, including PDF export capabilities and the Math equation editor.

In this lesson, you will become acquainted with using Writer to create and format a resume. Upon completion of this lesson, you will have learned the three fundamental types of resumes, how to use Writer to insert and format text to create a winning resume, how to use Writer's built-in spell check tool to search for potential spelling errors, how to save and print a Writer document and more.

Types of Resumes

There are three common types of resumes: chronological, modified chronological and functional. Each one has its advantages and disadvantages. In case you are not familiar with the differences in the style and purpose of these types of resumes, let's review each one so you can decide which style best meets your needs when you later develop your own resume.

- *Chronological* – This type of resume is most suitable for individuals who already have substantial work experience in the field in which they are seeking employment. Chronological resumes focuses the reader's attention on prior work experience, including the company and dates of prior employment, significant responsibilities the job candidate was entrusted with in their position and career accomplishments. While professional skills, education and other relevant information are presented in the resume, chronological resumes focus primarily on prior work history and experience.

- *Modified Chronological* – This type of resume is nearly identical to a chronological resume with the exception of the work experience section. In a modified chronological resume, the work experience section allows individuals to focus on prior employment that is most relevant to the position they are seeking rather than strictly adhering to listing their employment history in reverse chronological order by date.

- *Functional* – This type of resume is most suitable for individuals who have relevant skills for the position they are seeking but lack work experience in the related career field. However, functional resumes are also suitable for individuals who wish to minimize repeating employment descriptions under several job listings, or who have so many employability skills that it could take three pages or more to complete a resume. While work experience, education and other relevant information are presented in resume, functional resumes focus the reader's attention on the candidate's qualifications and relevant skills rather than employment history.

In this lesson, we will first learn the fundamentals of creating a resume by formatting an existing functional resume. As stated above, a functional resume will highlight someone's relevant qualifications for a position despite having little or no work experience in a career field. While this lesson will not describe step-by-step how to create a chronological or modified chronological resume, the concepts of developing a resume using OpenOffice.org is the same for those styles of resumes. For additional information regarding these three types of resumes, see the section **"Preparing Your Own Resume"** that can be found later in this lesson.

Getting Started

The fastest and least troublesome way to prepare any word processing document is to input the document text first, then format the document afterwards. Therefore, we will begin this lesson by entering in the text and information needed for our resume.

Before we do so, we need to open the Lesson Two file that is available for use with this book. To open the file, follow these steps:

1   If you have not already downloaded the lesson files for this book, use a web browser to go to **http://documentation.openoffice.org/conceptualguide/OpenOfficeOrg3LessonFiles.zip**. This will provide a direct link for your browser to begin an automatic download of the lesson files. If a dialog window appears asking where you would like to save the file to be downloaded, select your computer workstation's desktop and begin downloading the file.

2   When the file appears on your computer's desktop, double-click the file icon to unzip its contents and access the files associated with each lesson. Double-click the Lesson Files folder icon that contains the available lesson files, locate the Lesson 02 folder and double-click on it to access the file for this lesson. When you have opened the folder, double-click the file named **lesson_02_start.odt** to open the file.

3   When the file has been opened, it is suggested that you make the line numbers viewable for the document. This will aid you in following the directions to correctly format the document. To view the line numbers for the document, click on the Tools menu and select Line Numbering from the menu options that appear. When the Line Numbering selection window appears, click in the checkbox "Show Numbering" to activate line numbering. Also, in the Interval selection box located under the View selection area, change the interval to 1. Then click the OK button to view the line numbers within the file.

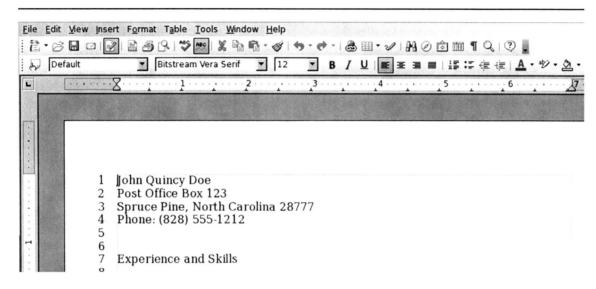

Inserting Text

Now that we have opened the lesson file, we will begin by inserting additional text within John Q. Doe's resume. John has already provided a lot of information within his resume. However, he has yet to enter information regarding his computer skills as well as his email address within his heading at the top of the document. We will assist him by entering the information within the document.

1 Place your pointer at the beginning of line 5 within the resume. When you move the pointer within the editing area of a word processing document, the pointer transforms itself into an I-bar. An I-bar symbolizes that text within the area is available for editing. Click once to place a cursor at the beginning of the line.

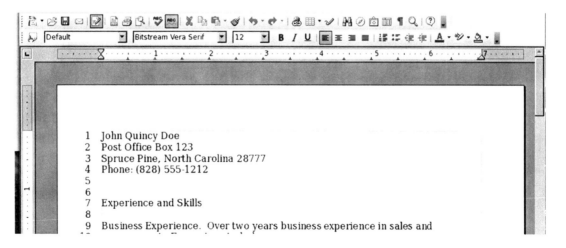

2   In line 5 of the resume, we are going to add John's email address. Formatting the text the same way as the rest of his resume header, add his email address jqdoe@hisisp.com to the resume header as shown below.

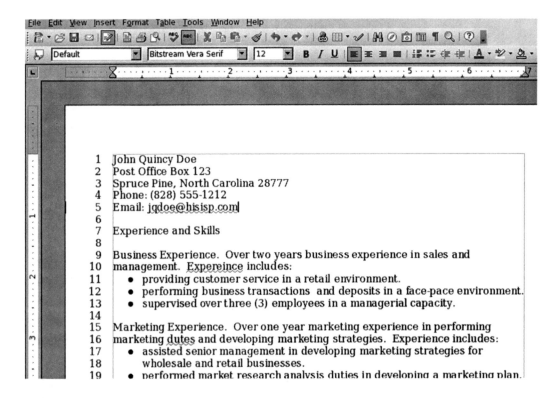

3   Now that John's email address has been added to his header, we will now add information about his computer skills within the resume. The first section of the resume describes John's professional experience and skills. Place your pointer at the beginning of line 22 within the resume. The pointer will transform itself into an I-bar again. At this point, click once to place a cursor at the beginning of the line.

4   Now that we have a flashing cursor at the beginning of line 22, we can begin entering text that details John's computer experience. John's computer experience includes three (3) years proficient use of Windows, Linux and Macintosh operating systems. His experience also includes proficient use of the Microsoft Office, OpenOffice.org and AppleWorks office suites, as well as proficient use of the QuickBooks accounting software application. Formatting this information similar to his business and marketing experience, begin typing the information within the resume. When you enter text into a word processor, the application will automatically shift the text down one line when you reach the end of the right-hand margin. Therefore, you only need to press the ENTER or RETURN key on your keyboard when you wish to begin a new paragraph or list. When completed, the text should look similar to the image shown on the next page.

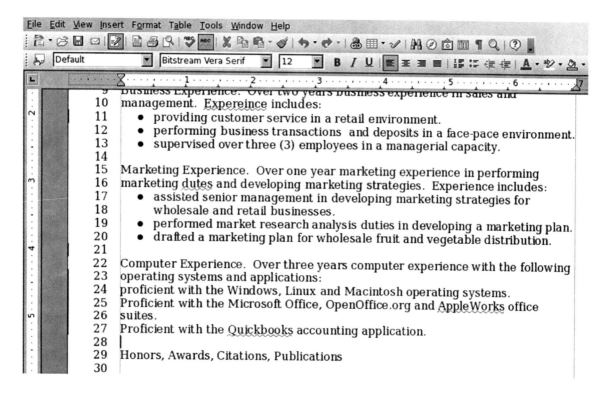

5 Now that you have entered the text as show above, you may notice that the first character of lines 25 and 27 has been capitalized. OpenOffice.org automatically did this because it was recognizing that the previous line ended with a period, and that the ENTER or RETURN key was pressed to begin a new line item or paragraph. Because the previous line items begin in lowercased characters, we will manually edit the first characters in lines 25 and 27 to change them to lower-case characters. Place the pointer at the beginning of line 25. When the I-bar appears, hold down the left mouse button and drag the I-bar over the first character in the line to select it.

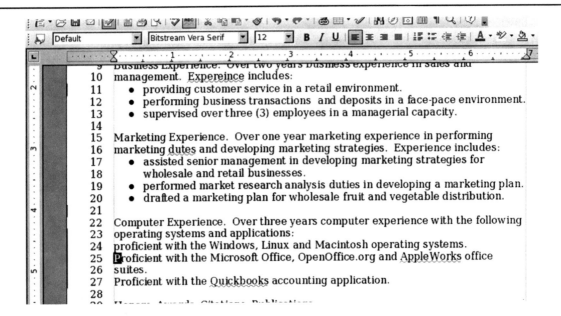

6 When the text you wish to edit has been selected, you may begin typing the information you wish to change. In this case, press the P key on your keyboard to enter the lower-case character into the document.

7 Next, place the pointer at the beginning of line 27. When the I-bar appears, hold down the left mouse button and drag the I-bar over the first character in the line to select it. Then press the P key on your keyboard to enter the lower-case character into the document. The first characters for lines 25 and 27 have now been edited.

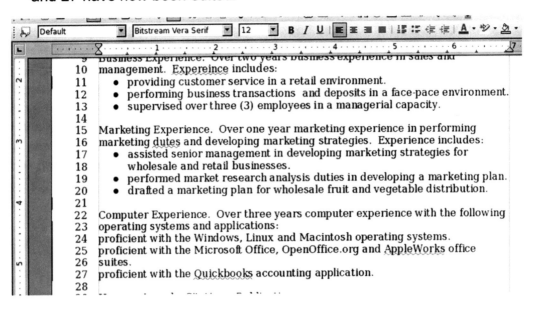

Bulleting and Numbering Text

Next, we need to change the computer experience lists to bulleted lists. To do so, perform the following steps:

1 Using your mouse, place the pointer at the beginning of line 24. Holding down the left mouse button, drag over lines 24 through 27 to select the text list.

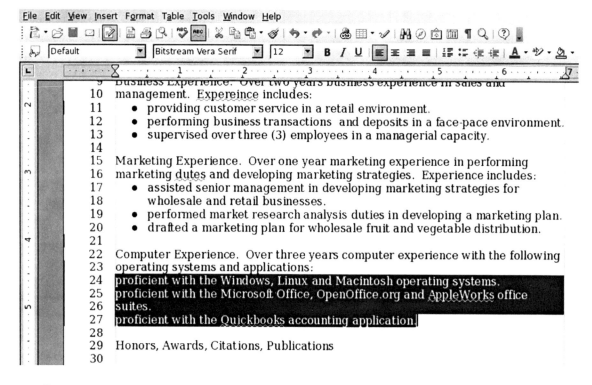

2 Click on the Format menu and select Bullets and Numbering from the menu option that appears.

3 Within the window that appears, you have numerous bullet and numbering format options available to you that are sorted within tabs that are presented along the top. Click on the Bullets tab, which presents the various bullet formats. Select the large bullet format from the options available.

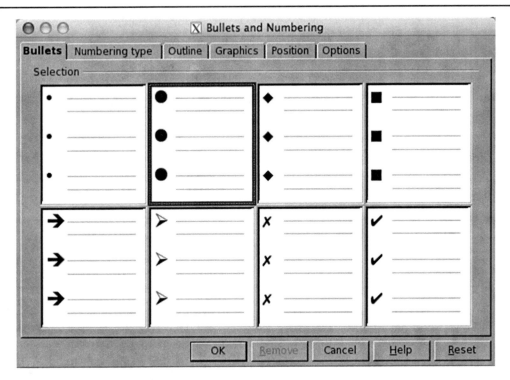

4 Click the OK button to complete the selection. The computer experience list should now be formatted as a bulleted list as shown below. Click your pointer anywhere within the editing area to deselect the text.

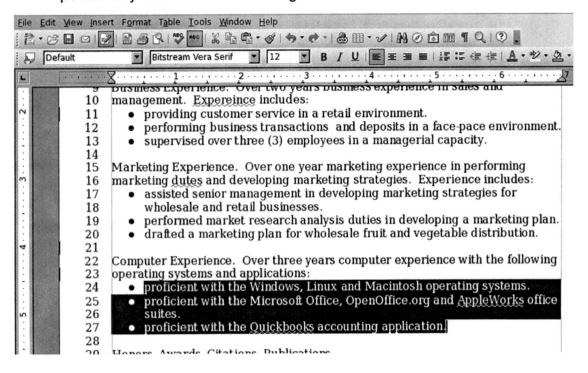

Cut, Copy and Paste

Whenever a resume is created, the generally accepted method of formatting your work history and education is by listing it in reverse-chronological order. That is, the first listing under such a section should begin with the most recent school attended or job held. Then list the next most recent school attended or job held, and so on.

As you notice in John's resume, he has listed his education experience correctly by beginning with his most recent school attended (Mayland Community College) followed by the next most recent school attended (Mitchell High School). However, his work history is not correctly formatted. His most recent job held, an internship with Autumn Harvest, is listed third rather than at the beginning. Rather than retyping the text at the beginning of the Work Experience section, we will cut and paste the listing to move it to the beginning of the section. To do so, perform the following steps:

1 Using your mouse, place the pointer at the beginning of line 54. Holding down the left mouse button, drag over lines 53 through 59 to select the text that will be moved.

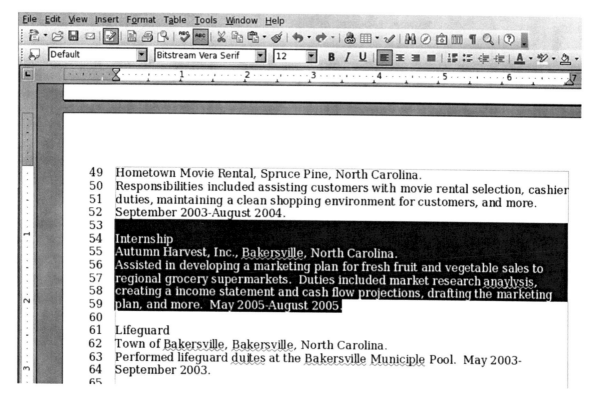

2   To eliminate the text to reinsert in another location in the document, click the Edit menu and choose the Cut menu option.

3   Using your mouse, place the pointer at the beginning of line 40. Click the left mouse button once. When you do so, you will see a cursor flashing indicating that the document is ready to be edited. In the Edit menu, choose the Paste menu option. The text referring to John's internship will now be placed at the beginning. Press the ENTER or RETURN key on your keyboard to insert a line space between the internship and shift manager employment listings.

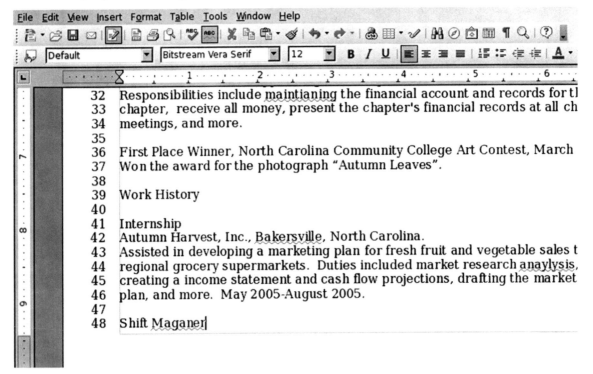

```
32   Responsibilities include maintianing the financial account and records for th
33   chapter,  receive all money, present the chapter's financial records at all ch
34   meetings, and more.
35
36   First Place Winner, North Carolina Community College Art Contest, March
37   Won the award for the photograph "Autumn Leaves".
38
39   Work History
40
41   Internship
42   Autumn Harvest, Inc., Bakersville, North Carolina.
43   Assisted in developing a marketing plan for fresh fruit and vegetable sales t
44   regional grocery supermarkets.  Duties included market research anaylysis,
45   creating a income statement and cash flow projections, drafting the market
46   plan, and more.  May 2005-August 2005.
47
48   Shift Maganer
```

4   Locate line 60 in the document. You will notice that when you cut the text referring to the internship, an additional line was left where the text was originally located. To eliminate this additional line, place the pointer at the beginning of line 60. Click the left mouse button once. When the flashing cursor appears at the beginning of line 60, press the DELETE key once on your keyboard and the additional line will be eliminated.

Text Alignment

Next, we are going to align the resume heading so that it is in the center of the first page. To do so, follow these steps:

1 Using your mouse, place the pointer at the beginning of line 1. Holding down the left mouse button, drag over lines 1 through 5 to select the text that will be aligned.

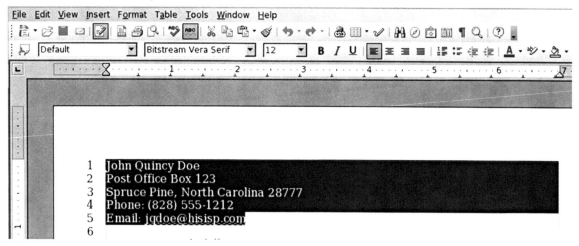

2 Click on the Format menu and select Paragraph from the menu options that appear.

3 Click on the Alignment tab in the window that appears. Select the center alignment by clicking on the radio button next to your desired selection.

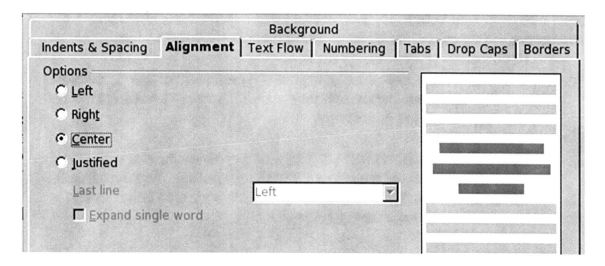

4 Click the OK button to complete the selection.

You may also change the paragraph alignment by using the appropriate alignment buttons located within the Formatting toolbar, as seen below.

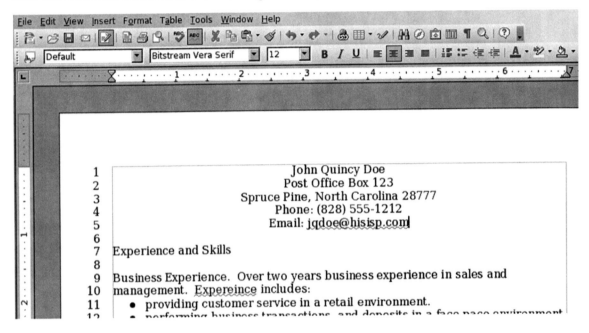

Formatting Text

Now that the text for John's resume has been entered, lists positioned in the correct order and the resume header aligned, we can now begin formatting the text. First, we need to bold some of the text within the resume, including the header and section titles. To do so, perform the following steps:

1 Using your mouse, place the pointer at the beginning of line 1. Holding down the left mouse button, drag over lines 1 through 5 to select the text that will be formatted in bold font.

2 Holding down the CONTROL (CTRL) key on your keyboard, use your left mouse button to select lines 7, 29, 39, 66 and 74 only. As you will notice, holding down your CONTROL (CTRL) key allows you to select text in different areas of a document at the same time.

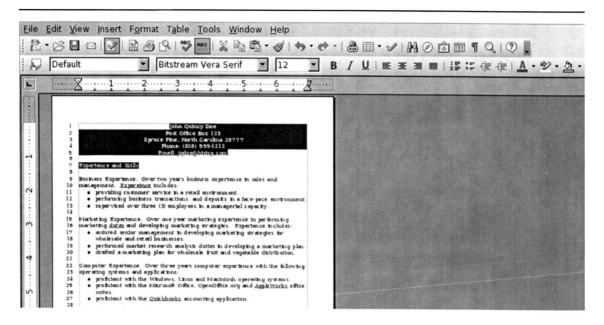

3 Click on the Format menu and select Character from the menu options that appear.

4 If it is not already selected, click the Font tab within the window that appears. Select the Bold font style within the window list. Click the OK button to complete the selection.

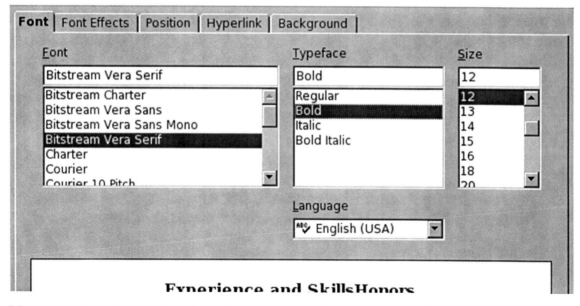

You may also change the font style by using the appropriate Font Style buttons located within the Formatting toolbar, as seen and the next page.

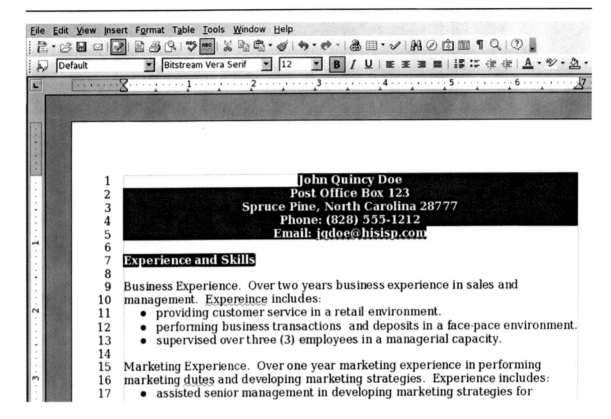

Next, we are going to create hanging indents for the text located below each primary section of the resume. This will allow the section titles to stand out in the resume and make for easier reading. To create the hanging indents, perform these steps:

5 Using your mouse, place the pointer at the beginning of line 9. Holding down the left mouse button, drag over lines 9 through 27 to select the text that will be indented.

6 Holding down the CONTROL (CTRL) key on your keyboard, use your left mouse button to select lines 31 through 37, 41 through 64, 68 through 72, and line 76. Again, holding down your CONTROL (CTRL) key allows you to select text in different areas of a document at the same time.

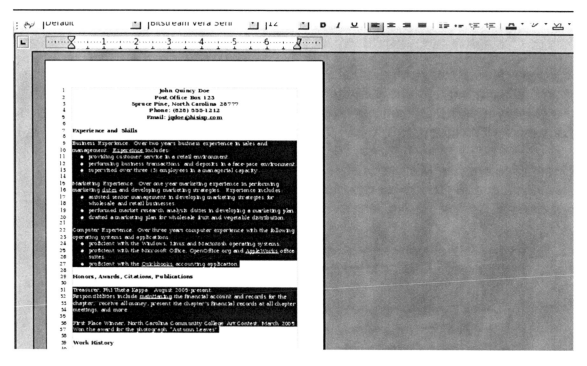

7 Locate the ruler within the OpenOffice.org application. The ruler is located between the toolbar and the document area. If the ruler is not visible, go to the View menu and select Ruler from the menu list. Then drag the bottom-left triangle within the ruler to the 1.0" location. This will create the indent for the text selected.

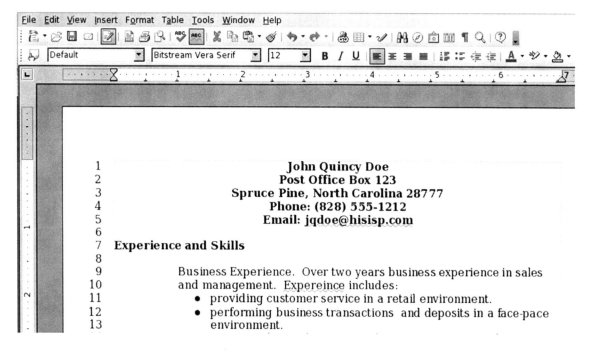

Checking Document Spelling

You may have already noticed that John's resume contains a few spelling and/or grammatical errors. It is very important that a resume contain no errors. One of the primary reasons prospective employers throw out a resume is due to mistakes contained within them.

OpenOffice.org, like Microsoft Office and many other office productivity suites, contains a spelling tool to reduce or eliminate spelling errors made within your documents. To spell check John's resume, follow these steps:

1   If you wish to spell check a specific word or sentence, select the text you wish to spell check. Otherwise, proceed to Step #2.

2   Go to the Tools menu and select Spellcheck from the menu options that appear. You may also press the F7 key on your keyboard to begin checking for spelling errors.

3   If any potential spelling errors appear, OpenOffice.org will indicate the potential error and give you a list of possible suggestions to correct the spelling.

4   If you see a spelling suggestion that would correct the error, select it from the Suggestions list and click the CHANGE button.

5   If you believe that the word in question is spelled correctly, you can click the IGNORE ONCE button to proceed to the next potential spelling error. If the word in question is spelled correctly and you use it often when creating documents, you may click the ADD button to add it to the Spellcheck's dictionary.

When you have completed checking for potential spelling errors, click the CLOSE button to exit and return to the document.

Saving the Document

Now that the resume has been completed, the document file needs to be saved like any other word processing document. OpenOffice.org supports over 20 file formats for opening and saving word processing documents, including Microsoft Word. To save the document to your computer's hard drive or removable disk, follow these steps:

1   Click on the File menu and choose Save As from the menu options that appear.

2   A window will appear and prompt you to choose a location to save your document. Choose the location you want to save a document to in the Save In popup field.

3   In the field File Name, type the name you would like to save the file as.

4   In the Save As Type popup menu, select the file format you wish to save the document as, including the OpenDocument Text (.odt) or Microsoft Word (.doc) file format.

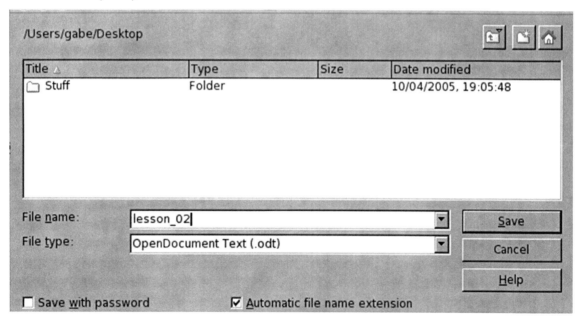

5   Click the button SAVE to complete the operation.

(NOTE: If you are given a window prompt that warns you about saving the document as a Microsoft Word file, click the YES button. The OpenOffice.org development team has gone to great lengths to help ensure that your document saved in the Word format will open properly with Microsoft Word. However, because the programming code utilized to create the Word file format is proprietary and not available to the OpenOffice.org team to view for ensuring full compatibility with Microsoft Word, not all of your document's formatting may open up 100% correctly when it is opened using the Microsoft Word application.)

Exporting the Document in the PDF Format

One of the many useful features OpenOffice.org has built-in to the office suite is the ability to export documents as a Portable Document Format (PDF) file. OpenOffice.org documents, saved as a PDF file, is a convenient way to share read-only documents to other users that have a PDF reader application installed on their computer. However, OpenOffice.org cannot edit a document that has been saved as a PDF file. Therefore, if you wish to save a document for editing at a later date, save the document in its Native OpenDocument file format.

To save a document as a read-only PDF file, follow these steps:

1 Click on the File menu and choose Export As PDF from the menu options that appear.

2 When the Export As PDF window appears, OpenOffice.org will provide you with some additional options for you to select. Among these options are the page range and image compression quality. If you choose Lossless Compression, the file will be exported in the highest quality possible but the file size will be larger. Sending large file sizes via email, for example, will result in longer receiving and download times. You also have the option to select JPEG compression to decrease the file size and, therefore, reduce the amount of time it takes to upload and download a file. OpenOffice. org allows you to use the popup menu provided to select the compression quality on a scale from 1% to 100%, with 1% being the lowest quality. After you have selected your additional export options, click the EXPORT button.

3 A window will appear and prompt you to choose a location to save your document. Choose the location you want to save a document to in the Save In popup field.

4 In the field File Name, type the name you would like to save the file as.

5 In the File Format popup menu, make sure Portable Document Format (PDF) is selected.

Printing the Document

If you are creating a resume, odds are you will sooner or later need to print it on quality bond paper to distribute to prospective employers. To print the document within OpenOffice.org Writer, follow these steps:

1 With the file open within OpenOffice.org, click on the File menu and select Print from the menu options that appear. You may also hold down the CONTROL (CTRL) key and press P on the keyboard to prompt for the Print window.

2 If you have more than one printer that your computer can send print jobs to, select the printer you wish to send the document to in the Printer selection area.

3 In the Print Range selection area, use the radio buttons to select which pages you wish to print. If you choose the Pages option, enter the page range you wish to print (example: 1-5 will print pages one through 5; 1,2,5 will print pages one, two and five). If you choose the Selection option, OpenOffice.org will only print the text you have selected (highlighted) within your document.

4 In the Copies selection area, enter the number of copies you wish to print of the document.

5 If you wish to customize the print job, click on the OPTIONS button and select or deselect the print options you wish to choose. If you do not want to customize any print settings, skip to Step #6.

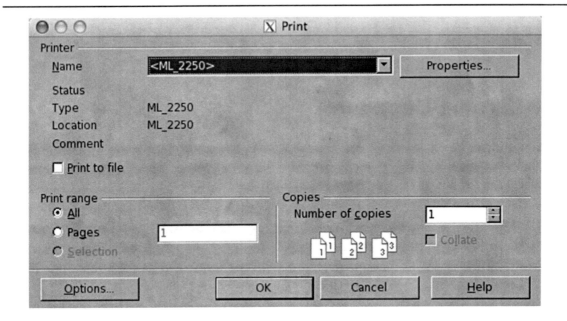

6 Once you have completed specifying your print settings, click the OK button to begin printing.

Preparing Your Own Resume

Now that you have learned how to format a resume using OpenOffice.org, you can create your own resume if you wish to do so. Before you begin creating your own resume, you may want to organize some of the information that will be needed to complete it. Information that you will need to have within your resume includes:

- Experience and Skills – Make a list of professional skills and experience you possess that employers would have an interest in. This would include computer skills, business-related tasks and other specific skills related to the position you are applying for. For computer skills, you will want to list computer applications you are proficient in, such as the OpenOffice. org office suite or various operating systems such as Linux, Windows® or Macintosh® OS X.

- Work History – You will need to list employers that you have previously worked for, beginning with the most recent. Information that will be presented in the resume includes job title, employer's name and location, the beginning and ending date of employment (month and year is usually sufficient) and a brief description of your duties while employed. If you have held positions with many employers in your career, you may want to narrow your list of employers to three (3) or four (4) where the duties you performed are most relevant to the position you are seeking. Typically, a resume should be no longer than two (2) pages in length.

- Education and Training – Make a list of the educational institutions you attended, as well as any additional training you received, and sort by the most recent institutions you attended followed by those that enhance your employability for the position you are seeking. For example, let's say you have a high school diploma, a two-year Associates degree from a community college in Network Administration and received a certification for successfully passing the Linux+ Certification exam. When you list the education and training you have received, you would list it in the following order: two-year Associates degree, high school diploma and finally the successfully completion of the certification exam.

- Finally, if you have received any honors or awards, you may list them on your resume as well. This would include being elected as an officer for a school club, articles that you had written and were published, awards received, and being a member of a volunteer or civic organization.

Once you have organized the information above, you are ready to proceed with creating your resume. If you need additional information regarding preparing a resume, the University of Waterloo Career Services Division has detailed information online about the three types of resumes above and how to prepare a resume. Their website is **http://www.cdm.uwaterloo.ca/**, and resume information can be found under Networks and Contacts located in the menu of the left side of the homepage.

Additional Resources

The Riley Guide: Resumes and Cover Letters
http://www.rileyguide.com/letters.html

University of Waterloo Career Development eManual: Resumes
http://www.cdm.uwaterloo.ca/step4_2.asp

Alec's Career Advice
http://www.alec.co.uk/

OpenOffice.org User Guides: Writer
http://documentation.openoffice.org/

Review Questions

1   Which key would you press on your keyboard to allow you to select text within different areas of a document at the same time?

2   Which primary menu item would you select within OpenOffice.org to change font styles and types, as well as to insert bulleted and numbered lists?

3   Approximately how many file formats does OpenOffice.org support for opening and saving word processing documents?

4   (True or False) Text can be formatted in bold type by either selecting the Format | Character menu option or by pressing the Bold format button located in the Formatting toolbar.

5   (True or False) Documents exported in the Portable Document Format (PDF) file type can be edited later with OpenOffice.org.

LESSON

3

Formatting a Research Paper Using Writer

Lesson Objectives

In this lesson, you will learn the following:

1   How to display nonprinting characters and line numbers to aid in formatting documents.

2   How to create headers to automatically number pages within the upper corner of each page within a document.

3   How to insert page and section numbers within a document.

4   How to sort paragraphs in alphanumerical order.

Overview

In the previous lesson, you learned how to use Writer to create a winning resume. Another task students often utilize a word processor for is to complete a research paper assignment. Research papers can often be very detailed, lengthy documents that require complex formatting. Writer has all of the capabilities to successfully complete the creation of a research paper. Moreover, the licensing terms for the open source word processor application provide students a full-featured, low cost solution to complete their assignments at school or home.

In this lesson, you will learn how to use Writer to perform the fundamental tasks of formatting a research paper. While this lesson will refer to the MLA writing style regarding the proper formatting of a research paper, the skills learned in this lesson can also be applied for preparing research papers in the APA style, as well as other research paper styles. Upon completion of this lesson, you will have learned how to use Writer to display nonprinting characters and line numbers, insert headers for page numbering, formatting hanging indents, inserting footnotes and more.

Getting Started

Before we do so, we need to open the Lesson Three file that is available for use with this book. To open the file, follow these steps:

1 If you have not already downloaded the lesson files for this book, use a web browser to go to **http://documentation.openoffice.org/ conceptualguide/OpenOfficeOrg3LessonFiles.zip**. This will provide a direct link for your browser to begin an automatic download of the lesson files. If a dialog window appears asking where you would like to save the file to be downloaded, select your computer workstation's desktop and begin downloading the file.

2 When the file appears on your computer's desktop, double-click the file icon to unzip its contents and access the files associated with each lesson. Double-click the Lesson Files folder icon that contains the available lesson files, locate the Lesson 03 folder and double-click on it to access the file for this lesson. When you have opened the folder, double-click the file named **lesson_03_start.odt** to open the file.

Display Nonprinting Characters and Line Numbers

When the lesson file is open, it will be helpful when completing this lesson to display nonprinting characters and to make line numbers viewable. This will aid you in following the directions to correctly format the document. To display nonprinting characters and view the line numbers for the document, follow these steps:

1 Click on the Tools menu and select Line Numbering from the menu options that appear.

2 When the Line Numbering selection window appears, click in the checkbox "Show Numbering" to activate line numbering. Also, in the Interval selection box located under the View selection area, change the interval to 1. Then click the OK button to view the line numbers within the file.

3 To display nonprinting characters, such as paragraph marks and line spacing, click on the View menu and select Nonprinting Characters from the menu options that appear. You could also hold down the CONTROL (CTRL) key on your keyboard while pressing the F10 key to activate viewing nonprinting characters as well.

Formatting Text

One of the first thing that needs to be done to format this research paper in accordance with the MLA writing style is to format the text properly. This would include double-spacing each line, selecting 12-point font size for all text within the document and format paragraph indents. To properly format the text within this research paper, follow these steps:

1   Click the Edit menu and choose Select All from the menu options that appear.

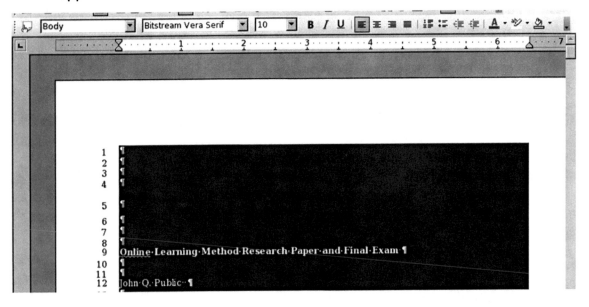

2   Click the Format menu and choose Character from the menu options that appear.

3   Click on the Font tab in the window that appears. Select the Bitstream Vera Serif font, regular typeface and 12-point font size. Then click the OK button.

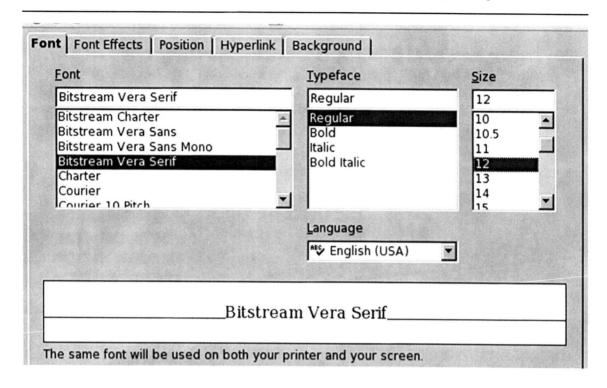

4   With the entire document remaining selected, click the Format menu and choose Paragraph from the menu options that appear.

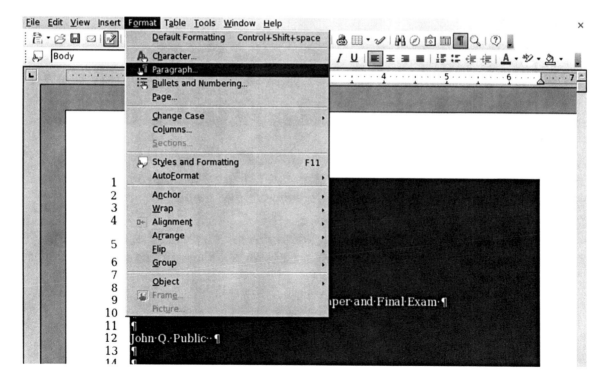

5 Click on the Indents & Spacing tab in the window appears. In the Indent selection area, use the First Line selection field to configure each paragraph to indent the first line by 0.5". In the Line Spacing selection area, select Double from the popup menu provided. In the Register-True selection area, place a checkmark within the checkbox provided to activate the feature. Then click the OK button.

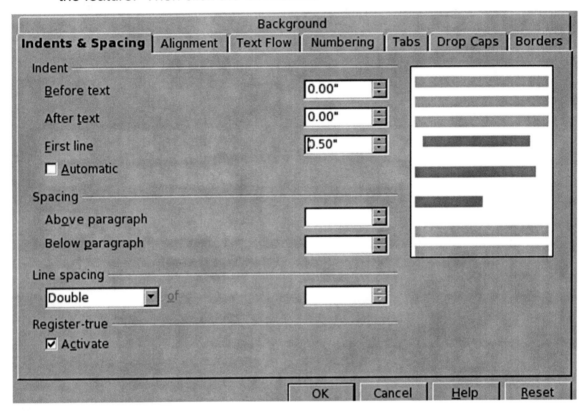

A few lines within the document do not need to be formatted with a paragraph indent. This would include the cover page, the works cited page as well as section headings. To format these areas, follow these steps:

6 Using your mouse, place the pointer at the beginning of line 1. Holding down the left mouse button, drag over lines 1 through 23 to select the cover page text.

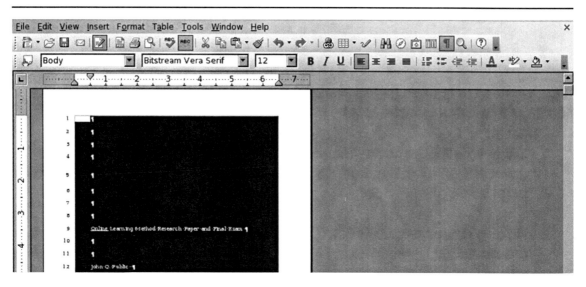

7 Holding down the CONTROL (CTRL) key on your keyboard, use your left mouse button to select lines 54, 111, 193, 240, 315, 355, 449 and 524 through 556 only. As you will notice, holding down your CONTROL (CTRL) key allows you to select text in different areas of a document at the same time.

8 Click on the Format menu and choose Paragraph from the menu options that appear.

9 Click on the Indents & Spacing tab in the window appears. In the Indent selection area, use the First Line selection field to configure each paragraph to indent the first line by 0.0". Then click the OK button.

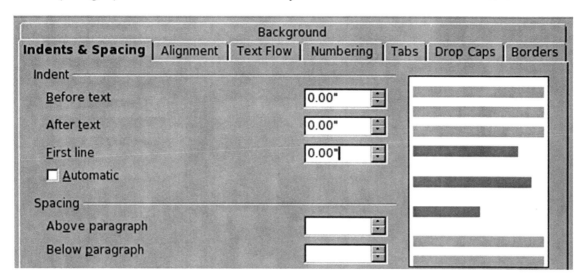

Text Alignment

Next, we need to change the text alignment for the cover page and section headings from left alignment to center alignment. To do so, follow these steps:

1 Using your mouse, place the pointer at the beginning of line 1. Holding down the left mouse button, drag over lines 1 through 23 to select the cover page text.

2 Holding down the CONTROL (CTRL) key on your keyboard, use your left mouse button to select lines 54, 111, 193, 240, 315, 355, 449 and 524. As you will notice, holding down your CONTROL (CTRL) key allows you to select text in different areas of a document at the same time.

3 Click on the Format menu and choose Paragraph from the menu options that appear.

4 Click on the Alignment tab in the window appears. In the Options selection area, choose the Center alignment option by clicking your mouse button within the radio button provided. Then click the OK button.

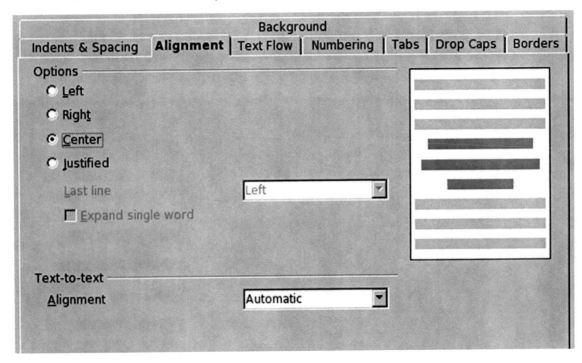

Inserting a Header for Page Numbering

For large documents, such as this research paper, it is helpful for readers to refer back to certain sections by having page numbers printed on each page. While you could manually number each page yourself, an easier method is to have the word processor insert page numbers automatically. For this document, we will insert a header and place the page number within it. To do so, follow these steps:

1 Click the Insert menu, select Header from the menu options that appear and select Default from the submenu options that appear.

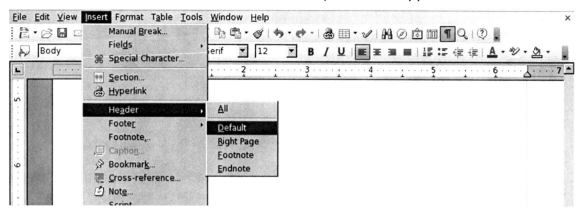

2 When the option is selected, you will notice that the word processor places a separate text area at the top of each page within the document. If you had selected Footer from the Insert menu, the text area would have been placed at the bottom of each page. When you type text within a header or footer, the text appears on each page of the document. In this exercise, type **Online Learning Method**. Because you are typing within the header area, the text is automatically formatted in bold.

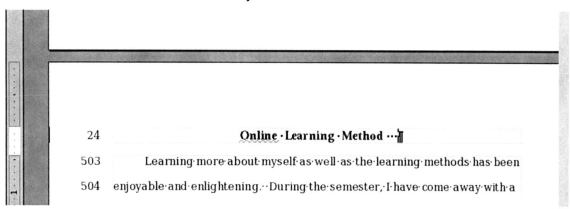

3 Press the SPACE BAR key three times to place some space between the text and where the page number will be positioned. Then click the Insert menu, select Fields from the menu options that appear and select Page Number from the submenu options that appear. When doing so, the field that is inserted into the header automatically numbers each page within the document.

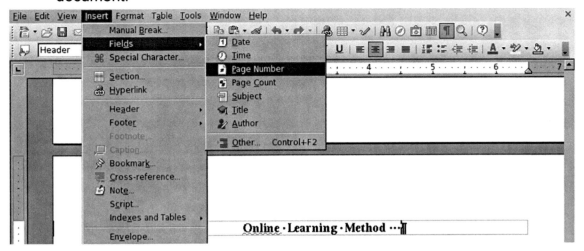

4 Finally, we need to change the alignment of the text within the header from center to right alignment. To do so, click the Format menu and choose Paragraph from the menu options that appear.

5 Click on the Alignment tab in the window appears. In the Options selection area, choose the Right alignment option by clicking your mouse button within the radio button provided. Then click the OK button.

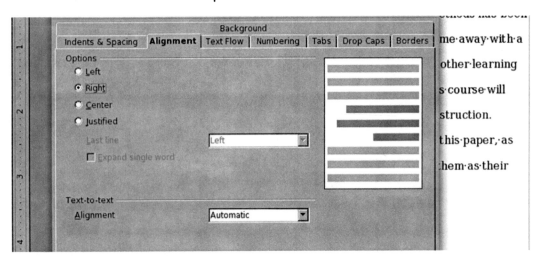

Inserting Footnotes

Footnotes, used for embedding explanatory notes within a research paper formatted in the MLA documentation style, are considered optional. The research paper we are formatting for this exercise does not need a footnote. However, if you ever need to include a footnote within a research paper in the future, you may do so using Writer by following these steps:

1 Place your cursor within the page you wish the footnote to appear. For this example, place your cursor at the end of the sentence in line 482 by clicking at the location with your left mouse button.

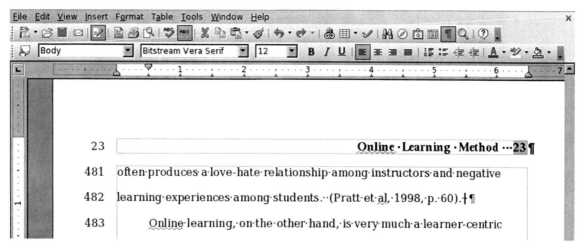

2 Go to the Insert menu and select Footnote from the menu options that appear.

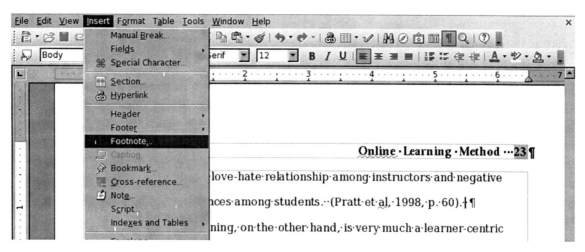

3   In the Insert Footnote window that appears, select Automatic within the
Numbering selection area for the footnotes to be listed numerically at the
bottom of the page.

4   Select Footnote within the Type selection area.

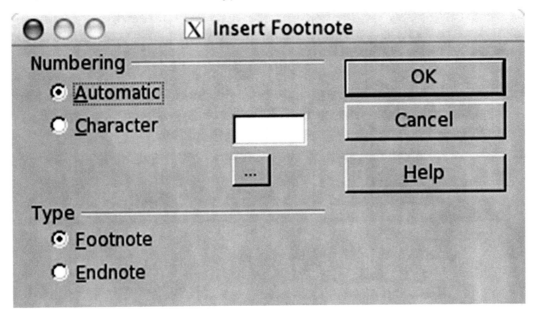

5   Click the OK button to complete the operation. A superscript will be
placed at the end of the sentence in line 482 and the footnote will appear
at the bottom of the page. You can then type notes you wish to add. To
immediately remove the footnote, click on the Edit menu and choose Undo:
Insert Footnote from the menu options that appear.

Inserting Page Breaks

Within the research paper, we need to be assured that the cover page and the
works cited page are both on a separate page from the rest of the document.
Rather than using the ENTER or RETURN key on the keyboard to place spaces
and move those sections to their respective pages, we can insert page breaks at
the end of the cover page and the beginning of the works cited page. That way,
whenever you add text or make formatting changes to the body of the document,
the cover page and works cited page would remain on its own individual page. To
insert page breaks within this document, follow these steps:

1 Place your cursor at the beginning on line 8 within the document. Press the DELETE key on your keyboard three (3) times to remove some of the empty lines within the cover page.

2 Place the cursor at the beginning of line 21 by clicking at the beginning of the line with your left mouse button.

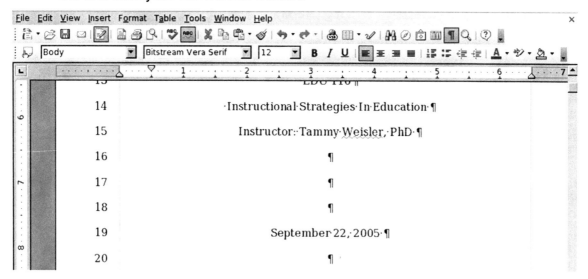

3 Go to the Insert menu and select Manual Break from the menu options that appear.

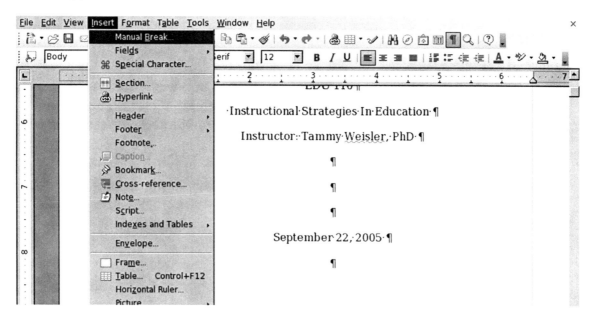

4   When the Manual Break window appears, click on the Page Break radio button within the Type selection area.

5   If you are creating the page break for a specific purpose, you may select one of the formatting options from the Style popup menu. If you wish to have a standard page break, as we want for this exercise, leave the popup menu selected None.

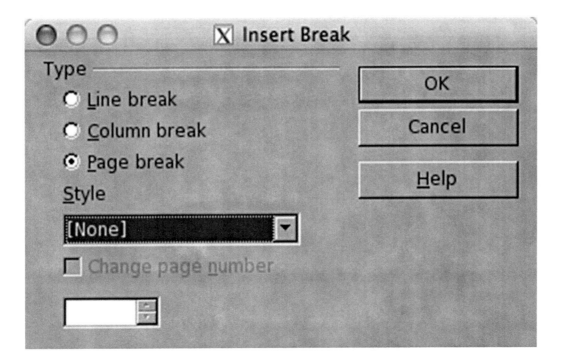

6   When you have selected the formatting options you wish the new page to have, click the OK button to complete the operation. A page break is then placed at the end of line 21. A page break is represented with a blue line running across the document editing area.

7   Place your cursor at the beginning on line 522 within the document. Press the ENTER or RETURN key on your keyboard three (3) times to remove the Works Cited heading down three lines onto the next page.

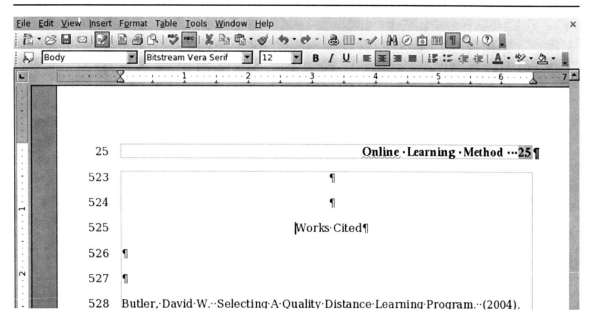

8 Place the cursor at the beginning of line 523. Then go to the Insert menu and select Manual Break from the menu options that appear.

9 When the Manual Break window appears, click on the Page Break radio button within the Type selection area.

10 If you are creating the page break for a specific purpose, you may select one of the formatting options from the Style popup menu. If you wish to have a standard page break, as we want for this exercise, leave the popup menu selected None.

11 When you have selected the formatting options you wish the new page to have, click the OK button to complete the operation. A page break is then placed at the end of line 523.

(NOTE: Instead of selecting the Insert menu, you can also create a new page break by holding down the CONTROL (CTRL) key and press the Enter key on the keyboard.)

Creating Hanging Indents

Now that the works cited page has been formatted with a page break, the text within the section needs to be formatted with a hanging indent. A hanging indent is formatted the opposite of a normal paragraph indent; the first line is left aligned while the second and subsequent lines are indented. To format the Works Cited section with hanging indents, follow these steps:

1   Using your mouse, place the pointer at the beginning of line 529. Holding down the left mouse button, drag over lines 529 through 558 to select the works cited text.

2   Locate the ruler at the top of the text editing area. On the left side of the ruler, you will the Hanging Indent marker. The Hanging Indent marker looks much like an hourglass.

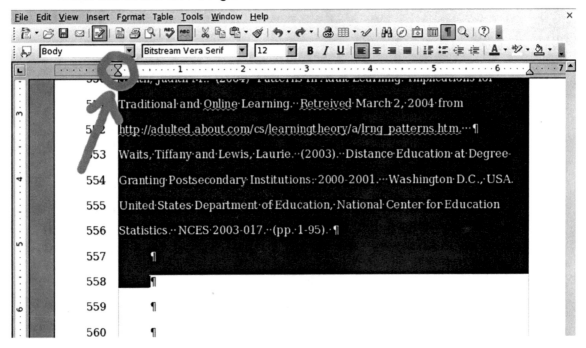

3   Place your pointer at the bottom-half of the Hanging Indent marker. Holding down your left mouse button, drag the Hanging Indent marker within the ruler to the 0.5" mark. When doing so, the top-half of the Hanging Indent marker also drags to the 0.5" mark. To reposition the top-half of the Hanging Indent marker to the 0.0" mark, place your pointer on the top-half of the marker and drag it back to the 0.0" position. When completed, 0.5" hanging indents are created for the Works Cited section.

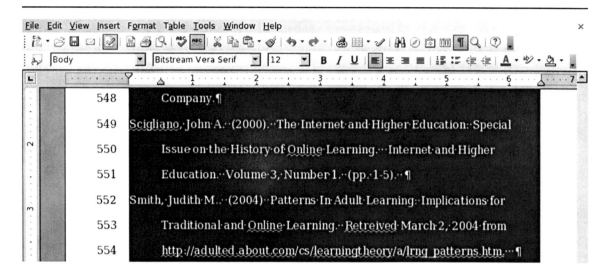

Sorting Paragraphs

According to the MLA documentation style, the works listed within the Works Cited section need to be listed in alphabetical order. Rather than cutting and pasting the works into the correct order, we can select paragraphs and sort them in alphabetical order. While our Works Cited section is still selected from creating the hanging indents, we can easily sort the works in the correct order. To sort paragraphs in alphabetical order, follow these steps:

1 With the Works Cited section selected, click the Tools menu and select Sort from the menu options that appear.

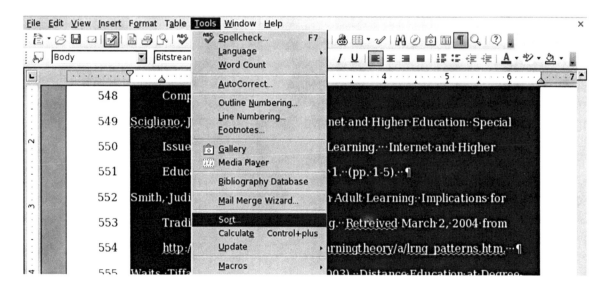

2   When the Sort window appears, select Key 1 by clicking within the checkbox provided. This indicates the first sort order you are specifying for the selected text.

3   For the Key Type, select Alphanumeric within the popup menu provided.

4   Finally, choose Ascending Order within the Sort Criteria selection area by clicking within the radio button provided. Once the appropriate selection criteria have been specified, click the OK button.

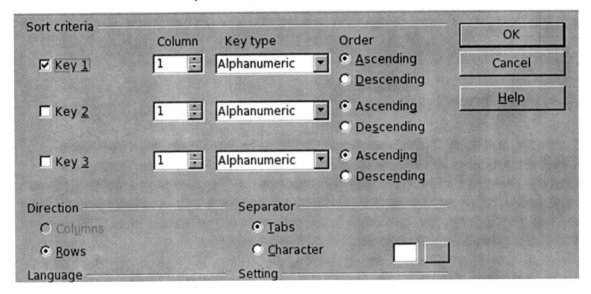

Using Word Count

Often times when receiving a research paper assignment, the instructor will provide a list of requirements that the final paper must meet. One of the most common requirements specified for a research paper if for it to have a minimum number of words. OpenOffice.org Writer has a word count feature that can assist users in determining the number of words contained within a document.

To use the word count feature, simply click the Tools menu and select Word Count from the menu options that appear. The word count feature will display the number of words within a document or selected text, as well as the number of characters typed within the document. To close the Word Count window, simply click the OK button.

Checking Document Spelling

One of the most important steps in completing a research paper is to check the document for grammatical and spelling errors. Although OpenOffice.org currently does not have a grammar check tool, you can speed up the process of checking for document errors within Writer by utilizing the Spellcheck tool. To check for spelling errors within this research paper, follow these steps:

1 If you wish to spell check a specific word or sentence, select the text you wish to spell check. Otherwise, proceed to Step #2.

2 Go to the Tools menu and select Spellcheck from the menu options that appear. You may also press the F7 key on your keyboard to begin checking for spelling errors.

3 If any potential spelling errors appear, OpenOffice.org will indicate the potential error and give you a list of possible suggestions to correct the spelling.

4 If you see a spelling suggestion that would correct the error, select it from the Suggestions list and click the CHANGE button.

5 If you believe that the word in question is spelled correctly, you can click the IGNORE ONCE button to proceed to the next potential spelling error. If the word in question is spelled correctly and you use it often when creating documents, you may click the ADD button to add it to the Spellcheck's dictionary.

When you have completed checking for potential spelling errors, click the CLOSE button to exit and return to the document.

Saving the Document

Now that the research paper has been completed, it is time to save the document. To save the document to your computer's hard drive or removable disk, follow these steps:

1   Click on the File menu and choose Save As from the menu options that appear.

2   A window will appear and prompt you to choose a location to save your document. Choose the location you want to save a document to in the Save In popup field.

3   In the field File Name, type the name you would like to save the file as.

4   In the Save As Type popup menu, select the file format you wish to save the document as, including the OpenDocument Text (.odt) or Microsoft Word (.doc) file format.

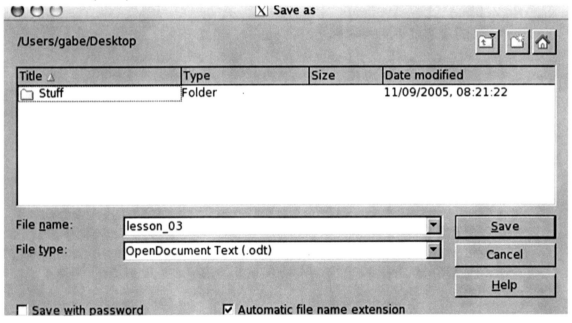

5   Click the button SAVE to complete the operation.

(NOTE: If you are given a window prompt that warns you about saving the document as a Microsoft Word file, click the YES button. The OpenOffice.org development team has gone to great lengths to help ensure that your document saved in the Word format will open properly with Microsoft Word. However, because the programming code utilized to create the Word file format is proprietary and not available to the OpenOffice.org team to view for ensuring full compatibility with Microsoft Word, not all of your document's formatting may open up 100% correctly when it is opened using the Microsoft Word application.)

Exporting the Document in the PDF Format

As mentioned in the previous lesson regarding creating a resume, one of the many useful features OpenOffice.org has built-in to the office suite is the ability to export documents as a Portable Document Format (PDF) file. Saving a research paper as a PDF file has a number of possible advantages, including being able to share the document as read-only, making it difficult for others to alter the contents within the paper. Moreover, a research paper saved in the PDF format could be read by anyone who has one of a number of free PDF reader applications, as opposed to saving the document in a format that requires a specific application to read it. Remember, however, OpenOffice.org cannot edit a document that has been saved as a PDF file. Therefore, if you wish to save a document for editing at a later date, save the document in its Native OpenDocument file format.

To save a document as a read-only PDF file, follow these steps:

1 Click on the File menu and choose Export As PDF from the menu options that appear.

2 When the Export As PDF window appears, OpenOffice.org will provide you with some additional options for you to select. Among these options are the page range and image compression quality. If you choose Lossless Compression, the file will be exported in the highest quality possible but the file size will be larger. Sending large file sizes via email, for example, will result in longer receiving and download times. You also have the option to select JPEG compression to decrease the file size and, therefore, reduce the amount of time it takes to upload and download a file. OpenOffice. org allows you to use the popup menu provided to select the compression quality on a scale from 1% to 100%, with 1% being the lowest quality. After you have selected your additional export options, click the EXPORT button.

3 A window will appear and prompt you to choose a location to save your document. Choose the location you want to save a document to in the Save In popup field.

4 In the field File Name, type the name you would like to save the file as.

5 In the File Format popup menu, make sure Portable Document Format (PDF) is selected.

Printing the Document

The final step in completing a research paper assignment is to print the document. To print the document within OpenOffice.org Writer, follow these steps:

1 With the file open within OpenOffice.org, click on the File menu and select Print from the menu options that appear. You may also hold down the CONTROL (CTRL) key and press P on the keyboard to prompt for the Print window.

2 If you have more than one printer that your computer can send print jobs to, select the printer you wish to send the document to in the Printer selection area.

3 In the Print Range selection area, use the radio buttons to select which pages you wish to print. If you choose the Pages option, enter the page range you wish to print (example: 1-5 will print pages one through 5; 1,2,5 will print pages one, two and five). If you choose the Selection option, OpenOffice.org will only print the text you have selected (highlighted) within your document.

4 In the Copies selection area, enter the number of copies you wish to print of the document.

5 If you wish to customize the print job, click on the OPTIONS button and select or deselect the print options you wish to choose. If you do not want to customize any print settings, skip to Step #6.

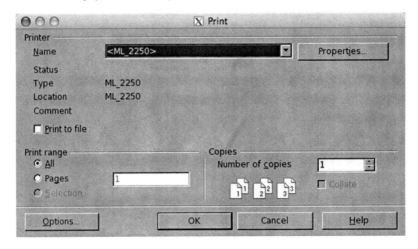

6 Once you have completed specifying your print settings, click the OK button to begin printing.

Additional Resources

Writing a Thesis with OpenOffice.org
http://documentation.openoffice.org/HOW_TO/word_processing/How_to_Write_a_Thesis_in_OOo.pdf

I. Lee: How to Write Footnotes and Endnotes in MLA Style
http://www.aresearchguide.com/7footnot.html

Purdue University Online Writing Lab: Using Modern Language Association (MLA) Format
http://owl.english.purdue.edu/handouts/research/r_mla.html

Review Questions

1 Which primary menu item would you select within OpenOffice.org to make nonprinting characters visible when editing a document?

2 What is the name of the separate text area at the top of each page that is often used to insert page number fields within a research paper?

3 What type of document formatting option allows you to embed explanatory notes within a research paper, where the notes are placed at the bottom of the page?

4 (True or False) A page break is represented with a blue line running across the document editing area.

5 (True or False) Paragraphs can be sorted into alphabetical order without having to use the cut-and-paste method.

LESSON

4 Creating a Brochure Using Writer

Lesson Objectives

In this lesson, you will learn the following:

1   How to change the page size and orientation for an OpenOffice.org Writer
    document.

2   How to add and format columns within a Writer document.

3   How to insert and format graphics within a Writer document.

4   The advantages and disadvantages of exporting a document as a Portable
    Document Format (PDF) file.

Overview

In the last two lessons, we have learned how Writer has a vast array of features
that allow users to create the most complex text documents. However, Writer can
create much more than text documents. Writer has the features and capabilities
to create documents with elaborate layouts and graphics, including newsletters,
brochures, web pages and much more.

In this lesson, you will become acquainted with Writer's formatting capabilities
to create a travel brochure. Upon completing this lesson, you will have learned
the fundamentals in creating complex layouts, including formatting text columns,
adjusting page orientation and margins, elaborately formatting text and inserting
high resolution graphics.

Getting Started

Before we do so, we need to open the Lesson Four file that is available for use
with this book. To open the file, follow these steps:

1   If you have not already downloaded the lesson files for this book,
    use a web browser to go to **http://documentation.openoffice.org/**

conceptualguide/OpenOfficeOrg3LessonFiles.zip. This will provide a direct link for your browser to begin an automatic download of the lesson files. If a dialog window appears asking where you would like to save the file to be downloaded, select your computer workstation's desktop and begin downloading the file.

2 When the file appears on your computer's desktop, double-click the file icon to unzip its contents and access the files associated with each lesson. Double-click the Lesson Files folder icon that contains the available lesson files, locate the Lesson 04 folder and double-click on it to access the file for this lesson. When you have opened the folder, double-click the file named **lesson_04_start.odt** to open the file.

Changing Page Size and Orientation

Once you have opened the lesson file, you will notice that much of the text for this brochure has already been provided. Like virtually any other text document, it is easier to enter the text within the document first before proceeding with adjusting the formatting of the document. To create this brochure, we will need to adjust the page size, margins and orientation so that, when printed, the pages can be folded properly for distribution.

To change the page size, margins and orientation, follow these steps:

1 Click on the Format menu and select Page from the menu options that appear.

2 When the Page Style window appears, click on the Page tab at the top of the window (if it isn't already selected).

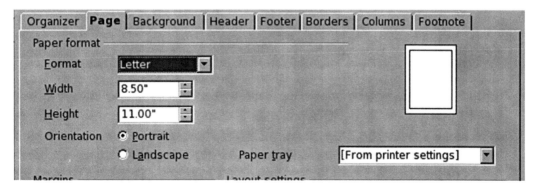

3 Using the Format popup menu, select the predefined paper size you will print your document on. For this brochure, select Letter. When you select an option, the width and height will automatically change to format itself to the predefined paper format. Because the paper size format Letter was chosen, the width and height was automatically formatted 8.5" and 11.0" respectively. If this had been another type of document and you had wished to select a custom paper size, you could have utilized the Width and Height menus to enter the appropriate page size.

4 In the Margins selection area, specify your page margins for your document by entering the appropriate measurements. For this brochure, enter 0.79" for the left, right, top and bottom margins.

5 Because a tri-fold brochure is being created, the page orientation also needs to be adjusted. Using the Orientation radio buttons located within the Paper Format selection area, select Landscape.

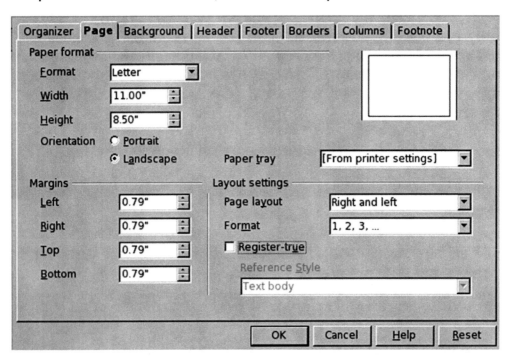

6 In the Layout selection area, you have the option to select the register-true format feature. When you select this feature, it can make pages easier to read by preventing gray shadows from appearing between the lines of text. This could be a useful feature if your document will be printed on the front and back of pages, such as this brochure. To select this feature, click inside the checkbox. When a checkmark appears within the box, the feature is enabled. In the Reference Style popup menu located beneath the Register-True checkbox, select Text Body from the options provided.

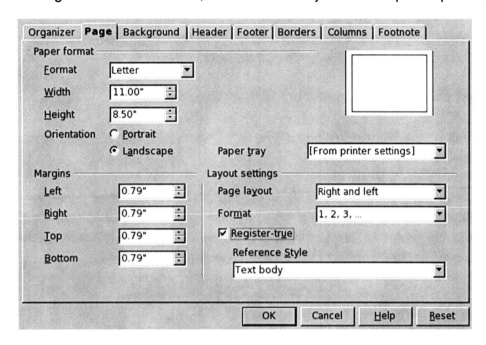

7 Once you have selected your page style formatting options, click the OK button to complete the selection.

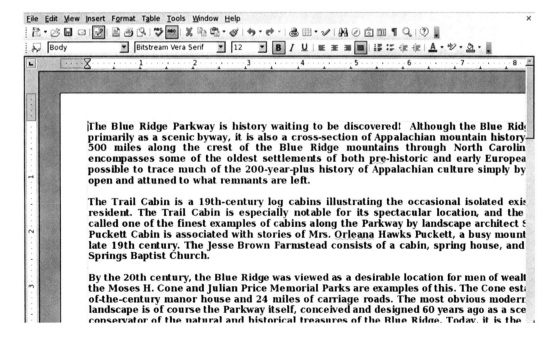

Adding Columns

After changing the page size and orientation of the document, the next thing that needs to be done is to format the text within columns. This brochure will be a tri-fold, which will result in three columns of text formatted between folds. Therefore, we need to add three columns to this document.

To create columns for this document, follow these steps:

1 Click on the Format menu and select Columns from the menu options that appear.

2 Within the Settings selection area, you may click on one of the predefined column formats available to you or enter the number of columns you wish your document to have. For this brochure, select the predefined three (3) column format or enter (3) into the Columns format field.

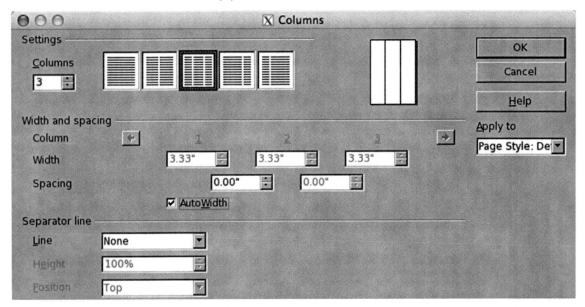

3 If you want to customize the width and spacing of the columns within your document or add a separator line, utilize the fields available within the appropriate selection areas. For this brochure, enter 0.10" within the spacing selection field and press the TAB key on your keyboard. You should notice the column width for each of the three columns change from 3.14" to 3.08".

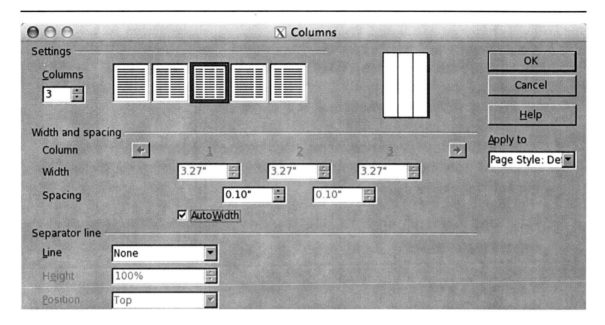

4 Click the OK button to complete the selection.

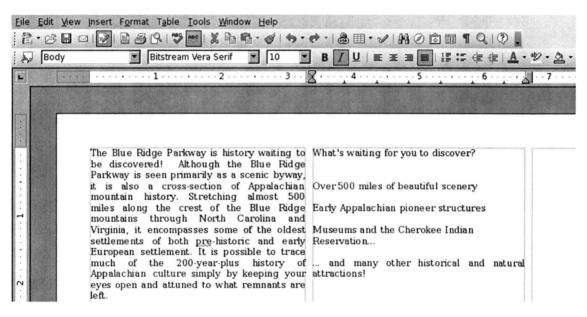

Formatting Text (changing font type, size, alignment and style)

The next step in completing the brochure is to format the text. For a brochure, the text needs to be very legible and easy on the eyes when reading. To accomplish this, we will choose a font that is legible when reading, increase the size of some of the text so that certain points catches the readers attention and bold the text throughout the brochure to make it easy on the eyes when reading.

To format the text within the brochure, follow these steps:

1   With the brochure document open, click on the Edit menu and choose Select All from the menu options that appear. When doing so, the text in the entire document is selected.

2   Next, click on the Format menu and select Character from the menu options that appear.

3   If it is not already selected, click the Font tab within the window that appears. Select the Bitstream Vera Serif font within the Font window list. In the Typeface selection area, choose the Bold font style. In the Size selection area, select size 12. Once you have made these selections, click the OK button.

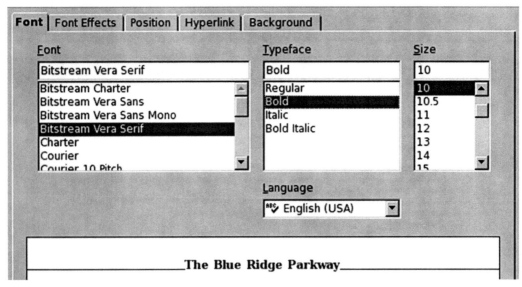

4   Now that the main body of text has been formatted, a few lines of text need some additional formatting. Look at column two of the brochure document. Using your mouse, select the text **What's waiting for you to discover**. Within the Formatting toolbar located just above the ruler at the top of the document, locate the Font Size popup menu and select 24. The size of the selected text will be formatted accordingly.

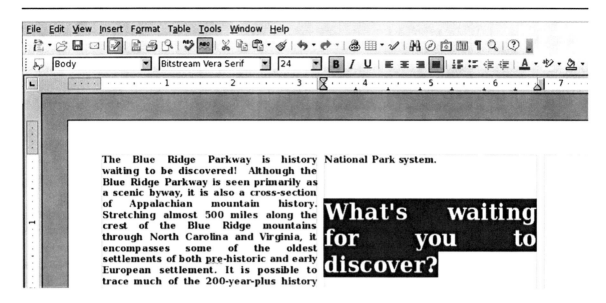

5 With the text still selected from Step #4, locate the Paragraph Alignment buttons within the Formatting toolbar. Click the Centered alignment button and the text will be centered within the column it appears in. This will format the heading for our inside bulleted list.

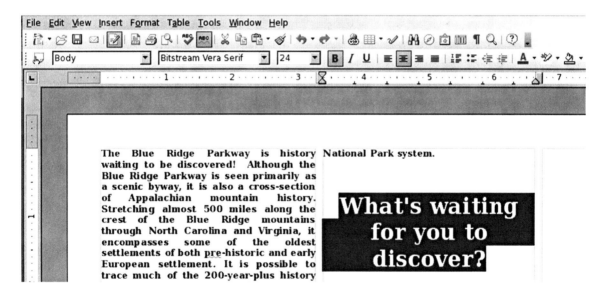

6 Below the heading that we just formatted, you will find a text list containing four points. This needs some additional formatting. To select the text, place your mouse pointer at the beginning of the first point. Holding down the left mouse button, drag over the next nine lines to select for editing.

The Blue Ridge Parkway is history waiting to be discovered! Although the Blue Ridge Parkway is seen primarily as a scenic byway, it is also a cross-section of Appalachian mountain history. Stretching almost 500 miles along the crest of the Blue Ridge mountains through North Carolina and Virginia, it encompasses some of the oldest settlements of both pre-historic and early European settlement. It is possible to trace much of the 200-year-plus history of Appalachian culture simply by keeping your eyes open and attuned to what remnants are left.

The Trail Cabin is a 19th-century log cabins illustrating the occasional isolated existence of mountain resident. The Trail Cabin is especially notable for its spectacular location, and the Caudill Cabin was called one of the finest examples of cabins along the Parkway by landscape architect Stanley Abbott. The

National Park system.

What's waiting for you to discover?

Over 500 miles of beautiful scenery

Early Appalachian pioneer structures

Museums and the Cherokee Indian Reservation...

... and many other historical and natural attractions!

7 After selecting the text, locate the Font Size popup menu within the Formatting toolbar and select 16 from the size options provided. While the text is still selected, locate the Paragraph Alignment buttons within the Formatting toolbar and click the Left alignment button.

Stretching almost 500 miles along the crest of the Blue Ridge mountains through North Carolina and Virginia, it encompasses some of the oldest settlements of both pre-historic and early European settlement. It is possible to trace much of the 200-year-plus history of Appalachian culture simply by keeping your eyes open and attuned to what remnants are left.

The Trail Cabin is a 19th-century log cabins illustrating the occasional isolated existence of mountain resident. The Trail Cabin is especially notable for its spectacular location, and the Caudill Cabin was called one of the finest examples of cabins along the Parkway by landscape architect Stanley Abbott. The Puckett Cabin is associated with stories of Mrs. Orleana Hawks Puckett, a busy mountain mid-wife of the late 19th century. The Jesse Brown Farmstead consists of a cabin, spring house, and the relocated Cool Springs Baptist Church.

By the 20th century, the Blue Ridge was viewed as a desirable location for men of wealth to build retreats; the Moses H.

What's waiting for you to discover?

Over 500 miles of beautiful scenery

Early Appalachian pioneer structures

Museums and the Cherokee Indian Reservation...

... and many other historical and natural attractions!

8 Because the text we formatted in Step #7 will be a list located within the inside of the brochure, it would be helpful to format the text as a bulleted list. With the text remaining selected, click on the Format menu and choose Bullets and Numbering from the menu options that appear. When the window appears, select the Bullets tab. A number of bullet formats will be presented. For this brochure, select the second arrow format located on the lower row within the options provided. Then click the OK button to complete the formatting.

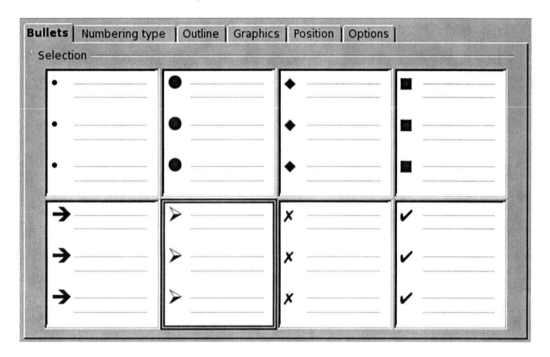

9 The final text remaining to be formatted is that which will appear on the front of the brochure. Below the bulleted list we just formatted, you will find the text that will appear on the cover of the brochure. Using your mouse, select the text **The Blue Ridge Parkway**. After selecting the text, locate the Font Size popup menu within the Formatting toolbar and select 36 from the size options provided. While the text is still selected, locate the Paragraph Alignment buttons within the Formatting toolbar and click the Centered alignment button.

10 Finally, use your left mouse button select the last line of text **History Waiting To Be Discovered!** . After selecting the text, locate the Font Size popup menu within the Formatting toolbar and select 18 from the size options provided. While the text is still selected, locate the Paragraph

Alignment buttons within the Formatting toolbar and click the Centered alignment button.

Inserting and Formatting Graphics

All of the text that will be present in the brochure has been formatted. The brochure may look anything but desirable at this point. However, the brochure will take shape as we begin with the last major process of completing the formatting of the brochure: inserting and formatting images within the document.

When you accessed the file associated with this lesson, you may have noticed an extra folder labeled "Images" within the lesson folder. Inside the folder contains four images that we will insert into the brochure. Upon completing the insertion of these images within the brochure, the document should be near completion for saving.

To insert the images within the brochure, follow these steps:

1   The first image that will be inserted into the brochure will be placed at the beginning of the first paragraph that currently appears within the document. Using your mouse, place the pointer in front of the first character of the paragraph. When the I-bar appears, click your left mouse button and a cursor will be flashing in front of the paragraph. Press the ENTER or RETURN key on the keyboard to insert and additional line in front of the first paragraph, allowing space to insert the first image.

2 In the center of your keyboard, located to the left of the numeric keypad, find the arrow keys and press the key that points up. This will position the cursor into the front of the first, empty line you just created.

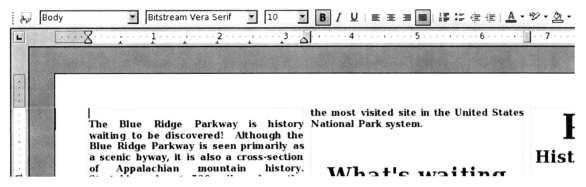

3 Click on the Insert menu, select Picture from the menu options that appear and then select From File within the submenu options that appear.

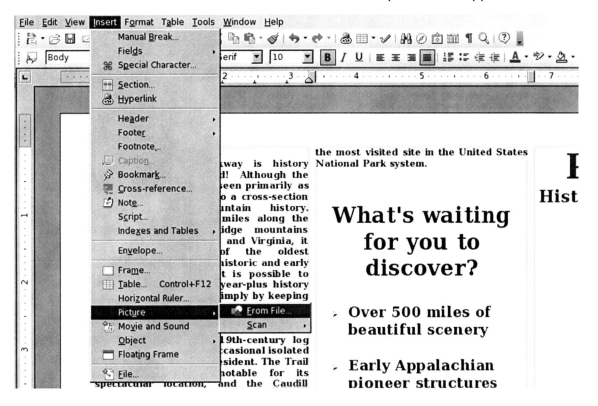

4 When the Insert Picture window appears, use the navigation buttons located in the upper-right corner of the window to locate the image files associated with this lesson. These photos can be found in the Lesson 04 folder, which is contained within the downloadable Lesson Files folder associated with this book. Once you have located the images, use your mouse to click on the image file lesson_04_image01.jpg to select it. If you wish to see a preview of the image within the Insert Picture window, make sure the Preview checkbox is selected by clicking within it. To insert it within the brochure, click the OPEN button.

(NOTE: The LINK checkbox located within the Name and Type selection area allows you to place an image within the brochure without actually embedding the image into the document file. When a checkmark appears within the box provided, this means the Link formatting option is selected. This method allows you to reduce the file size of the document. However, if you send a document to another user and want the images to be included properly, you must either embed the images within the document itself by deselecting the Link option or by exporting the entire document as a PDF file.)

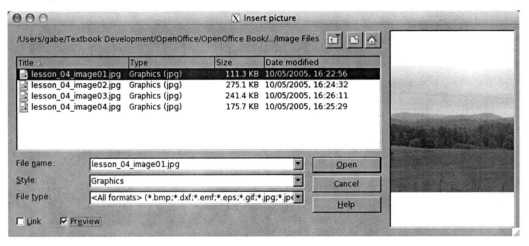

5 Next, we are going to insert the second image into the brochure. The second image will be placed below the second paragraph. If there is an empty line at the top of the second column (or before the second paragraph), place your mouse button at the beginning of the empty line. When the I-bar appears, click your left mouse button and a cursor will be flashing in front of the paragraph. Press the DELETE key on the keyboard to remove the empty line.

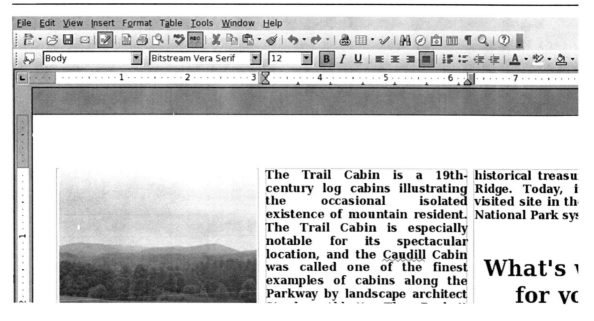

6 Using your mouse, place the pointer at the empty line located beneath the second paragraph. When the I-bar appears, click your left mouse button and a cursor will be flashing in front of the paragraph.

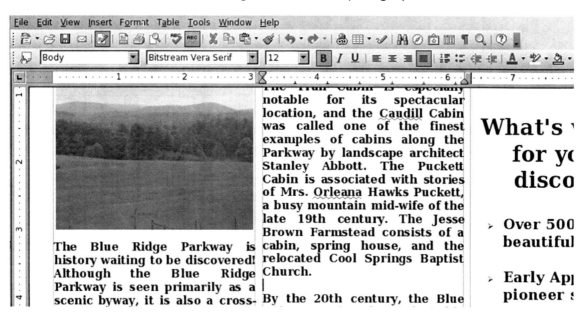

7 Click on the Insert menu, select Picture from the menu options that appear and then select From File within the submenu options that appear. When the Insert Picture window appears, use the navigation buttons located in the upper-right corner of the window to again locate the image files associated with this lesson. Once you have located the images, use your mouse to click on the image file lesson_04_image02.jpg to select it. To insert it within the brochure, click the OPEN button.

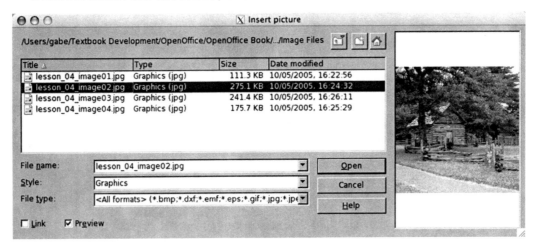

8 The third image that will be inserted into the brochure will be placed at the beginning of the third paragraph that currently appears within the document. Using your mouse, place the pointer in front of the first character of the third paragraph. When the I-bar appears, click your left mouse button and a cursor will be flashing in front of the paragraph. Press the ENTER or RETURN key on the keyboard to insert and additional line in front of the third paragraph, allowing space to insert the third image.

9 In the center of your keyboard, located to the left of the numeric keypad, find the arrow keys and press the key that points up. This will position the cursor into the front of the empty line you just created.

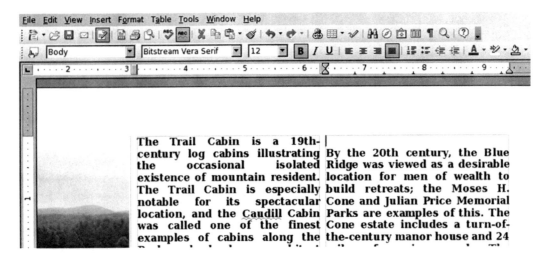

10 Click on the Insert menu, select Picture from the menu options that appear and then select From File within the submenu options that appear. When the Insert Picture window appears, use the navigation buttons located in the upper-right corner of the window to again locate the image files associated with this lesson. Once you have located the images, use your mouse to click on the image file lesson_04_image03.jpg to select it. To insert it within the brochure, click the OPEN button. When completed, the first page of the brochure should look similar to below.

11 The final image that will be placed into the brochure will be located in the third column on the second page, in between the brochure title **The Blue Ridge Parkway** and the tag line **History Waiting To Be Discovered!**. Before we can insert the image, however, we need to position the brochure title and tag line within the third column. Locate the first line of the brochure title, within the first column of the second page. Using your mouse, place the pointer in front of the first character. When the I-bar appears, click your left mouse button and a cursor will be flashing in front of the text.

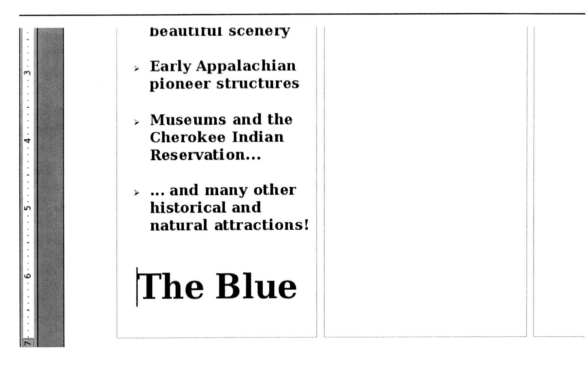

12 Press down on the ENTER or RETURN key on the keyboard. Continue to hold down the key to insert additional lines in front of brochure title. When the beginning of the brochure title reaches the second line of the third column, release the key. The brochure title is now in its proper position.

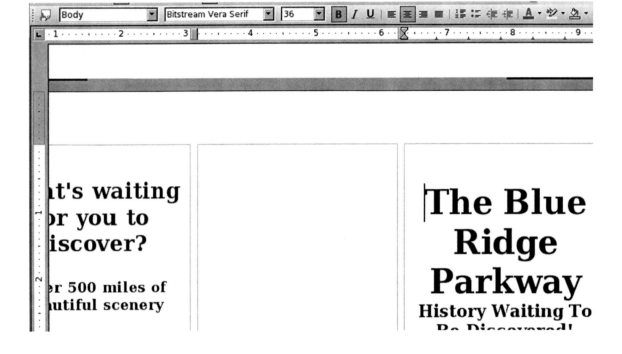

13 Three additional lines needs to be added between the brochure title and the tag line to allow space for the image, as well as to center the image between them. To do so, use your mouse to place the pointer in front of the first word of the tagline (History). When the I-bar appears, click your left mouse button and a cursor will be flashing in front of the text. Press the ENTER or RETURN key three (3) times to place the appropriate number of lines between the title and tag line.

14 In the center of your keyboard, located to the left of the numeric keypad, find the arrow keys and press the key that points up two (2) times. This will position the cursor in the center of the title and tag line.

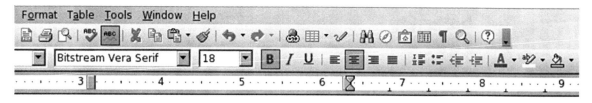

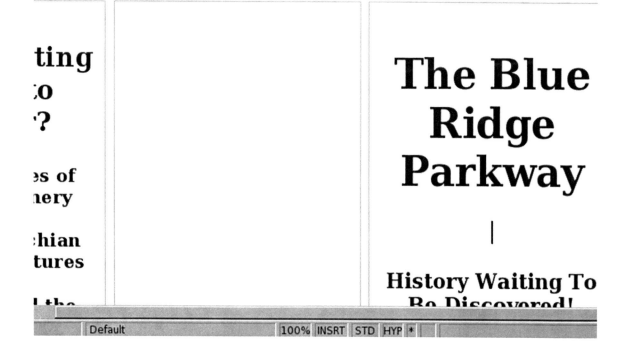

15 Click on the Insert menu, select Picture from the menu options that appear and then select From File within the submenu options that appear. When the Insert Picture window appears, use the navigation buttons located in the upper-right corner of the window to again locate the image files associated with this lesson. Once you have located the images, use your mouse to click on the image file lesson_04_image04.jpg to select it. To insert it within the brochure, click the OPEN button. When completed, the second page of the brochure should look similar to the illustration on the following page.

What's waiting for you to discover?

> Over 500 miles of beautiful scenery

> Early Appalachian pioneer structures

> Museums and the Cherokee Indian Reservation...

> ... and many other historical and natural attractions!

The Blue Ridge Parkway

History Waiting To Be Discovered!

16 Finally, we are going to add a shadow effect to each of the images inserted into the brochure. To add a drop shadow to an image, click once on an image using the left mouse button to select it. Then click on the Format menu and select Picture from the menu options that appear. When the Picture window appears, click the Borders tab and select the Bottom-Right shadow position located in the Shadow Style selection area. Click the OK button, and repeat the process for each image within the brochure. The image formatting will then be complete.

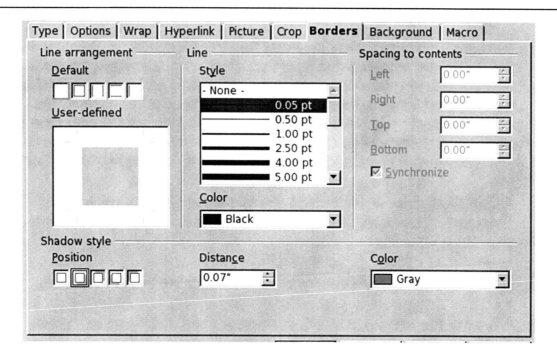

Exporting the Document in the PDF Format

Finally, we are going to save the brochure as a Portable Document Format (PDF) document. The PDF file format is one of the preferred formats among graphic artists and commercial printers. When sending documents to a printer to be mass-produced, like a brochure for example, PDF files retain the original formatting much better when transferred to other computers. Therefore, the formatting you see when you save a file on your computer in PDF format is what a graphic artist or commercial printer sees on their computer. However, when a file is saved in the PDF format, it is saved as read-only and cannot be edited later. Therefore, if you wish to edit a document later, you need to save a copy of the file in another format, such as the OpenDocument (.odt) format.

To save a document as a read-only PDF file, follow these steps:

1 Click on the File menu and choose Export As PDF from the menu options that appear.

2 When the Export As PDF window appears, OpenOffice.org will provide you with some additional options for you to select. Among these options are the page range and image compression quality. If you choose Lossless

Compression, the file will be exported in the highest quality possible but the file size will be larger. Sending large file sizes via email, for example, will result in longer receiving and download times. You also have the option to select JPEG compression to decrease the file size and, therefore, reduce the amount of time it takes to upload and download a file. OpenOffice. org allows you to use the popup menu provided to select the compression quality on a scale from 1% to 100%, with 1% being the lowest quality. After you have selected your additional export options, click the EXPORT button.

3 A window will appear and prompt you to choose a location to save your document. Choose the location you want to save a document to in the Save In popup field.

4 In the field File Name, type the name you would like to save the file as.

5 In the File Format popup menu, make sure Portable Document Format (PDF) is selected. Then click the SAVE button.

Additional Resources

OpenOffice.org Templates: Tri-Fold Brochure
http://documentation.openoffice.org/Samples_Templates/User/template/trifold_brochure.stw

OpenOffice.org Writer Guide: Working with Graphics
http://documentation.openoffice.org/manuals/oooauthors2/0208WG-WorkingWithGraphics.pdf

OpenOffice.org Getting Started Guide: Using Fontwork
http://documentation.openoffice.org/manuals/oooauthors2/0116GS-UsingFontWork.pdf

OpenOffice.org Getting Started Guide: Working with the Gallery
http://documentation.openoffice.org/manuals/oooauthors2/0114GS-WorkingWithTheGallery.pdf

Review Questions

1 Which page orientation would you normally select to create a brochure?

2 What is the name of the format feature that makes pages easier to read by preventing gray shadows from appearing between the lines of text?

3 What menu would you select to create columns within a Writer document?

4 (True or False) The PDF file format is one of the preferred formats among graphic artists and commercial printers.

5 (True or False) You can utilize the arrow keys located in the center of the keyboard to move the cursor within a word processing document.

5

Creating a Household Expense Spreadsheet Using Calc

Lesson Objectives

In this lesson, you will learn the following:

1   How to create a monthly household expense spreadsheet using the OpenOffice.org Calc spreadsheet application.

2   How to insert text and numbers within spreadsheet cells.

3   How to use the SUM function to quickly add values contained within a specified range of cells.

4   Learn how to create charts using data contained within a Calc worksheet.

Overview

The OpenOffice.org office productivity suite contains an easy-to-use, full-featured spreadsheet application called Calc. Calc has all of the fundamental features found in other major spreadsheet applications, plus features unavailable in any other application similar to it. In the next three lessons, we will learn how to use Calc to create both basic and more complex spreadsheet documents.

In this lesson, you will become acquainted with using Calc by creating a basic spreadsheet document for calculating household expenses on a monthly basis. Upon completion of this lesson, you will have learned the basics of entering text and numbers within cells, how to add values contained within a worksheet quickly and easily, how to create a bar graph that visually represents the data present within the Calc spreadsheet document and more.

Getting Started

Before we do so, we need to open the Lesson Five file that is available for use with this book. To open the file, follow these steps:

1   If you have not already downloaded the lesson files for this book, use a web browser to go to **http://documentation.openoffice.org/**

conceptualguide/OpenOfficeOrg3LessonFiles.zip. This will provide a direct link for your browser to begin an automatic download of the lesson files. If a dialog window appears asking where you would like to save the file to be downloaded, select your computer workstation's desktop and begin downloading the file.

2 When the file appears on your computer's desktop, double-click the file icon to unzip its contents and access the files associated with each lesson. Double-click the Lesson Files folder icon that contains the available lesson files, locate the Lesson 05 folder and double-click on it to access the file for this lesson. When you have opened the folder, double-click the file named **lesson_05_start.ods** to open the file.

Renaming the Worksheet

The first thing we are going to do is rename the worksheet we are working in. By default, Calc automatically creates three (3) worksheets when you create a new spreadsheet document. However, you can delete worksheets or add additional worksheets within a Calc spreadsheet document, if desired. These default spreadsheets are automatically named Sheet1, Sheet2 and Sheet3. While this naming scheme may not be a problem when working with basic worksheets, it can cause confusion when working with larger, more complex spreadsheet documents.

To rename the worksheet we will be working with, follow these steps:

1 Select the worksheet that is to be renamed by clicking on the worksheet tab located just above the Status Bar.

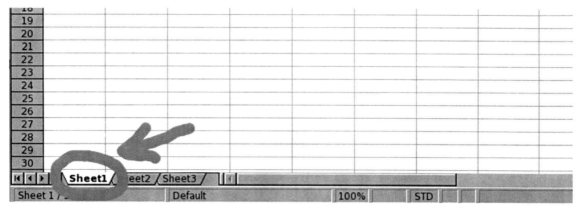

2   Click the Format menu, select Sheet from the menu options that appear and select Rename from the submenu options that appear.

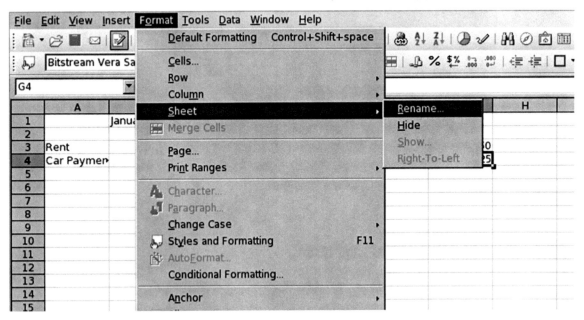

3   When the Rename Sheet window appears, type the name **Budget**. This will become the name of the worksheet.

4   Click the OK to complete the operation.

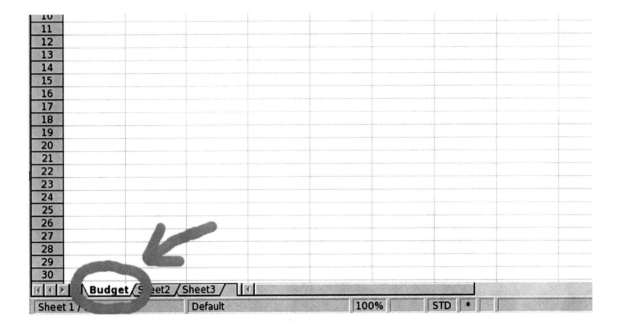

Entering Text and Numbers Within Cells

Spreadsheet document layouts are organized by columns (labeled alphabetically) and rows (labeled numerically). The intersection of a row and column within the spreadsheet creates a cell. Cells are identified by their column and row location within the spreadsheet. For example, cell A1 is located within the spreadsheet where column A intersects with row 1.

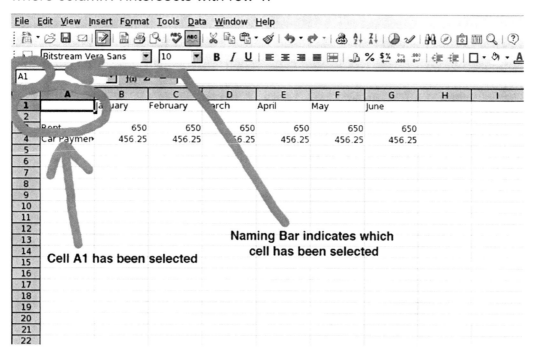

Cell A1 has been selected

Naming Bar indicates which cell has been selected

Before any formatting or calculations are performed within a spreadsheet, often you must first select the cells associated with the operation you are trying to perform. To select an individual cell, simply click on the cell location with the left mouse button. To select multiple cells, hold down the left mouse button while selecting the range of cells.

To enter text and numbers within spreadsheet cells, simply select a cell and begin typing. The text and numbers will appear within the Formula Bar located just above the spreadsheet layout. Press the TAB key on the keyboard to select the cell in the next column, or press the ENTER or RETURN key to select the cell in the next row.

For this lesson, we are creating a spreadsheet that will help keep track of monthly household expenses. Only a couple of expenses have been recorded so far, and only six months are currently entered into the spreadsheet. Therefore, we need to complete the spreadsheet by entering the remaining months and related household expenses. To do so, follow these steps:

1 Select cell H1 within the Budget worksheet. Once the cell has been selected, type *July* for the month that will be entered into the cell. Then press the TAB key on your keyboard.

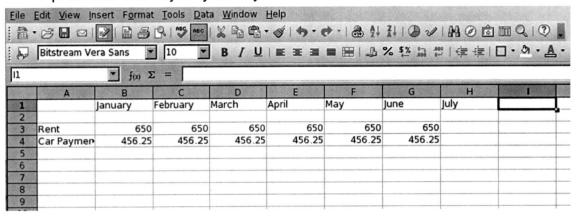

2 When you pressed the TAB key, you noticed that July was entered into cell H1 and Calc automatically proceeded to select cell I1 in the next column. With cell I1 automatically selected for you, type *August* and press the TAB key. Repeat this process for each month of the year. When you have reached the month of December, it should be entered into cell M1. In cell N1, type TOTAL in capital letters. If any of the words appear to get chopped off within the cell, it will be okay, as we will format the text and cells later.

3   Next, select cell A5 within the **Budget** worksheet. Once the cell has been selected, type *Insurance* for the type of expense that will be entered into the cell. Then press the ENTER or RETURN key on your keyboard.

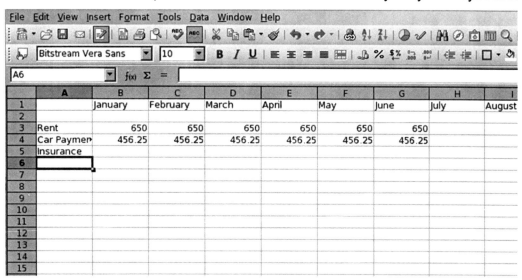

4   When you pressed the ENTER or RETURN key, you noticed that *Insurance* was entered into cell A5 and Calc automatically proceeded to select A6 in the next row. With A6 automatically selected for you, type *Phone* and press the ENTER or RETURN key. Then in cells A7, A8 and A9, type *Electric*, *Cable* and *Food* respectively. In cell A10, type *TOTAL* in capital letters. Again, if any of the words appear to get chopped off within the cell, it will be okay, as we will format the text and cells later.

	A	B	C	D	E	F	G	H	I
1		January	February	March	April	May	June	July	August
2									
3	Rent	650	650	650	650	650	650		
4	Car Paymen	456.25	456.25	456.25	456.25	456.25	456.25		
5	Insurance								
6	Phone								
7	Electric								
8	Cable								
9	Food								
10	TOTAL								
11									
12									
13									
14									
15									
16									

N4		▾	f(x) Σ =											
	A	B	C	D	E	F	G	H	I	J	K	L	M	N
		January	February	March	April	May	June	July	August	September	October	November	December	TOTAL
1														
2														
3	Rent	650	650	650	650	650	650	650	650	650	650	650	650	
4	Car Payme	456.25	456.25	456.25	456.25	456.25	456.25	456.25	456.25	456.25	456.25	456.25	456.25	
5	Insurance													
6	Phone													
7	Electric													
8	Cable													
9	Food													
10	TOTAL													
11														
12														
13														
14														
15														
16														
17														
18														
19														
20														
21														
22														
23														
24														
25														
26														
27														
28														
29														
30														

5   Now that we have created the rows and columns, we now need to provide the worksheet some data to calculate. As you have noticed, the rent and car payment amounts have already been entered for months January through June. Since those amounts will not change for the remainder of the year, enter 650.00 and 456.25 for the remainder of the year. When you enter 650.00, the decimal place will be dropped because the cells are currently formatted that way. We will be changing this format later in the lesson. Be sure not to enter any data within the TOTAL column, as it will be used later to calculate the yearly total for each household expense.

		▾	f(x) Σ =											
A	B	C	D	E	F	G	H	I	J	K	L	M	N
	January	February	March	April	May	June	July	August	September	October	November	December	TOTAL	
t	650	650	650	650	650	650	650	650	650	650	650	650		
Payme	456.25	456.25	456.25	456.25	456.25	456.25	456.25	456.25	456.25	456.25	456.25	456.25		
irance														
ne														
tric														
le														
d														
AL														

6   Next, we need to enter payment amounts for the other expenses. Beginning with cell B5, enter 100.00 for cells B5, C5, D5, E5, F5, G5, H5, I5, J5, K5 and M5 to reflect the amounts paid each month for insurance.

7   For the phone service expenses, enter the following amounts within the respective cells associated with the months the expenses were incurred: 42.25 (cell B6), 48.46 (cell C6), 46.18 (cell D6), 52.75 (cell E6), 45.52 (cell F6), 47.10 (cell G6), 49.19 (cell H6), 56.98 (cell I6), 54.14 (cell J6), 55.10 (cell K6), 58.55 (cell L6) and 60.17 (cell M6).

N6   f(x) Σ =

	A	B	C	D	E	F	G	H	I	J	K	L	M	N
		January	February	March	April	May	June	July	August	September	October	November	December	TOTAL
1														
2														
3	Rent	650	650	650	650	650	650	650	650	650	650	650	650	
4	Car Payme	456.25	456.25	456.25	456.25	456.25	456.25	456.25	456.25	456.25	456.25	456.25	456.25	
5	Insurance	100	100	100	100	100	100	100	100	100	100	100	100	
6	Phone	42.25	48.46	46.18	52.75	45.52	47.1	49.19	56.98	54.14	55.1	58.55	60.17	
7	Electric													
8	Cable													
9	Food													
10	TOTAL													

8   For the electric service expenses, enter the following amounts within the respective cells associated with the months the expenses were incurred: 178.18 (cell B7), 188.72 (cell C7), 165.12 (cell D7), 117.32 (cell E7), 128.98 (cell F7), 145.22 (cell G7), 176.54 (cell H7), 195.47 (cell I7), 168.65 (cell J7), 125.05 (cell K7), 145.34 (cell L7) and 162.27 (cell M7).

9   Beginning in cell B8, enter 48.15 for cells B8, C8, D8, E8, F8, G8, H8, I8, J8, K8 and M8 to reflect the amounts paid each month for cable television service.

	A	B	C	D	E	F	G	H	I	J	K	L	M	N
		January	February	March	April	May	June	July	August	September	October	November	December	TOTAL
1														
3	Rent	650	650	650	650	650	650	650	650	650	650	650	650	
4	Car Payme	456.25	456.25	456.25	456.25	456.25	456.25	456.25	456.25	456.25	456.25	456.25	456.25	
5	Insurance	100	100	100	100	100	100	100	100	100	100	100	100	
6	Phone	42.25	48.46	46.18	52.75	45.52	47.1	49.19	56.98	54.14	55.1	58.55	60.17	
7	Electric	178.18	188.72	165.12	117.32	128.98	145.22	176.54	195.47	168.65	125.05	145.34	162.27	
8	Cable	48.15	48.15	48.15	48.15	48.15	48.15	48.15	48.15	48.15	48.15	48.15	48.15	
9	Food													
10	TOTAL													

10 Lastly, for the food expenses, enter the following amounts within the respective cells associated with the months the expenses were incurred: 225.15 (cell B9), 200.25 (cell C9), 182.56 (cell D9), 176.98 (cell E9), 215.48 (cell F9), 202.33 (cell G9), 199.87 (cell H9), 201.47 (cell I9), 164.77 (cell J9), 214.22 (cell K9), 210.99 (cell L9) and 223.57 (cell M9).

	A	B	C	D	E	F	G	H	I	J	K	L	M	N
		January	February	March	April	May	June	July	August	September	October	November	December	TOTAL
1														
3	Rent	650	650	650	650	650	650	650	650	650	650	650	650	
4	Car Payme	456.25	456.25	456.25	456.25	456.25	456.25	456.25	456.25	456.25	456.25	456.25	456.25	
5	Insurance	100	100	100	100	100	100	100	100	100	100	100	100	
6	Phone	42.25	48.46	46.18	52.75	45.52	47.1	49.19	56.98	54.14	55.1	58.55	60.17	
7	Electric	178.18	188.72	165.12	117.32	128.98	145.22	176.54	195.47	168.65	125.05	145.34	162.27	
8	Cable	48.15	48.15	48.15	48.15	48.15	48.15	48.15	48.15	48.15	48.15	48.15	48.15	
9	Food	225.15	200.25	182.56	176.98	215.48	202.33	199.87	201.47	164.77	214.22	210.99	223.57	
10	TOTAL													

Using SUM to Add Values Within a Worksheet

Now that we have completed entering the text and values needed for the spreadsheet, we are ready to begin totaling up our expenses for each month and expense category. To do this, we will use the SUM function button located in the Function Bar. The SUM function button is similar to the AUTOSUM function button in Microsoft Excel. Using the SUM function button in Calc, you can automatically add the numbers in the cell range you select. The SUM function cannot be used to subtract, multiply or divide values within a selected cell range. To add the expenses to receive a total for each month and category, follow these steps:

1 Using your mouse, select the cell B10.

2 Click the SUM function button located in the Function Bar. When you click the button, Calc automatically suggests a cell range. In this step, Calc automatically selects cell range B3 through B9, which is the cell range we wish to add the expenses of. If Calc had incorrectly chose the cell range you wish to add, you could simply hold down your left mouse button and drag over the desired cell range to make the appropriate selection. Once the desired cell range has been selected, press the ENTER or RETURN key and Calc adds the values within the cell range selected. The results are then produced within the cell originally selected.

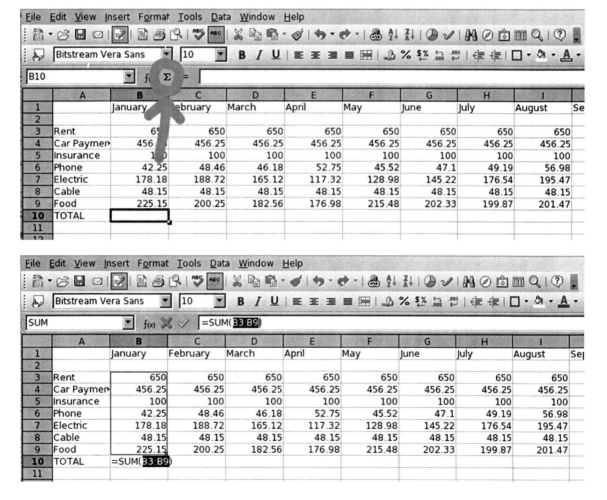

3 Repeat Step #1 by selecting, one at a time, each of the following cells: C10, D10, E10, F10, G10, H10, I10, J10, K10, L10, M10, N3, N4, N5, N6, N7, N8, N9 and N10. After selecting an individual cell, follow the instructions in Step #2 to obtain the results for the appropriate cell range. When you reach cell N3 and click the SUM function button, Calc should automatically select cell range B3 through M3 (represented in the formula as B3:M3). This is the correct cell range to add the total yearly expense for rent. When you have completed adding the cell ranges specified above, the spreadsheet should look like the illustration below.

N11			$f_{(x)}$ Σ =											
	A	B	C	D	E	F	G	H	I	J	K	L	M	N	O
1		January	February	March	April	May	June	July	August	September	October	November	December	TOTAL	
2															
3	Rent	650	650	650	650	650	650	650	650	650	650	650	650	7800	
4	Car Payme	456.25	456.25	456.25	456.25	456.25	456.25	456.25	456.25	456.25	456.25	456.25	456.25	5475	
5	Insurance	100	100	100	100	100	100	100	100	100	100	100	100	1200	
6	Phone	42.25	48.46	46.18	52.75	45.52	47.1	49.19	56.98	54.14	55.1	58.55	60.17	616.39	
7	Electric	178.18	188.72	165.12	117.32	128.98	145.22	176.54	195.47	168.65	125.05	145.34	162.27	1896.86	
8	Cable	48.15	48.15	48.15	48.15	48.15	48.15	48.15	48.15	48.15	48.15	48.15	48.15	577.8	
9	Food	225.15	200.25	182.56	176.98	215.48	202.33	199.87	201.47	164.77	214.22	210.99	223.57	2417.64	
10	TOTAL	1699.98	1691.83	1648.26	1601.45	1644.38	1649.05	1680	1708.32	1641.96	1648.77	1669.28	1700.41	19983.69	

Formatting Text and Numbers Within Cells

As we have been adding the expenses for each month and category, you have noticed that not all of the values are formatted the same. For instance, all of the figures represented in this household expense worksheet are dollar amounts. When we typically write a dollar amount on paper, we write it with a dollar sign in front of the value, and cents are represented two decimal places behind the dollar amount. Currently, however, the amounts represented for the rent do not contain the cents amount. Nor do any of the values within the spreadsheet have the dollar sign placed in front of them.

In the following steps, we will format the cells so that the values contained within are represented in U.S. dollar amounts. We will also adjust the width of the cells within the spreadsheet so that characters and values within the cells are not chopped off. To perform these formatting changes, follow these steps:

1 Beginning on cell B3, hold down your left mouse button and drag over all of the numeric values contained within the worksheet to select them for editing.

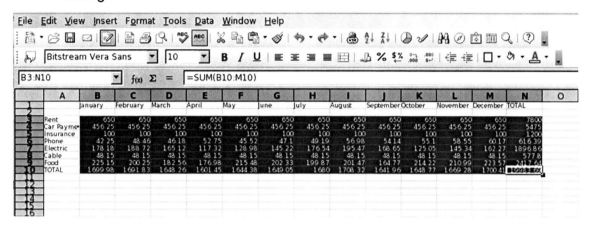

2 Click on the Format menu and select Cells from the menu options that appear.

3 When the Format Cells window appears, click on the Numbers tab located at the top of the window.

4 In the Category selection area, select Currency.

5 Once a category has been selected, select a format type located within the Format selection area. By default, Calc will choose -$1,234.00. The minus (-) sign represented in front of the dollar amount represents a negative amount, as is a standard format spreadsheet applications use if a dollar amounts happens to be negative. This format type is acceptable, and should be selected if it isn't already.

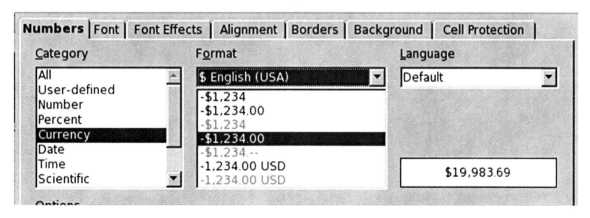

6   Click the OK button to complete the operation.

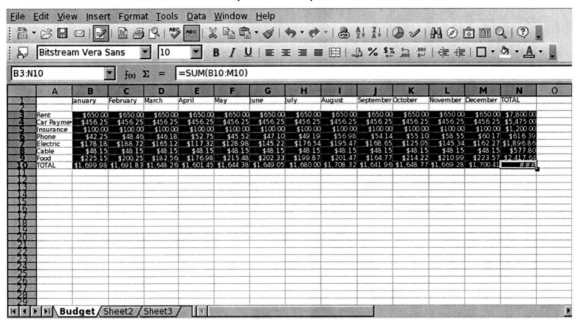

7   If you look carefully at cell N10, you will notice that the dollar value has disappeared and has been replaced by pound signs (###). This is because the cell isn't wide enough to display all of the characters of the value that is currently there. Therefore, we need to adjust the column width for the worksheet. To do so, go to the Edit menu and choose Select All from the menu options that appear. This will select all of the cells within the worksheet.

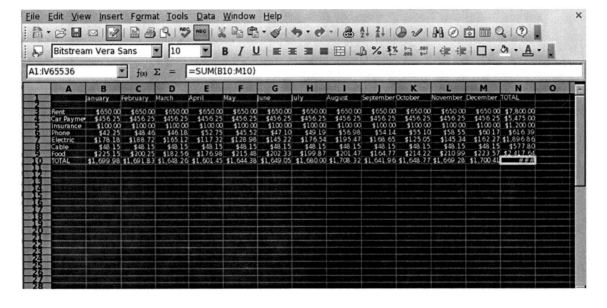

8 Click on the Format menu, select Columns from the menu options that appear and select Optimal Width from the submenu options that appear.

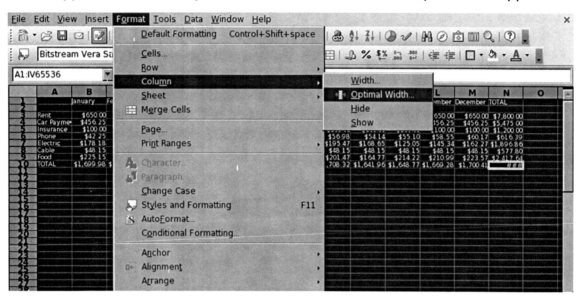

9 When the Optimal Column Width window appears, it automatically detects that an additional 0.1" needs to be added to the width of each column. Click the OK button to complete the operation. When the column width has been adjusted, all of the characters and values within the worksheet should appear correctly, including cell N10. Click on any cell within the spreadsheet to deselect the cells.

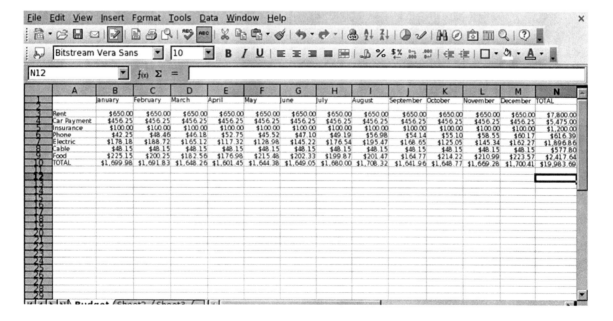

Adding a Bar Graph Within a Spreadsheet

To create a bar graph within a Calc spreadsheet document, follow these steps:

1 Using your mouse, select the column range N3 through N9. After selecting the column range, hold down the CONTROL (CTRL) key on your keyboard and select the column range A3 through A9. By selecting column range A3 through A9, the bar graph, when completed, will contain a legend that will properly label each bar with the associated expense amount.

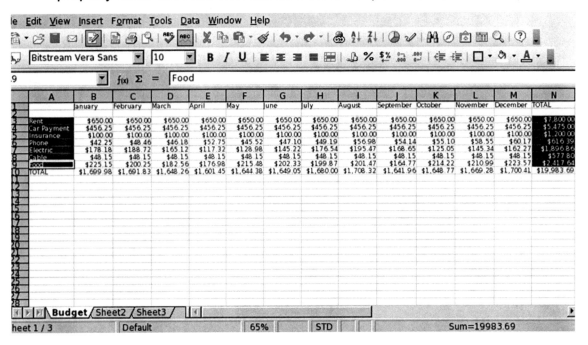

2 Go to the Insert menu and select Chart from the menu options that appear.

3 When the AutoFormat Chart window appears, the selection made in Step #1 should appear in the range field. If the selection is correct, make sure the checkbox 'First Column as label" is selected. Then click the NEXT button at the bottom of the window. If the selection is not correct, click the Shrink button located next to the range field to enter back into the worksheet and select the appropriate cells containing the data to appear within the chart.

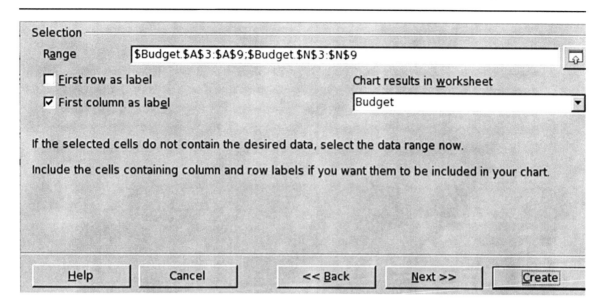

4   In the next window to appear, select the appropriate Chart Type. Use the
scroll bar located on the right side of the window to view all of the available
selections, including the bar graph. Also select the Rows from the Data
Series radio button located below the Chart Type selections, and click the
checkbox Show Text Elements In Preview to view how the chart will be
labeled. The click the NEXT button.

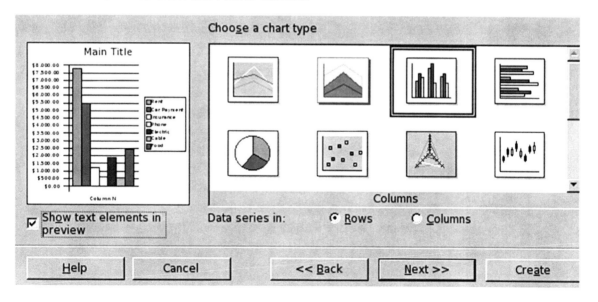

5   The next window will allow you to choose from a selection of variant chart
formats for the bar graph. For this lesson, select the first variant displayed
(if it isn't already selected) and click the NEXT button.

6 In the Display selection area that appears in the next window, type *Household Expenses* as the chart title within the text field provided. Make sure the checkboxes are selected for both the Chart Title and Legend. Select the checkboxes for both the X Axis and Y Axis titles. In the text fields provided, type *Expenses* for the X Axis and *Amount ($)* for the Y Axis. Make sure the radio button for formatting the data series in rows is selected.

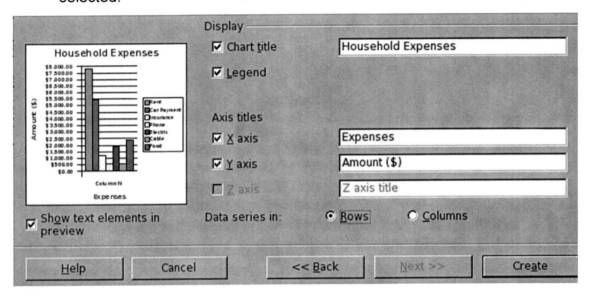

7 Click the CREATE button to complete the operation. The completed chart should appear within the worksheet. Once the chart appears within the spreadsheet, click any cell to deselect the cells that were used to create the chart. Then you can move the chart to another location within the worksheet by placing your pointer in the middle of the chart, hold down your left mouse button and drag it to the desired location. You may also enlarge or reduce the size of the chart by placing your pointer on top of one of the green boxes on the corners of the chart, hold down your mouse button and drag the corner of the box until the chart reaches the desired size.

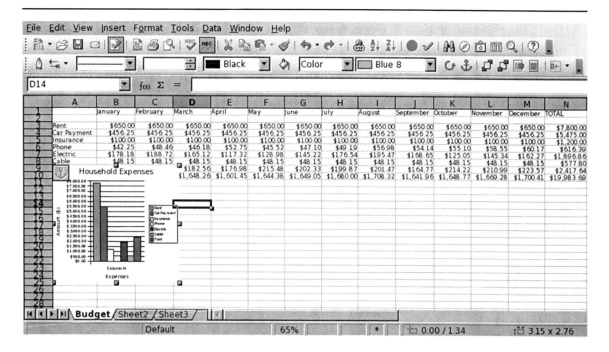

Saving a Spreadsheet Document

Now that the spreadsheet has been completed, the document file needs to be saved like any other spreadsheet document. OpenOffice.org supports over 20 file formats for opening and saving spreadsheet documents, including Microsoft Excel. To save the document to your computer's hard drive or removable disk, follow these steps:

1   Click on the File menu and choose Save As from the menu options that appear.

2   A window will appear and prompt you to choose a location to save your document. Choose the location you want to save a document to in the Save In popup field.

3   In the field File Name, type the name you would like to save the file as.

4   In the Save As Type popup menu, select the file format you wish to save the document as, including the OpenDocument Spreadsheet (.ods) or Microsoft Excel (.xls) file format.

5 Click the button SAVE to complete the operation.

(NOTE: If you are given a window prompt that warns you about saving the document as a Microsoft Excel file, click the YES button. The OpenOffice.org development team has gone to great lengths to help ensure that your document saved in the Excel format will open properly with Microsoft Excel. However, because the programming code utilized to create the Excel file format is proprietary and not available to the OpenOffice.org team to view for ensuring full compatibility with Microsoft Excel, not all of your document's formatting may open up 100% correctly when it is opened using the Microsoft Excel application.)

Printing a Calc Spreadsheet Document

Printing a Calc spreadsheet document is very similar to printing a Writer word processing document. However, because spreadsheets can be very long in width, often you will need to customize the orientation and scaling print configuration options before sending the document to the printer. To print a spreadsheet document within OpenOffice.org Calc, follow these steps:

1 With the file open within OpenOffice.org, click on the File menu and select Print from the menu options that appear. You may also hold down the Control (CTRL) key and press P on the keyboard to prompt for the Print window.

2 If you have more than one printer that your computer can send print jobs to, select the printer you wish to send the document to in the Printer selection area.

3 In the Print Range selection area, use the radio buttons to select which pages you wish to print. If you choose the Pages option, enter the page range you wish to print (example: 1-5 will print pages one through 5; 1,2,5 will print pages one, two and five). If you choose the Selection option, OpenOffice.org will only print the text you have selected (highlighted) within your document.

4 In the Copies selection area, enter the number of copies you wish to print of the document.

5 If you wish to customize the print job, click on the OPTIONS button and select or deselect the print options you wish to choose. If you do not want to customize any print settings, skip to Step #6.

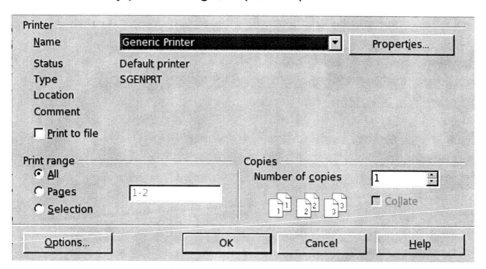

6 When printing spreadsheets, you will often need to change the page orientation to Landscape and scale the page to less that 100% so that all of the columns that contain data on a worksheet will be printed on the same sheet of paper. You may also want to consider printing the worksheets on 8.5" x 14" US Legal size paper if there are many columns containing data within the worksheet. To configure the options, click on the PROPERTIES button within the print window and configure the appropriate selections using the popup menus provided.

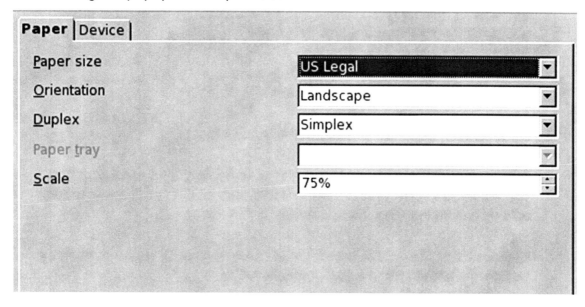

7 Once you have completed specifying your print settings, click the OK button to begin printing.

Additional Resources

OpenOffice.org: Getting Started with Calc
http://documentation.openoffice.org/manuals/oooauthors2/0107GS-GettingStartedWithCalc.pdf

OpenOffice.org: Entering, Editing and Formatting Data
http://documentation.openoffice.org/manuals/oooauthors2/0302CG-EnterEditFormatData.pdf

OpenOffice.org: Creating Charts and Graphs
http://documentation.openoffice.org/manuals/oooauthors2/0304CG-CreatingChartsAndGraphs.pdf

Janice Holm Lloyd – N.C. Cooperative Extension Service: Budgeting for Home Ownership
http://www.ces.ncsu.edu/depts/fcs/housing/pubs/fcs432.pdf

Review Questions

1 By default, how many worksheets does a Calc spreadsheet document contain when you create a new document?

2 Columns are labeled _____ while rows are labeled _____ within the layout of a spreadsheet document.

3 What do the pound signs (###) within a cell indicate?

4 (True or False) Because spreadsheets can be very long in width, often you will need to customize the orientation and scaling print configuration options before sending the document to the printer.

5 (True or False) The SUM function can be used to add, subtract, multiply and divide values within a selected cell range.

LESSON

6

Creating a Balance Sheet Using Calc

Lesson Objectives

In this lesson, you will learn the following:

1   How to create a balance sheet and why they are important for monitoring the financial status of an individual or business.

2   How to resize cells using the mouse pointer.

3   How to add worksheets to a spreadsheet document.

4   How to add values among worksheets.

5   How to use the SUM function to add values among multiple cells throughout a worksheet.

Overview

In the last lesson, we learned how to use Calc to create a basic spreadsheet for calculating monthly household expenses. Using Calc can help keep track of where money is being spent each month and where money could be saved or expenditures eliminated. However, Calc has the ability to create even more complex spreadsheet documents, including calculating financial data for business plans, creating business reports and more.

In this lesson, you will become acquainted with features within Calc to create a balance sheet. Upon completion of this lesson, you will have learned to fundamentals of creating more complex formulas. This includes creating formulas manually to calculate values listed throughout a worksheet, and even among multiple worksheets. Ending the lesson will include instruction regarding how to understand and analyze the data contained within a balance sheet.

Getting Started

Before we do so, we need to open the Lesson Six file that is available for use with this book. To open the file, follow these steps:

1   If you have not already downloaded the lesson files for this book, use a web browser to go to **http://documentation.openoffice.org/ conceptualguide/OpenOfficeOrg3LessonFiles.zip**. This will provide a direct link for your browser to begin an automatic download of the lesson files. If a dialog window appears asking where you would like to save the file to be downloaded, select your computer workstation's desktop and begin downloading the file.

2   When the file appears on your computer's desktop, double-click the file icon to unzip its contents and access the files associated with each lesson. Double-click the Lesson Files folder icon that contains the available lesson files, locate the Lesson 06 folder and double-click on it to access the file for this lesson. When you have opened the folder, double-click the file named **lesson_06_start.ods** to open the file.

Entering Text and Numbers Within Cells

The first thing we need to for this lesson is to enter the remaining text and values needed to complete the personal balance sheet. If you are unfamiliar with selecting cells within a Calc spreadsheet document, you will need to refer to the section in Lesson 6 titled "Entering Text and Numbers Within Cells". You may also refer to the sections 'Selecting a Cell" and "Entering Text and Numbers" located within Appendix B.

To enter the remaining text and numbers needed to complete the personal balance sheet in this lesson, follow these steps:

1   With the lesson file lesson_06_start.ods open, select the personal balance sheet by clicking on the worksheet tab labeled **Personal** located above the status bar.

2   Select cell B8. Once the cell has been selected, type **_Furniture_** for the type of current asset that will be entered into the cell. Then press the ENTER or RETURN key on your keyboard.

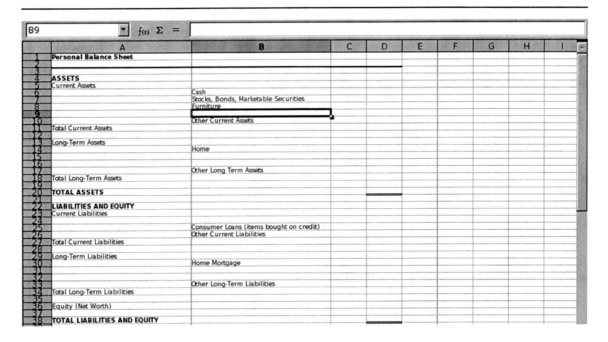

3 When you pressed the ENTER or RETURN key, you noticed that Furniture was entered into cell B8 and Calc automatically proceeded to select B9 in the next row. With B9 automatically selected for you, type *Jewelry* and press the ENTER or RETURN key. Then in cells B15, B16, B24, B31 and B32, type *Rental Property*, *Automobiles*, *Credit Card Balances*, *Rental Property Loan and Automobile Loan Balance* respectively.

4 Now that we have created the column that describes each type of asset or liability contained within the personal balance sheet, we now need to provide the worksheet some data to calculate. Enter the following amounts within the respective cells associated with the type of asset or liability: 300.00 (cell D6), 5000.00 (cell D7), 2500.00 (cell D8), 750.00 (cell D9), 550.00 (cell D10), 211000.00 (cell D14), 125000.00 (cell D15), 12000.00 (cell D16), 10000.00 (cell D17), 4200.00 (cell D24), 5000.00 (cell D25), 1500.00 (cell D26), 205000.00 (cell D30), 118000.00 (cell D31), 15000.00 (cell D32) and 15000.00 (cell D33).

D34		f{x} Σ =						
	A	B	C	D	E	F	G	H
1	Personal Balance Sheet							
2								
3								
4	ASSETS							
5	Current Assets							
6		Cash		300				
7		Stocks, Bonds, Marketable Securities		5000				
8		Furniture		2500				
9		Jewelry		750				
10		Other Current Assets		550				
11	Total Current Assets							
12								
13	Long-Term Assets							
14		Home		211000				
15		Rental Property		125000				
16		Automobiles		12000				
17		Other Long Term Assets		10000				
18	Total Long-Term Assets							
19								
20	TOTAL ASSETS							
21								
22	LIABILITIES AND EQUITY							
23	Current Liabilities							
24		Credit Card Balances		4200				
25		Consumer Loans (items bought on credit)		5000				
26		Other Current Liabilities		1500				
27	Total Current Liabilities							
28								
29	Long-Term Liabilities							
30		Home Mortgage		205000				
31		Rental Property Loan		118000				
32		Automobile Loan Balance		15000				
33		Other Long-Term Liabilities		15000				
34	Total Long-Term Liabilities							
36	Equity (Net Worth)							
38	TOTAL LIABILITIES AND EQUITY							
40								

Formatting Cells

As we have been entering the dollar amounts for the assets and liabilities, you have noticed that the values are not formatted properly. For instance, all of the figures represented in this personal balance sheet are dollar amounts. When we typically write a dollar amount on paper, we write it with a dollar sign in front of the value, and cents are represented two decimal places behind the dollar amount. Currently, however, the amounts represented do not contain the cents amount. Nor do any of the values within the spreadsheet have the dollar sign placed in front of them.

In the following steps, we will format the cells so that the values contained within are represented in U.S. dollar amounts. We will also format some of the cells so that they contain lines that signify where a subtotal is present for a specific asset or liability. This is often done to help in identifying the subtotals within a balance sheet. To perform these formatting changes, follow these steps:

1   Using your left mouse button, click on column label D located at the top of the worksheet. Doing so will select the entire column, but will leave all remaining columns within the worksheet unselected.

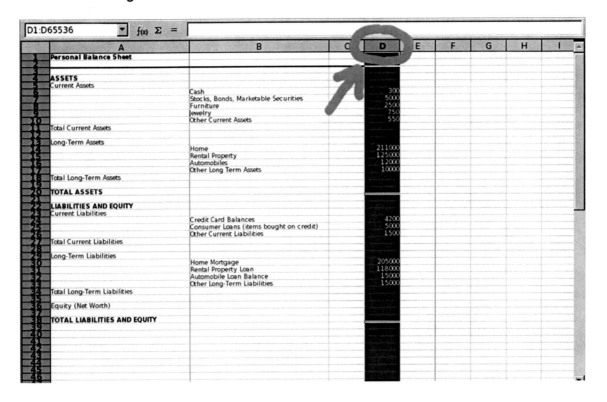

2   Click on the Format menu and select Cells from the menu options that appear.

3   When the Format Cells window appears, click on the Numbers tab located at the top of the window.

4   In the Category selection area, select Currency.

5   Once a category has been selected, select a format type located within the Format selection area. By default, Calc will choose -$1,234.00. The minus

(-) sign represented in front of the dollar amount represents a negative amount, as is a standard format spreadsheet applications use if a dollar amounts happens to be negative. This format type is acceptable, and should be selected if it isn't already.

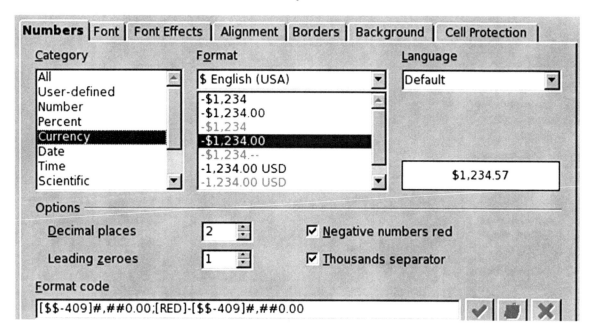

6   Click the OK button to complete the operation.

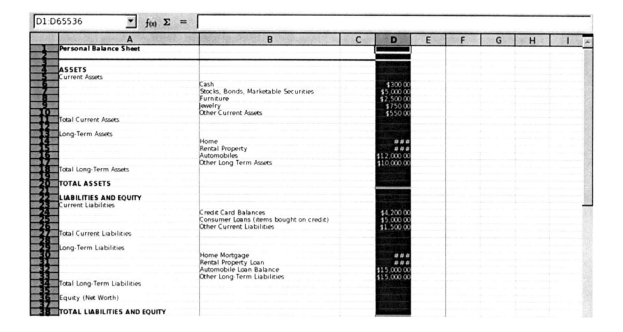

7 Next, we are going to format some of the cells so that they contain lines that signify where a subtotal is present for a specific asset or liability. To do so, select cell D10.

D33	▼	f(x) Σ =	15000						
A		B	C	D	E	F	G	H	I
Personal Balance Sheet									
ASSETS									
Current Assets									
		Cash		$300.00					
		Stocks, Bonds, Marketable Securities		$5,000.00					
		Furniture		$2,500.00					
		Jewelry		$750.00					
		Other Current Assets		$550.00					
Total Current Assets									
Long-Term Assets									
		Home		###					
		Rental Property		###					
		Automobiles		$12,000.00					
		Other Long Term Assets		$10,000.00					
Total Long-Term Assets									
TOTAL ASSETS									
LIABILITIES AND EQUITY									
Current Liabilities									
		Credit Card Balances		$4,200.00					
		Consumer Loans (items bought on credit)		$5,000.00					
		Other Current Liabilities		$1,500.00					
Total Current Liabilities									
Long-Term Liabilities									
		Home Mortgage		###					
		Rental Property Loan		###					
		Automobile Loan Balance		$15,000.00					
		Other Long-Term Liabilities		$15,000.00					
Total Long-Term Liabilities									
Equity (Net Worth)									
TOTAL LIABILITIES AND EQUITY									

8 Click on the Format menu and select Cells from the menu options that appear.

9 When the Format Cells window appears, click on the Borders tab located at the top of the window.

10 In the Line Arrangement selection area, select the border arrangement by clicking on the second default arrangements provided. Customize the border arrangement by double-clicking with your left mouse button on the top, left and right borders until they are deleted using the User-Defined configuration area provided.

11 In the Line selection area, select the 1.00pt border thickness using the Styles selections and choose the Black border color using the Color popup menu.

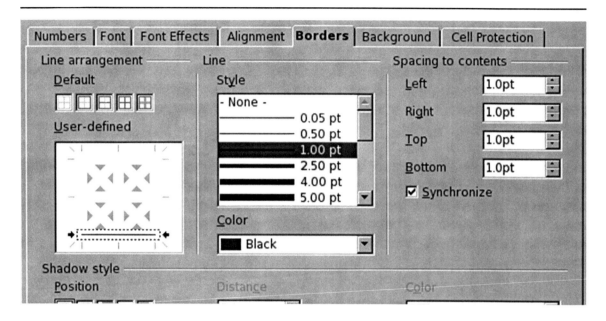

12 In the Spacing To Contents area, select the appropriate border spacing for each side of the selected cells (optional).

13 Once all formatting selections have been made, click the OK button to complete the operation.

14 Repeat steps #7 through #13 for cells D17, D26 and D33. After doing so, cell formatting for the personal balance sheet will be complete.

	A	B	C	D	E	F	G	H	I
1	Personal Balance Sheet								
2									
3									
4	ASSETS								
5	Current Assets								
6		Cash		$300.00					
7		Stocks, Bonds, Marketable Securities		$5,000.00					
8		Furniture		$2,500.00					
9		Jewelry		$750.00					
10		Other Current Assets		$550.00					
11	Total Current Assets								
12									
13	Long-Term Assets								
14		Home		###					
15		Rental Property		###					
16		Automobiles		$12,000.00					
17		Other Long Term Assets		$10,000.00					
18	Total Long-Term Assets								
19									
20	TOTAL ASSETS								
21									
22	LIABILITIES AND EQUITY								
23	Current Liabilities								
24		Credit Card Balances		$4,200.00					
25		Consumer Loans (items bought on credit)		$5,000.00					
26		Other Current Liabilities		$1,500.00					
27	Total Current Liabilities								
28									
29	Long-Term Liabilities								
30		Home Mortgage		###					
31		Rental Property Loan		###					
32		Automobile Loan Balance		$15,000.00					
33		Other Long-Term Liabilities		$15,000.00					
34	Total Long-Term Liabilities								
35									

Resizing Cells Using the Mouse Pointer

If you look carefully at cells D14, D15, D30 and D31, you will notice that the dollar value has disappeared and has been replaced by pound signs (###). This is because the cell isn't wide enough to display all of the characters of the value that is currently there.

In Lesson 5, you may recall that we utilized the Format menu to increase the width of the columns so that text and numeric values would display properly. Not only can you utilize the Format menu to adjust the width of columns and the height of rows, but you can also use your mouse pointer within the column and row label area within a worksheet to make adjustments as well. To do so, follow these steps:

1 Place your mouse pointer at the top of the worksheet within the column label area along the border between two columns. In this example, place your mouse pointer within the column label area where column D and E border each other.

2 When you place your mouse pointer where column D and E border each other, your mouse pointer transforms into a line with two arrows pointing left and right. When it does, hold down the left mouse button and drag it to the right to increase the width of the column. If the width of the column had needed to be decreased, you would have dragged the mouse to the left. When the column has been adjusted to the desired width, release the left mouse button.

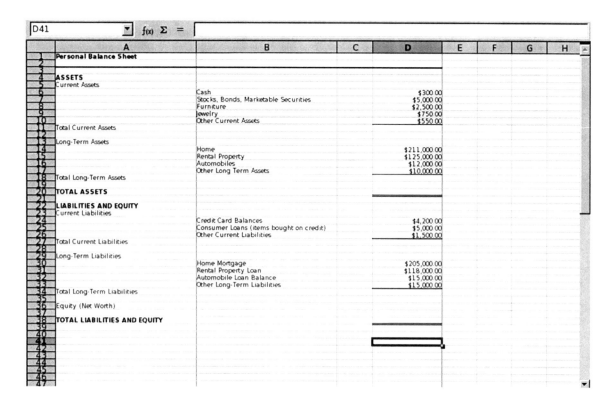

3 To perform a similar task to adjust the height of a row, place the mouse pointer in the row area on the left side of the worksheet and perform a similar operation by dragging the mouse up or down.

Creating Formulas Using the SUM Function

Now that our personal balance sheet has been formatted and values provided for the various asset and liability entries, we are now ready to use the SUM function to enable the worksheet to automatically calculate the values for us. To do so, follow these steps:

1 Using your mouse, select cell D11.

2 Click the SUM function button located in the Function Bar. When you click the button, Calc automatically suggests a cell range. In this step, Calc automatically selects cell range D6 through D10, which is the cell range we wish to calculate the total current assets. If Calc had incorrectly chose the cell range you wish to add, you could simply hold down your left mouse button and drag over the desired cell range to make the appropriate selection. Once the desired cell range has been selected, press the ENTER or RETURN key and Calc adds the values within the cell range selected. The results are then produced within cell D11.

D11		fx Σ =							
	A		B	C	D	E	F	G	H
1	Personal Balance Sheet								
2									
3									
4	ASSETS								
5	Current Assets								
6			Cash		$300.00				
7			Stocks, Bonds, Marketable Securities		$5,000.00				
8			Furniture		$2,500.00				
9			Jewelry		$750.00				
10			Other Current Assets		$550.00				
11	Total Current Assets								
12									
13	Long-Term Assets								
14			Home		$211,000.00				
15			Rental Property		$125,000.00				
16			Automobiles		$12,000.00				
17			Other Long Term Assets		$10,000.00				
18	Total Long-Term Assets								
19									
20	TOTAL ASSETS								
21									
22	LIABILITIES AND EQUITY								
23	Current Liabilities								
24			Credit Card Balances		$4,200.00				
25			Consumer Loans (items bought on credit)		$5,000.00				
26			Other Current Liabilities		$1,500.00				
27	Total Current Liabilities								

SUM		fx ✕ ✓	=SUM(D6:D10)						
	A		B	C	D	E	F	G	H
1	Personal Balance Sheet								
2									
3									
4	ASSETS								
5	Current Assets								
6			Cash		$300.00				
7			Stocks, Bonds, Marketable Securities		$5,000.00				
8			Furniture		$2,500.00				
9			Jewelry		$750.00				
10			Other Current Assets		$550.00				
11	Total Current Assets				=SUM(D6:D10)				
12									
13	Long-Term Assets								
14			Home		$211,000.00				
15			Rental Property		$125,000.00				
16			Automobiles		$12,000.00				
17			Other Long Term Assets		$10,000.00				
18	Total Long-Term Assets								
19									
20	TOTAL ASSETS								
21									
22	LIABILITIES AND EQUITY								
23	Current Liabilities								
24			Credit Card Balances		$4,200.00				
25			Consumer Loans (items bought on credit)		$5,000.00				
26			Other Current Liabilities		$1,500.00				
27	Total Current Liabilities								

3 Select cell D18. Then click the SUM function button located in the Function Bar. When doing so, cells D14 through D17 should be selected, which is the cell range we wish to select to calculate the total long-term assets.

Press the ENTER or RETURN key and Calc adds the values within the cell range selected. The results are then produced within cell D18.

SUM	▼	ƒ(x) ✕ ✓	=SUM(D14:D17)						
	A	B	C	D	E	F	G	H
1	Personal Balance Sheet							
2								
3								
4	ASSETS							
5	Current Assets							
6		Cash		$300.00				
7		Stocks, Bonds, Marketable Securities		$5,000.00				
8		Furniture		$2,500.00				
9		Jewelry		$750.00				
10		Other Current Assets		$550.00				
11	Total Current Assets			$9,100.00				
12								
13	Long-Term Assets							
14		Home		$211,000.00				
15		Rental Property		$125,000.00				
16		Automobiles		$12,000.00				
17		Other Long Term Assets		$10,000.00				
18	Total Long-Term Assets			=SUM(D14:D17)				
19								
20	TOTAL ASSETS							
21								
22	LIABILITIES AND EQUITY							
23	Current Liabilities							
24		Credit Card Balances		$4,200.00				
25		Consumer Loans (items bought on credit)		$5,000.00				
26		Other Current Liabilities		$1,500.00				
27	Total Current Liabilities							
28								
29	Long-Term Liabilities							
30		Home Mortgage		$205,000.00				
31		Rental Property Loan		$118,000.00				
32		Automobile Loan Balance		$15,000.00				
33		Other Long-Term Liabilities		$15,000.00				
34	Total Long-Term Liabilities							
35								

4 Next, we need to calculate the total assets that are presented within the personal balance sheet. We do so by adding together the total current assets and total long term assets. Because the cells we need to add are not adjacent to one another within the worksheet, we will need to create the formula manually to obtain the correct result. To do so, select cell D20. Then proceed with Step #5.

5 After selecting cell D20, type **=sum** followed by a beginning parenthesis. To type a beginning parenthesis, hold down the SHIFT key and press nine (9) within the main keyboard area (not within the numeric keypad area). After doing so, use your left mouse button to click cell D11. When doing so, the cell is entered into the formula. Then type the plus "+" sign, and then use the left mouse button to click cell D18 to enter the cell into the formula. End the formula by typing an ending parenthesis. To type an ending parenthesis, hold down the SHIFT key and press zero (0) within the main keyboard area (not within the numeric keypad area). When completed, the formula should read:

=sum(D11+D18)

Press the ENTER or RETURN key. The values contained within cells D11 and D18 will be added, and the result will be produced within cell D20.

| | SUM | | ▼ | f(x) ✕ ✓ | =sum(D11+D18) | | | | | |

	A	B	C	D	E	F	G	H
1	Personal Balance Sheet							
2								
3								
4	ASSETS							
5	Current Assets							
6		Cash		$300.00				
7		Stocks, Bonds, Marketable Securities		$5,000.00				
8		Furniture		$2,500.00				
9		Jewelry		$750.00				
10		Other Current Assets		$550.00				
11	Total Current Assets			$9,100.00				
12								
13	Long-Term Assets							
14		Home		$211,000.00				
15		Rental Property		$125,000.00				
16		Automobiles		$12,000.00				
17		Other Long Term Assets		$10,000.00				
18	Total Long-Term Assets			$358,000.00				
19								
20	TOTAL ASSETS			=sum(D11+D18)				
21								
22	LIABILITIES AND EQUITY							
23	Current Liabilities							
24		Credit Card Balances		$4,200.00				
25		Consumer Loans (items bought on credit)		$5,000.00				
26		Other Current Liabilities		$1,500.00				
27	Total Current Liabilities							
28								
29	Long-Term Liabilities							
30		Home Mortgage		$205,000.00				
31		Rental Property Loan		$118,000.00				
32		Automobile Loan Balance		$15,000.00				
33		Other Long-Term Liabilities		$15,000.00				
34	Total Long-Term Liabilities							
35								
36	Equity (Net Worth)							
37								
38	TOTAL LIABILITIES AND EQUITY							
39								
40								

6 Select cell D27. Then click the SUM function button located in the Function Bar. When doing so, cells D24 through D26 should be selected, which is the cell range we wish to select to calculate the total current liabilities. Press the ENTER or RETURN key and Calc adds the values within the cell range selected. The results are then produced within cell D27.

| | SUM | | ▼ | f(x) ✕ ✓ | =SUM(D24:D26) | | | | | |

	A	B	C	D	E	F	G	H
1	Personal Balance Sheet							
2								
3								
4	ASSETS							
5	Current Assets							
6		Cash		$300.00				
7		Stocks, Bonds, Marketable Securities		$5,000.00				
8		Furniture		$2,500.00				
9		Jewelry		$750.00				
10		Other Current Assets		$550.00				
11	Total Current Assets			$9,100.00				
12								
13	Long-Term Assets							
14		Home		$211,000.00				
15		Rental Property		$125,000.00				
16		Automobiles		$12,000.00				
17		Other Long Term Assets		$10,000.00				
18	Total Long-Term Assets			$358,000.00				
19								
20	TOTAL ASSETS			$367,100.00				
21								
22	LIABILITIES AND EQUITY							
23	Current Liabilities							
24		Credit Card Balances		$4,200.00				
25		Consumer Loans (items bought on credit)		$5,000.00				
26		Other Current Liabilities		$1,500.00				
27	Total Current Liabilities			=SUM(D24:D26)				
28								
29	Long-Term Liabilities							
30		Home Mortgage		$205,000.00				
31		Rental Property Loan		$118,000.00				
32		Automobile Loan Balance		$15,000.00				
33		Other Long-Term Liabilities		$15,000.00				
34	Total Long-Term Liabilities							
35								
36	Equity (Net Worth)							
37								
38	TOTAL LIABILITIES AND EQUITY							
39								
40								

7 Select cell D34. Then click the SUM function button located in the Function Bar. When doing so, cells D30 through D33 should be selected, which is the cell range we wish to select to calculate the total long-term liabilities. Press the ENTER or RETURN key and Calc adds the values within the cell range selected. The results are then produced within cell D34.

	A	B	C	D	E	F	G	H
SUM				=SUM(D30:D33)				
1	Personal Balance Sheet							
2								
3								
4	ASSETS							
5	Current Assets							
6		Cash		$300.00				
7		Stocks, Bonds, Marketable Securities		$5,000.00				
8		Furniture		$2,500.00				
9		Jewelry		$750.00				
10		Other Current Assets		$550.00				
11	Total Current Assets			$9,100.00				
12								
13	Long-Term Assets							
14		Home		$211,000.00				
15		Rental Property		$125,000.00				
16		Automobiles		$12,000.00				
17		Other Long Term Assets		$10,000.00				
18	Total Long-Term Assets			$358,000.00				
19								
20	TOTAL ASSETS			$367,100.00				
21								
22	LIABILITIES AND EQUITY							
23	Current Liabilities							
24		Credit Card Balances		$4,200.00				
25		Consumer Loans (items bought on credit)		$5,000.00				
26		Other Current Liabilities		$1,500.00				
27	Total Current Liabilities			$10,700.00				
28								
29	Long-Term Liabilities							
30		Home Mortgage		$205,000.00				
31		Rental Property Loan		$118,000.00				
32		Automobile Loan Balance		$15,000.00				
33		Other Long-Term Liabilities		$15,000.00				
34	Total Long-Term Liabilities			=SUM(D30:D33)				
35								
36	Equity (Net Worth)							
37								
38	TOTAL LIABILITIES AND EQUITY							
39								
40								
41								
42								

8 Next, we need to calculate the total equity, often referred to as an individuals net worth within a personal balance sheet. We do so by subtracting the total assets from the total of current and long-term liabilities. Again, because the cells we need to add are not adjacent to one another within the worksheet, we will need to create the formula manually to obtain the correct result. To do so, select cell D36. Then proceed with Step #9.

9 After selecting cell D36, type = followed by a beginning parenthesis. Because we will be subtracting some values within the formula, we cannot use the SUM function and obtain the correct value. To type a beginning parenthesis, hold down the SHIFT key and press nine (9) within the main keyboard area (not within the numeric keypad area). After doing so, use your left mouse button to click cell D20. When doing so, the cell is entered into the formula. Then type the minus "-" sign, followed by another beginning parenthesis. Use the left mouse button to click cell D27 to enter the cell into the formula. Type the plus "+" sign, then use the left mouse button to click cell D34. End the formula by typing two ending parentheses. To type the ending parentheses, hold down the SHIFT key and press the zero (0) key twice within the main keyboard area (not within the numeric keypad area). When completed, the formula should read:

$$=(D20-(D27+D34))$$

Press the ENTER or RETURN key. The values contained within the formula will be calculated, and the result will be produced within cell D36. Like when calculating the result using standard arithmetic, Calc adds the values D27 and D34 first, then subtracts the total value from the value contained within cell D20.

| | SUM | ▼ | fx ✕ ✓ | =(D20-(D27+D34)) | | | | |

	A	B	C	D	E	F
1	Personal Balance Sheet					
2						
3						
4	ASSETS					
5	Current Assets					
6		Cash		$300.00		
7		Stocks, Bonds, Marketable Securities		$5,000.00		
8		Furniture		$2,500.00		
9		Jewelry		$750.00		
10		Other Current Assets		$550.00		
11	Total Current Assets			$9,100.00		
12						
13	Long-Term Assets					
14		Home		$211,000.00		
15		Rental Property		$125,000.00		
16		Automobiles		$12,000.00		
17		Other Long Term Assets		$10,000.00		
18	Total Long-Term Assets			$358,000.00		
19						
20	TOTAL ASSETS			$367,100.00		
21						
22	LIABILITIES AND EQUITY					
23	Current Liabilities					
24		Credit Card Balances		$4,200.00		
25		Consumer Loans (items bought on credit)		$5,000.00		
26		Other Current Liabilities		$1,500.00		
27	Total Current Liabilities			$10,700.00		
28						
29	Long-Term Liabilities					
30		Home Mortgage		$205,000.00		
31		Rental Property Loan		$118,000.00		
32		Automobile Loan Balance		$15,000.00		
33		Other Long-Term Liabilities		$15,000.00		
34	Total Long-Term Liabilities			$353,000.00		
35						
36	Equity (Net Worth)			=(D20-(D27+D34))		
37						
38	TOTAL LIABILITIES AND EQUITY					
39						
40						
41						
42						
43						
44						
45						
46						
47						

| ◄ ◄ ► ►| \ Personal / Business / | | ◄ | |

| eet 1 / 2 | Default | 65% | INSRT | STD | * | | Sum=$0.00 |

10 Finally, we need to calculate the total liabilities and equity. We do so by adding together the total current liabilities, total long-term liabilities and equity (net worth). To do so, select cell D38. Then proceed with Step #11.

11 After selecting cell D38, type **=sum** followed by a beginning parenthesis. To type a beginning parenthesis, hold down the SHIFT key and press nine (9) within the main keyboard area (not within the numeric keypad area). After doing so, use your left mouse button to click cell D27. When doing so, the cell is entered into the formula. Then type the plus "+" sign, and then use the left mouse button to click cell D34 to enter the cell into the formula, followed by typing another plus "+" sign. Use the left mouse button to click cell D36 to enter the cell into the formula. End the formula by typing an ending parenthesis. To type an ending parenthesis, hold down the SHIFT key and press zero (0) within the main keyboard area (not within the numeric keypad area). When completed, the formula should read:

$$=sum(D27+D34+D36)$$

Press the ENTER or RETURN key. The values contained within cells D27, D34 and D36 will be added, and the result will be produced within cell D38.

	A	B	C	D	E	F	G	H
SUM				=sum(D27+D34+D36)				
1	Personal Balance Sheet							
2								
3								
4	ASSETS							
5	Current Assets							
6		Cash		$300.00				
7		Stocks, Bonds, Marketable Securities		$5,000.00				
8		Furniture		$2,500.00				
9		Jewelry		$750.00				
10		Other Current Assets		$550.00				
11	Total Current Assets			$9,100.00				
12								
13	Long-Term Assets							
14		Home		$211,000.00				
15		Rental Property		$125,000.00				
16		Automobiles		$12,000.00				
17		Other Long Term Assets		$10,000.00				
18	Total Long-Term Assets			$358,000.00				
19								
20	TOTAL ASSETS			$367,100.00				
21								
22	LIABILITIES AND EQUITY							
23	Current Liabilities							
24		Credit Card Balances		$4,200.00				
25		Consumer Loans (items bought on credit)		$5,000.00				
26		Other Current Liabilities		$1,500.00				
27	Total Current Liabilities			$10,700.00				
28								
29	Long-Term Liabilities							
30		Home Mortgage		$205,000.00				
31		Rental Property Loan		$118,000.00				
32		Automobile Loan Balance		$15,000.00				
33		Other Long-Term Liabilities		$15,000.00				
34	Total Long-Term Liabilities			$353,000.00				
35								
36	Equity (Net Worth)			$3,400.00				
37								
38	TOTAL LIABILITIES AND EQUITY			=sum(D27+D34+D36)				
39								
40								
41								
42								
43								
44								
45								
46								
47								

Personal / Business

Sheet 1 / 2   Default   65%   INSRT   STD   Sum=$0.00

Adding Values Among Worksheets

Not only can you calculate values within an individual worksheet, but you can also calculate values contained within multiple worksheets as well. In this simple example, we will calculate the total amount of cash present in both the personal balance sheet and the opening business balance sheet. To do so, follow these steps:

1   Select the personal balance sheet by clicking on the worksheet tab labeled **Personal** located above the status bar.

2   Select cell B42 and type **Total Personal and Business Cash**. Then press the ENTER or RETURN key on your keyboard.

3   Next, select cell D42. Then type **=sum** followed by a beginning parenthesis. To type a beginning parenthesis, hold down the SHIFT key and press nine (9) within the main keyboard area (not within the numeric keypad area). After doing so, use your left mouse button to click cell D6. When doing so, the cell is entered into the formula. Then type the plus "+" sign.

4   Select the opening business balance sheet by clicking on the worksheet tab labeled **Business** located above the status bar. Within the Business worksheet, use your left mouse button to click cell D6. When doing so, the cell is entered into the formula. End the formula by typing an ending parenthesis. To type an ending parenthesis, hold down the SHIFT key and press zero (0) within the main keyboard area (not within the numeric keypad area). When completed, the formula should read:

=sum(D6+Business.D6)

Press the ENTER or RETURN key. The values contained within cell D6 of the Personal worksheet and cell D6 of the Business worksheet will be added, and the result will be produced within cell D42 of the Personal worksheet.

Other Current Assets		$550.00
Total Current Assets		$9,100.00
Long-Term Assets		
	Home	$211,000.00
	Rental Property	$125,000.00
	Automobiles	$12,000.00
	Other Long Term Assets	$10,000.00
Total Long-Term Assets		$358,000.00
TOTAL ASSETS		**$367,100.00**
LIABILITIES AND EQUITY		
Current Liabilities		
	Credit Card Balances	$4,200.00
	Consumer Loans (items bought on credit)	$5,000.00
	Other Current Liabilities	$1,500.00
Total Current Liabilities		$10,700.00
Long-Term Liabilities		
	Home Mortgage	$205,000.00
	Rental Property Loan	$118,000.00
	Automobile Loan Balance	$15,000.00
	Other Long-Term Liabilities	$15,000.00
Total Long-Term Liabilities		$353,000.00
Equity (Net Worth)		$3,400.00
TOTAL LIABILITIES AND EQUITY		**$367,100.00**
	Total Personal and Business Cash	=sum(D6+Business D6)

Personal / Business

Sheet 1 / 2   Default   65%   INSRT   STD   Sum=$0.00

Adding Worksheets to a Spreadsheet Document

When opening this Calc spreadsheet lesson file, you will notice that two worksheets are present. These worksheets are labeled Personal and Business. However, additional worksheets can be created within this or any Calc spreadsheet document. To create a new worksheet within a Calc spreadsheet document, follow these steps:

1 Click the Insert menu and select Sheet from the menu options that appear.

2 In the Position selection area, choose whether the new worksheet should be positioned before or after the current worksheet by selecting the appropriate radio button.

3 In the Sheet selection area, select the number of worksheets to be added by using the selection field provided. If only one new worksheet is to be created, type the name the new worksheet should be labeled as using the Name text field provided. In this example, select to create one (1) new worksheet and enter your first name as the worksheet name.

4 Click OK to complete the operation. The new worksheet should appear within the worksheet list located just above the Status Bar at the bottom of the spreadsheet window.

Exporting a Spreadsheet as a Portable Document Format (PDF) File

Like the Writer word processing application bundled with OpenOffice.org, Calc has the ability to export spreadsheet documents as a Portable Document Format (PDF) file. As you recall, saving a document as a PDF file is a convenient way to share read-only documents to other users that have a PDF reader application installed on their computer. However, OpenOffice.org cannot edit a document that has been saved as a PDF file. Therefore, if you wish to save a document for editing at a later date, save the document in its Native OpenDocument file format.

To save a document as a read-only PDF file, follow these steps:

1 Click on the File menu and choose Export As PDF from the menu options that appear.

2 When the Export As PDF window appears, OpenOffice.org will provide you with some additional options for you to select. Among these options are the page range and image compression quality. If you choose Lossless Compression, the file will be exported in the highest quality possible but the file size will be larger. Sending large file sizes via email, for example, will result in longer receiving and download times. You also have the option to select JPEG compression to decrease the file size and, therefore, reduce the amount of time it takes to upload and download a file. OpenOffice. org allows you to use the popup menu provided to select the compression quality on a scale from 1% to 100%, with 1% being the lowest quality. After you have selected your additional export options, click the EXPORT button.

3 A window will appear and prompt you to choose a location to save your document. Choose the location you want to save a document to in the Save In popup field.

4 In the field File Name, type the name you would like to save the file as.

5   In the File Format popup menu, make sure Portable Document Format (PDF) is selected.

Understanding the Data Contained Within the Personal Balance Sheet

The personal balance sheet is complete. However, you may now be asking yourself, "Why would I need to create a balance sheet for myself?" or "What is the value of maintaining a personal balance sheet?" To answer these questions, let me first explain what a balance sheet is and why it is formatted the way it is. Then we will examine the personal balance sheet completed in this lesson to understand what the document is telling us. By doing so, this will hopefully develop an appreciation of how a personal balance sheet can help in analyzing the present financial status of an individual or family and, therefore, help in determining strategies to improve the financial status in the future.

Simply put, a personal balance sheet is a way for yourself or lenders to determine what your personal net worth is. Net worth, or can be referred to as equity, is calculated by adding up the value of all of the property a person or family owns and subtracting all of the money owed to lenders or individuals. Property that an individual or family owns are classified as assets, and are listed within the top half of a balance sheet. Money owed to lenders or individuals is called a liability. Liabilities, or the amount owed to multiple lenders or individuals, are listed within the bottom half of a balance sheet.

Assets and liabilities can be divided into subcategories. If you look at the personal balance sheet completed for this lesson, the assets are divided into two subcategories: current assets and long-term assets. Current assets refer to property that can be sold and converted to cash quickly, usually within one (1) year or less. Cash is the most basic asset an individual can have, and is often listed first within the assets category. Sometimes cash is referred to as a liquid asset, because it is an asset that doesn't have to be converted to money. Long-term assets refer to property that, while could be sold to convert to money, cannot be done so as quickly or easily. Real estate and automobiles are the most common types of long-term assets an individual may own. While technically a house or automobile could be sold and converted to money within a (1) year period, it is traditionally listed as a long-term asset because many individuals finance the purchases of such assets for more than a year.

Like the assets listed within the personal balance sheet, the liabilities are also divided into two subcategories: current liabilities and long-term liabilities. Current liabilities represent money that is owed to lenders or individuals which is due for payment-in-full within one (1) year. Again, you will note that some types of debt, such as credit card payments, may not be due for payment-in-full within one (1) year because payment plans may extend beyond that time. However, most lenders regard it as a current liability because such a liability needs to be paid as quickly as possible to reduce the amount of money being paid in interest to finance the debt. Long-term liabilities represent money that is owed to lenders and individuals to be paid off in installments over a term greater than one (1) year. For example, a home mortgage is often paid off over a thirty-year (30) period, or an automobile for a four (4) year period or longer. While a lender may not require an individual to divide the assets and liabilities into subcategories within a personal balance sheet submitted with a loan application, it may help an individual to do so to identify which liabilities need to be established as a priority for paying off, or which assets could be sold quickly to turn to cash.

The document is called a balance sheet because the amount of assets an individual or family has listed in the top half of the document must balance with the total calculated for the liabilities and equity in the bottom half of the document. If you look at the completed personal balance sheet for this lesson, you will note that the Total Assets and the Total Liabilities and Equity balance to $367,100.00. If the Total Assets and Total Liabilities and Equity do not balance when preparing a personal balance sheet, each section should be analyzed to determine where the calculation error is. Preparing a personal balance sheet with the Calc spreadsheet application, however, can help you significantly reduce errors. By creating formulas in their proper location within the spreadsheet, Calc can keep track of the calculations for you.

For example, select cell D31 within the completed personal balance sheet and change the liability value for the rental property to $122,000.00. Watch what happens to the Equity (Net Worth) value and the Total Liabilities and Equity value. The Total Liabilities and Equity remains at $367,100.00, as it should because the Total Assets remain at the same figure. The formulas we had created within Calc for this exercise was designed to do this. However, because this individual's liabilities increased and their assets remained unchanged, their net worth had to decrease. In fact, after changing the amount owed on the rental property, this individual now has a negative net worth of $600.00. This means that this individual now owes more money than they have in assets. The house and rental property are all worth more (see the value listed in the assets section) than they owe to the lenders for the respective property (as listed in the liabilities section). This individual could have a nice home, drive a decent car and have a large screen television in the living room. Yet, if they had to sell everything they own, they still wouldn't have enough money to pay off their debts in full.

How can this happen? For young people, it is not uncommon for them to have a negative net worth because they have yet to accumulate enough assets, or they have not accumulated enough equity in the assets they own for them to be worth more than they owe. Moreover, some assets can be more of a liability than they are worth. Automobiles are a prime example of this. In terms of money spent, automobiles are one of the most significant purchases an individual can make. Yet, they depreciate in value worse than any other asset an individual can own. It is not uncommon to purchase a car and have it lose its value up to 30% as soon as it is driven off the car lot. Examining the personal balance sheet completed for this lesson, you will note that the asset value listed for this individual's automobile is $12,000.00 (cell D16), yet this individual still owes the auto finance company $15000.00 (cell D32) for the automobile.

Other liabilities that can negatively affect an individual's net worth are credit card loans and consumer loans. Consumer debt refers to those owed for purchases such as furniture, appliances, and electronics where credit is obtained through in-store financing, check cashing businesses or consumer credit lenders. Debt incurred through such loans are often for purchasing items that are considered consumable, which have little or no value to a lender. Electronics, such as computers or televisions for example, are usually not accepted as assets of value by lenders on a personal balance sheet because they lose their value very quickly after purchase. Therefore, as collateral for a loan, it is worthless to a lender because they could not sell off such property at an auction and obtain nearly the amount of money that it cost when it was new. Yet, when an individual purchases these items new on credit, the money that was loaned for purchasing such items still has to be repaid. Moreover, credit card loans and consumer loans usually carry with it higher interest rates, which can further negatively affect an individual's finances.

So why would you need to prepare and maintain a personal balance sheet? Let's use purchasing a home as an example. When you apply for a mortgage loan at a bank to obtain financing to buy a new house, the bank is likely to ask that you present to them a copy of your personal balance sheet along with the application. Just as we did with the personal balance sheet completed for this lesson, examining a personal balance sheet is to assist the banker in determining how much equity (and what kind) you have accumulated to offer as collateral for the loan. Collateral is money, or assets that can be sold and converted to money, that the bank can seize in the event an individual defaults on repaying a loan. The greater an individual's net worth, the less of a credit risk they are to lenders. Increased equity means that, in the event that an individual defaults on a loan, there is an increased chance of being able to sell the assets and recoup the money owed on a loan. Moreover, greater equity means that an individual has a chance to turn that equity into money to keep their payments to lenders current in the event of loss of income, such as due to an illness, an injury at work or loss of employment. Other reasons for a personal balance sheet to be presented to a lender include purchasing commercial or rental property and seeking a loan to start a small business.

Working With Business Balance Sheets

A business balance sheet is very similar to a personal balance sheet. It's purpose is the same, except that assets and liabilities declared on a business balance sheet are often different than that declared on an individual's balance sheet. If you look at the business balance sheet provided in the lesson file, you will note that a number of assets and liabilities listed are exclusively related to a business' operations. These include inventory, accounts receivables, accounts payables and more. However, the method of calculating assets, liabilities and equity for a business is the same as for an individual. If you wish, you can utilize the business balance sheet provided in the lesson file to further practice using Calc for formatting worksheets and performing calculations.

Additional Resources

OpenOffice.org: Description of Functions
http://documentation.openoffice.org/manuals/oooauthors2/0314CG-DescriptionOfFunctions.pdf

OpenOffice.org: Template for Creating Balance Sheets
http://documentation.openoffice.org/Samples_Templates/User/template/balancesheet.stc

U.S. Small Business Administration: Balance Sheets
http://www.sba.gov/managing/financing/balsheet.html

James Hartsfield – N.C. Cooperative Extension Service: Understanding Financial Risk
http://www.ces.ncsu.edu/sampson/pubs/farm_man/UndstandFinRisk.html

Review Questions

1 What menu would you select to add a new worksheet within a Calc spreadsheet document?

2 When subtracting values among cells, does the SUM function need to be utilized? Why?

3 What type of image compression would need to be selected to export a PDF file in the highest quality possible?

4 (True or False) Cells can be resized by utilizing either the mouse pointer within the column and row label area or by selecting the View menu.

5 (True or False) Like the Writer word processing application bundled with OpenOffice.org, Calc has the ability to export spreadsheet documents as a Portable Document Format (PDF) file.

LESSON

7

Creating a Cash Flow Statement Using Calc

Lesson Objectives

In this lesson, you will learn the following:

1   How to create a cash flow statement and how to interpret the data contained within.

2   How to add font styles to text contained within a spreadsheet document.

3   How to create formulas to add, subtract and multiply values within a worksheet.

Overview

In the last two lessons, we have used Calc to create a personal worksheet for tracking personal monthly household expenses and a personal balance sheet. In this lesson, we will learn how to create a cash flow statement, often used by businesses to keep track of incoming revenues and outgoing expenditures at a given point in time. Upon completion of this lesson, you will have learned how to format text with font styles within a Calc worksheet, how to create formulas for multiplying data contained within the document and how to interpret the data within the completed cash flow statement.

Getting Started

Before we do so, we need to open the Lesson Seven file that is available for use with this book. To open the file, follow these steps:

1   If you have not already downloaded the lesson files for this book, use a web browser to go to **http://documentation.openoffice.org/ conceptualguide/OpenOfficeOrg3LessonFiles.zip**. This will provide a direct link for your browser to begin an automatic download of the lesson files. If a dialog window appears asking where you would like to save the file to be downloaded, select your computer workstation's desktop and begin downloading the file.

2 When the file appears on your computer's desktop, double-click the file icon to unzip its contents and access the files associated with each lesson. Double-click the Lesson Files folder icon that contains the available lesson files, locate the Lesson 07 folder and double-click on it to access the file for this lesson. When you have opened the folder, double-click the file named **lesson_07_start.ods** to open the file.

Applying Font Styles to Text Contained Within a Spreadsheet Document

Like the Writer word processing application, Calc provides a wide array of formatting options for text contained within a spreadsheet document. In fact, many of the menu and toolbar options that are available within Writer are the same within Calc as well.

In this lesson, we need to apply the Bold font style to some of the text within the cash flow statement. To do so, follow these steps:

1 Using your left mouse button, click on row label 3 located on the left side of the worksheet. Doing so will select the entire row, but will leave all remaining rows within the worksheet unselected.

2 To apply the Bold font style to the selected text, you can simply click the BOLD button located within the Formatting toolbar. If the Formatting toolbar is not visible, you can make it so by clicking on the View menu, select the Toolbars menu option and then select Formatting from the submenu options that appear.

3 Repeat Steps #1 and #2 for row 4 within the worksheet. Applying the necessary font styles for this worksheet will then be complete.

You can also format font styles by clicking on the Format menu located at the top of the Calc application window and selecting the Cells menu option.

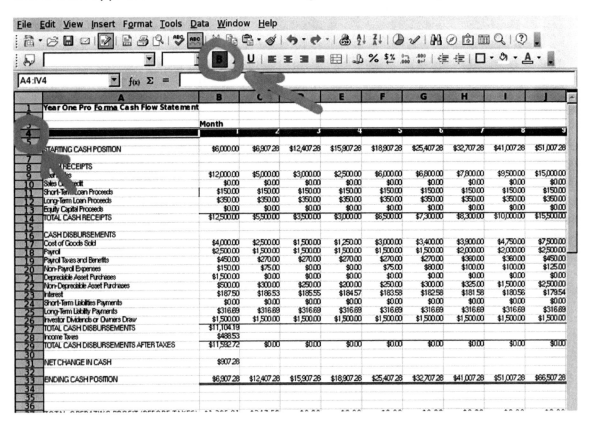

Creating Formulas to Add, Subtract and Multiply Values

We are now ready to begin to perform our calculations for the cash flow statement. Much of the information you need to perform the calculations has already been provided, while some of the basic calculations have already been performed. For each month, however, we need to perform additional calculations for three items: Total Cash Disbursements, Income Taxes and Net Change In Cash.

First, we are going to perform the calculations for the Total Cash Disbursements for each month. Total cash disbursements are calculated by simply adding together the cash disbursement values together to receive a total. To do so, follow these steps:

1 Using your mouse, select cell C27, which is the where the Total Cash Disbursements for Month Two (2) should be presented.

2 Click the SUM function button located in the Function Bar. When you click the button, Calc automatically suggests a cell range. In this step, Calc automatically selects cell range C17 through C26, which are the cash disbursement amounts we wish to add for Month Two (2). If Calc had incorrectly chose the cell range you wish to add, you could simply hold down your left mouse button and drag over the desired cell range to make the appropriate selection. Once the desired cell range has been selected, press the ENTER or RETURN key and Calc adds the values within the cell range selected. The results are then produced within the cell originally selected.

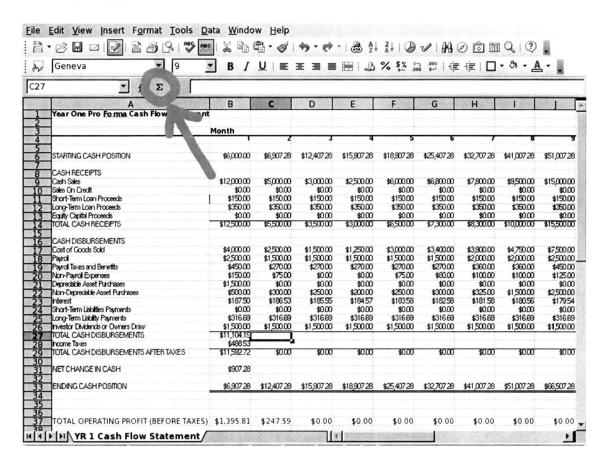

SUM $f_{(x)}$ ✗ ✓   =SUM(**C17:C26**)

	A	B	C	D	E	F	G	H	I	J
1	Year One Pro Forma Cash Flow Statement									
2										
3		Month								
4			1	2	3	4	5	6	7	8	9
5										
6	STARTING CASH POSITION	$6,000.00	$6,907.28	$12,407.28	$15,907.28	$18,907.28	$25,407.28	$32,707.28	$41,007.28	$51,007.28
7										
8	CASH RECEIPTS									
9	Cash Sales	$12,000.00	$5,000.00	$3,000.00	$2,500.00	$6,000.00	$6,800.00	$7,800.00	$9,500.00	$15,000.00
10	Sales On Credit	$0.00	$0.00	$0.00	$0.00	$0.00	$0.00	$0.00	$0.00	$0.00
11	Short-Term Loan Proceeds	$150.00	$150.00	$150.00	$150.00	$150.00	$150.00	$150.00	$150.00	$150.00
12	Long-Term Loan Proceeds	$350.00	$350.00	$350.00	$350.00	$350.00	$350.00	$350.00	$350.00	$350.00
13	Equity Capital Proceeds	$0.00	$0.00	$0.00	$0.00	$0.00	$0.00	$0.00	$0.00	$0.00
14	TOTAL CASH RECEIPTS	$12,500.00	$5,500.00	$3,500.00	$3,000.00	$6,500.00	$7,300.00	$8,300.00	$10,000.00	$15,500.00
15										
16	CASH DISBURSEMENTS									
17	Cost of Goods Sold	$4,000.00	$2,500.00	$1,500.00	$1,250.00	$3,000.00	$3,400.00	$3,900.00	$4,750.00	$7,500.00
18	Payroll	$2,500.00	$1,500.00	$1,500.00	$1,500.00	$1,500.00	$1,500.00	$2,000.00	$2,000.00	$2,500.00
19	Payroll Taxes and Benefits	$450.00	$270.00	$270.00	$270.00	$270.00	$270.00	$360.00	$360.00	$450.00
20	Non-Payroll Expenses	$150.00	$75.00	$0.00	$0.00	$75.00	$80.00	$100.00	$100.00	$125.00
21	Depreciable Asset Purchases	$1,500.00	$0.00	$0.00	$0.00	$0.00	$0.00	$0.00	$0.00	$0.00
22	Non-Depreciable Asset Purchases	$500.00	$300.00	$250.00	$200.00	$250.00	$300.00	$325.00	$1,500.00	$2,500.00
23	Interest	$187.50	$186.53	$185.55	$184.57	$183.58	$182.58	$181.58	$180.56	$179.54
24	Short-Term Liabilities Payments	$0.00	$0.00	$0.00	$0.00	$0.00	$0.00	$0.00	$0.00	$0.00
25	Long-Term Liability Payments	$316.69	$316.69	$316.69	$316.69	$316.69	$316.69	$316.69	$316.69	$316.69
26	Investor Dividends or Owners Draw	$1,500.00	$1,500.00	$1,500.00	$1,500.00	$1,500.00	$1,500.00	$1,500.00	$1,500.00	$1,500.00
27	TOTAL CASH DISBURSEMENTS	$11,104.19 =SUM(**C17:C26**)								
28	Income Taxes	$488.53								
29	TOTAL CASH DISBURSEMENTS AFTER TAXES	$11,592.72	$0.00	$0.00	$0.00	$0.00	$0.00	$0.00	$0.00	$0.00

3 Repeat Step #1 by selecting, one at a time, each of the following cells:
D27, E27, F27, G27, H27, I27, J27, K27, L27 and M27. After selecting an
individual cell, follow the instructions in Step #2 to obtain the results for
the appropriate month. When you have completed adding the cell ranges
specified above, the spreadsheet should look like the illustration on the
following page.

	A	B	C	D	E	F	G	H	I	J
1	Year One Pro Forma Cash Flow Statement									
2										
3		Month								
4			1	2	3	4	5	6	7	8	9
5										
6	STARTING CASH POSITION	$6,000.00	$6,907.28	$5,759.06	$3,736.82	$1,515.56	$920.29	$671.02	$287.75	-$419.50
7										
8	CASH RECEIPTS									
9	Cash Sales	$12,000.00	$5,000.00	$3,000.00	$2,500.00	$6,000.00	$6,800.00	$7,800.00	$9,500.00	$15,000.00
10	Sales On Credit	$0.00	$0.00	$0.00	$0.00	$0.00	$0.00	$0.00	$0.00	$0.00
11	Short-Term Loan Proceeds	$150.00	$150.00	$150.00	$150.00	$150.00	$150.00	$150.00	$150.00	$150.00
12	Long-Term Loan Proceeds	$350.00	$350.00	$350.00	$350.00	$350.00	$350.00	$350.00	$350.00	$350.00
13	Equity Capital Proceeds	$0.00	$0.00	$0.00	$0.00	$0.00	$0.00	$0.00	$0.00	$0.00
14	TOTAL CASH RECEIPTS	$12,500.00	$5,500.00	$3,500.00	$3,000.00	$6,500.00	$7,300.00	$8,300.00	$10,000.00	$15,500.00
15										
16	CASH DISBURSEMENTS									
17	Cost of Goods Sold	$4,000.00	$2,500.00	$1,500.00	$1,250.00	$3,000.00	$3,400.00	$3,900.00	$4,750.00	$7,500.00
18	Payroll	$2,500.00	$1,500.00	$1,500.00	$1,500.00	$1,500.00	$1,500.00	$2,000.00	$2,000.00	$2,500.00
19	Payroll Taxes and Benefits	$450.00	$270.00	$270.00	$270.00	$270.00	$270.00	$360.00	$360.00	$450.00
20	Non-Payroll Expenses	$150.00	$75.00	$0.00	$0.00	$75.00	$80.00	$100.00	$100.00	$125.00
21	Depreciable Asset Purchases	$1,500.00	$0.00	$0.00	$0.00	$0.00	$0.00	$0.00	$0.00	$0.00
22	Non-Depreciable Asset Purchases	$500.00	$300.00	$250.00	$200.00	$250.00	$300.00	$325.00	$1,500.00	$2,500.00
23	Interest	$187.50	$186.53	$185.55	$184.57	$183.58	$182.58	$181.58	$180.56	$179.54
24	Short-Term Liabilities Payments	$0.00	$0.00	$0.00	$0.00	$0.00	$0.00	$0.00	$0.00	$0.00
25	Long-Term Liability Payments	$316.69	$316.69	$316.69	$316.69	$316.69	$316.69	$316.69	$316.69	$316.69
26	Investor Dividends or Owners Draw	$1,500.00	$1,500.00	$1,500.00	$1,500.00	$1,500.00	$1,500.00	$1,500.00	$1,500.00	$1,500.00
27	TOTAL CASH DISBURSEMENTS	$11,104.19	$6,648.22	$5,522.24	$5,221.26	$7,095.27	$7,549.27	$8,683.27	$10,707.25	$15,071.23
28	Income Taxes	$488.53								
29	TOTAL CASH DISBURSEMENTS AFTER TAXES	$11,592.72	$6,648.22	$5,522.24	$5,221.26	$7,095.27	$7,549.27	$8,683.27	$10,707.25	$15,071.23
30										
31	NET CHANGE IN CASH	$907.28								
32										
33	ENDING CASH POSITION	$6,907.28	$5,759.06	$3,736.82	$1,515.56	$920.29	$671.02	$287.75	-$419.50	$9.27
34										
35										
36										
37	TOTAL OPERATING PROFIT (BEFORE TAXES)	$1,395.81	$247.59	$0.00	$0.00	$0.00	$0.00	$0.00	$0.00	$0.00

|◄ ◄ ► ►|\ YR 1 Cash Flow Statement /

Sheet 1 / 1   Default   75%   STD •   Sum=0

Next, we are going to perform the calculations for the Income Taxes that are to be paid for each month. The income taxes are calculated by multiplying the Total Operating Profit (Before Taxes) by the appropriate income tax rate. In this example, the income tax rate is 35% for federal, state and local taxes. Be aware that the Total Operating Profit is usually found on an income statement (also referred to as a Profit And Loss Statement or P&L Statement) and not on a cash flow statement. However, it has been listed on the worksheet to provide the necessary information to calculate the income tax payable for each month. To calculate the Income Taxes for each month, follow these steps:

4 Using your mouse, select cell C28, which is the where the Income Taxes for Month Two (2) should be presented.

5 After selecting cell C28, type the equal sign (**=**) followed by a beginning parenthesis. To type a beginning parenthesis, hold down the SHIFT key and press nine (9) within the main keyboard area (not within the numeric keypad area). After doing so, use your left mouse button to click the cell that contains the value for Total Operating Profit Before Taxes for the respective month. For Month Two (2), this value is displayed within cell C37. When doing so, the cell is entered into the formula. Then type the asterisk "*" sign, which represents the multiplication sign within spreadsheet applications. Then type 0.35 to tell Calc to multiply the Total Operating Profit Before Taxes for Month Two (2) by 35%. End the formula by typing an ending parenthesis. To type an ending parenthesis, hold down the SHIFT key and press zero (0) within the main keyboard area (not within the numeric keypad area). When completed, the formula should read:

=(C37*0.35)

Press the ENTER or RETURN key. The values will be added, and the amount of income tax to be paid for Month Two (2) will be calculated, with the result displayed within cell C28.

SUM ▾ | fx ✗ ✓ | =(C37*0.35)

	A	B	C	D	E	F	G	H	I	J
1	Year One Pro Forma Cash Flow Statement									
2										
3		Month								
4			1	2	3	4	5	6	7	8	9
5										
6	STARTING CASH POSITION	$6,000.00	$6,907.28	$5,759.06	$3,736.82	$1,515.56	$920.29	$671.02	$287.75	-$419.50
7										
8	CASH RECEIPTS									
9	Cash Sales	$12,000.00	$5,000.00	$3,000.00	$2,500.00	$6,000.00	$6,800.00	$7,800.00	$9,500.00	$15,000.00
10	Sales On Credit	$0.00	$0.00	$0.00	$0.00	$0.00	$0.00	$0.00	$0.00	$0.00
11	Short-Term Loan Proceeds	$150.00	$150.00	$150.00	$150.00	$150.00	$150.00	$150.00	$150.00	$150.00
12	Long-Term Loan Proceeds	$350.00	$350.00	$350.00	$350.00	$350.00	$350.00	$350.00	$350.00	$350.00
13	Equity Capital Proceeds	$0.00	$0.00	$0.00	$0.00	$0.00	$0.00	$0.00	$0.00	$0.00
14	TOTAL CASH RECEIPTS	$12,500.00	$5,500.00	$3,500.00	$3,000.00	$6,500.00	$7,300.00	$8,300.00	$10,000.00	$15,500.00
15										
16	CASH DISBURSEMENTS									
17	Cost of Goods Sold	$4,000.00	$2,500.00	$1,500.00	$1,250.00	$3,000.00	$3,400.00	$3,900.00	$4,750.00	$7,500.00
18	Payroll	$2,500.00	$1,500.00	$1,500.00	$1,500.00	$1,500.00	$1,500.00	$2,000.00	$2,000.00	$2,500.00
19	Payroll Taxes and Benefits	$450.00	$270.00	$270.00	$270.00	$270.00	$270.00	$360.00	$360.00	$450.00
20	Non-Payroll Expenses	$150.00	$75.00	$0.00	$0.00	$75.00	$80.00	$100.00	$100.00	$125.00
21	Depreciable Asset Purchases	$1,500.00	$0.00	$0.00	$0.00	$0.00	$0.00	$0.00	$0.00	$0.00
22	Non-Depreciable Asset Purchases	$500.00	$300.00	$250.00	$200.00	$250.00	$300.00	$325.00	$1,500.00	$2,500.00
23	Interest	$187.50	$186.53	$185.55	$184.57	$183.58	$182.58	$181.58	$180.56	$179.54
24	Short-Term Liabilities Payments	$0.00	$0.00	$0.00	$0.00	$0.00	$0.00	$0.00	$0.00	$0.00
25	Long-Term Liability Payments	$316.69	$316.69	$316.69	$316.69	$316.69	$316.69	$316.69	$316.69	$316.69
26	Investor Dividends or Owners Draw	$1,500.00	$1,500.00	$1,500.00	$1,500.00	$1,500.00	$1,500.00	$1,500.00	$1,500.00	$1,500.00
27	TOTAL CASH DISBURSEMENTS	$11,104.19	$6,648.22	$5,522.24	$5,221.26	$7,095.27	$7,549.27	$8,883.27	$10,707.25	$15,071.23
28	Income Taxes	$488.53	=(C37*0.35)							
29	TOTAL CASH DISBURSEMENTS AFTER TAXES	$11,592.72	$6,648.22	$5,522.24	$5,221.26	$7,095.27	$7,549.27	$8,883.27	$10,707.25	$15,071.23
30										
31	NET CHANGE IN CASH	$907.28								
32										
33	ENDING CASH POSITION	$6,907.28	$5,759.06	$3,736.82	$1,515.56	$920.29	$671.02	$287.75	-$419.50	$9.27
34										
35										
36										
37	TOTAL OPERATING PROFIT (BEFORE TAXES)	$1,395.81	$247.59	$0.00	$0.00	$0.00	$0.00	$0.00	$0.00	$0.00

|◄|◄|►|►|◄ YR 1 Cash Flow Statement /

6 Repeat Step #4 by selecting, one at a time, each of the following cells: D28, E28, F28, G28, H28, I28, J28, K28, L28 and M28. After selecting an individual cell, follow the instructions in Step #5 to obtain the results for the appropriate month. When you have completed adding the cell ranges specified above, the spreadsheet should look like the illustration below.

	A	B	C	D	E	F	G	H	I	J
1	Year One Pro Forma Cash Flow Statement									
2										
3		Month								
4			1	2	3	4	5	6	7	8	9
5										
6	STARTING CASH POSITION	$6,000.00	$6,907.28	$5,672.40	$3,850.16	$1,428.90	$833.63	$584.36	$201.09	-$506.16
7										
8	CASH RECEIPTS									
9	Cash Sales	$12,000.00	$5,000.00	$3,000.00	$2,500.00	$6,000.00	$6,800.00	$7,800.00	$9,500.00	$15,000.00
10	Sales On Credit	$0.00	$0.00	$0.00	$0.00	$0.00	$0.00	$0.00	$0.00	$0.00
11	Short-Term Loan Proceeds	$150.00	$150.00	$150.00	$150.00	$150.00	$150.00	$150.00	$150.00	$150.00
12	Long-Term Loan Proceeds	$350.00	$350.00	$350.00	$350.00	$350.00	$350.00	$350.00	$350.00	$350.00
13	Equity Capital Proceeds	$0.00	$0.00	$0.00	$0.00	$0.00	$0.00	$0.00	$0.00	$0.00
14	TOTAL CASH RECEIPTS	$12,500.00	$5,500.00	$3,500.00	$3,000.00	$6,500.00	$7,300.00	$8,300.00	$10,000.00	$15,500.00
15										
16	CASH DISBURSEMENTS									
17	Cost of Goods Sold	$4,000.00	$2,500.00	$1,500.00	$1,250.00	$3,000.00	$3,400.00	$3,900.00	$4,750.00	$7,500.00
18	Payroll	$2,500.00	$1,500.00	$1,500.00	$1,500.00	$1,500.00	$1,500.00	$2,000.00	$2,000.00	$2,500.00
19	Payroll Taxes and Benefits	$450.00	$270.00	$270.00	$270.00	$270.00	$270.00	$360.00	$360.00	$450.00
20	Non-Payroll Expenses	$150.00	$75.00	$0.00	$0.00	$75.00	$80.00	$100.00	$100.00	$125.00
21	Depreciable Asset Purchases	$1,500.00	$0.00	$0.00	$0.00	$0.00	$0.00	$0.00	$0.00	$0.00
22	Non-Depreciable Asset Purchases	$500.00	$300.00	$250.00	$200.00	$250.00	$300.00	$325.00	$1,500.00	$2,500.00
23	Interest	$187.50	$186.53	$185.55	$184.57	$183.58	$182.58	$181.58	$180.56	$179.54
24	Short-Term Liabilities Payments	$0.00	$0.00	$0.00	$0.00	$0.00	$0.00	$0.00	$0.00	$0.00
25	Long-Term Liability Payments	$316.69	$316.69	$316.69	$316.69	$316.69	$316.69	$316.69	$316.69	$316.69
26	Investor Dividends or Owners Draw	$1,500.00	$1,500.00	$1,500.00	$1,500.00	$1,500.00	$1,500.00	$1,500.00	$1,500.00	$1,500.00
27	TOTAL CASH DISBURSEMENTS	$11,104.19	$6,648.22	$5,522.24	$5,221.26	$7,095.27	$7,549.27	$8,883.27	$10,707.25	$15,071.23
28	Income Taxes	$488.53	$86.66	$0.00	$0.00	$0.00	$0.00	$0.00	$0.00	$0.00
29	TOTAL CASH DISBURSEMENTS AFTER TAXES	$11,592.72	$6,734.88	$5,522.24	$5,221.26	$7,095.27	$7,549.27	$8,883.27	$10,707.25	$15,071.23
30										
31	NET CHANGE IN CASH	$907.28								
32										
33	ENDING CASH POSITION	$6,907.28	$5,672.40	$3,850.16	$1,428.90	$833.63	$584.36	$201.09	-$506.16	-$77.38
34										
35										
36										
37	TOTAL OPERATING PROFIT (BEFORE TAXES)	$1,395.81	$247.59	$0.00	$0.00	$0.00	$0.00	$0.00	$0.00	$0.00

|◄|◄|►|►| YR 1 Cash Flow Statement /

Finally, we are going to perform the calculations for the Net Change In Cash for each month. The net change in cash is calculated by subtracting the Total Cash Disbursements After Taxes from the Total Cash Receipts for the respective month. To calculate the Net Change In Cash for each month, follow these steps:

7 Using your mouse, select cell C31, which is the where the Net Change In Cash for Month Two (2) should be presented.

8 After selecting cell C31, type the equal sign (**=**) followed by a beginning parenthesis. To type a beginning parenthesis, hold down the SHIFT key and press nine (9) within the main keyboard area (not within the numeric keypad area). After doing so, use your left mouse button to click the cell that contains the value for Total Cash Receipts for the respective month. For Month Two (2), this value is displayed within cell C14. When doing so, the cell is entered into the formula. Then type the minus "-" sign, and then use the left mouse button to click cell that contains the value for Total Cash Disbursements After Taxes for the respective month. For Month Two (2), the value is displayed within cell C29. End the formula by typing an ending parenthesis. To type an ending parenthesis, hold down the SHIFT key and press zero (0) within the main keyboard area (not within the numeric keypad area). When completed, the formula should read:

=(C14-C29)

Press the ENTER or RETURN key. The value contained within cells C29 will be subtracted from the value contained within cell C14, and the result will be produced within cell C31.

13	Equity Capital Proceeds	$0.00	$0.00	$0.00	$0.00	$0.00	$0.00	$0.00	$0.00	$0.00
14	TOTAL CASH RECEIPTS	$12,500.00	$5,500.00	$3,500.00	$3,000.00	$6,500.00	$7,300.00	$8,300.00	$10,000.00	$15,500.00
15										
16	CASH DISBURSEMENTS									
17	Cost of Goods Sold	$4,000.00	$2,500.00	$1,500.00	$1,250.00	$3,000.00	$3,400.00	$3,900.00	$4,750.00	$7,500.00
18	Payroll	$2,500.00	$1,500.00	$1,500.00	$1,500.00	$1,500.00	$1,500.00	$2,000.00	$2,000.00	$2,500.00
19	Payroll Taxes and Benefits	$450.00	$270.00	$270.00	$270.00	$270.00	$270.00	$360.00	$360.00	$450.00
20	Non-Payroll Expenses	$150.00	$75.00	$0.00	$0.00	$75.00	$80.00	$100.00	$100.00	$125.00
21	Depreciable Asset Purchases	$1,500.00	$0.00	$0.00	$0.00	$0.00	$0.00	$0.00	$0.00	$0.00
22	Non-Depreciable Asset Purchases	$500.00	$300.00	$250.00	$200.00	$250.00	$300.00	$325.00	$1,500.00	$2,500.00
23	Interest	$187.50	$186.53	$185.55	$184.57	$183.58	$182.58	$181.58	$180.56	$179.54
24	Short-Term Liabilities Payments	$0.00	$0.00	$0.00	$0.00	$0.00	$0.00	$0.00	$0.00	$0.00
25	Long-Term Liability Payments	$316.69	$316.69	$316.69	$316.69	$316.69	$316.69	$316.69	$316.69	$316.69
26	Investor Dividends or Owners Draw	$1,500.00	$1,500.00	$1,500.00	$1,500.00	$1,500.00	$1,500.00	$1,500.00	$1,500.00	$1,500.00
27	TOTAL CASH DISBURSEMENTS	$11,104.19	$6,648.22	$5,522.24	$5,221.26	$7,095.27	$7,549.27	$8,683.27	$10,707.25	$15,071.23
28	Income Taxes	$488.53	$86.66	$0.00	$0.00	$0.00	$0.00	$0.00	$0.00	$0.00
29	TOTAL CASH DISBURSEMENTS AFTER TAXES	$11,592.72	$6,734.88	$5,522.24	$5,221.26	$7,095.27	$7,549.27	$8,683.27	$10,707.25	$15,071.23
30										
31	NET CHANGE IN CASH		$907.28 =(C14-C29)							
32										
33	ENDING CASH POSITION	$6,907.28	$5,672.40	$3,650.16	$1,428.90	$833.63	$584.36	$201.09	-$506.16	-$77.39
34										
35										
36										
37	TOTAL OPERATING PROFIT (BEFORE TAXES)	$1,395.81	$247.59	$0.00	$0.00	$0.00	$0.00	$0.00	$0.00	$0.00

YR 1 Cash Flow Statement

Sheet 1 / 1   Default   75%   INSRT   STD   *   Sum=$0.00

9 Repeat Step #7 by selecting, one at a time, each of the following cells: D31, E31, F31, G31, H31, I31, J31, K31, L31 and M31. After selecting an individual cell, follow the instructions in Step #8 to obtain the results for the appropriate month. When you have completed adding the cell ranges specified above, the spreadsheet should look like the illustration on the following page.

Year One Pro Forma Cash Flow Statement	B	C	D	E	F	G	H	I	J
Month									
	1	2	3	4	5	6	7	8	9
STARTING CASH POSITION	$6,000.00	$6,907.28	$5,672.40	$3,650.16	$1,428.90	($833.63)	$584.36	$201.09	($506.18)
CASH RECEIPTS									
Cash Sales	$12,000.00	$5,000.00	$3,000.00	$2,500.00	$6,000.00	$6,800.00	$7,800.00	$9,500.00	$15,000.00
Sales On Credit	$0.00	$0.00	$0.00	$0.00	$0.00	$0.00	$0.00	$0.00	$0.00
Short-Term Loan Proceeds	$150.00	$150.00	$150.00	$150.00	$150.00	$150.00	$150.00	$150.00	$150.00
Long-Term Loan Proceeds	$350.00	$350.00	$350.00	$350.00	$350.00	$350.00	$350.00	$350.00	$350.00
Equity Capital Proceeds	$0.00	$0.00	$0.00	$0.00	$0.00	$0.00	$0.00	$0.00	$0.00
TOTAL CASH RECEIPTS	$12,500.00	$5,500.00	$3,500.00	$3,000.00	$6,500.00	$7,300.00	$8,300.00	$10,000.00	$15,500.00
CASH DISBURSEMENTS									
Cost of Goods Sold	$4,000.00	$2,500.00	$1,500.00	$1,250.00	$3,000.00	$3,400.00	$3,900.00	$4,750.00	$7,500.00
Payroll	$2,500.00	$1,500.00	$1,500.00	$1,500.00	$1,500.00	$1,500.00	$2,000.00	$2,000.00	$2,500.00
Payroll Taxes and Benefits	$450.00	$270.00	$270.00	$270.00	$270.00	$270.00	$360.00	$360.00	$450.00
Non-Payroll Expenses	$150.00	$75.00	$0.00	$0.00	$0.00	$75.00	$80.00	$100.00	$125.00
Depreciable Asset Purchases	$1,500.00	$0.00	$0.00	$0.00	$0.00	$0.00	$0.00	$0.00	$0.00
Non-Depreciable Asset Purchases	$500.00	$300.00	$250.00	$200.00	$250.00	$300.00	$325.00	$1,500.00	$2,500.00
Interest	$187.50	$186.53	$185.55	$184.57	$183.58	$182.58	$181.58	$180.56	$179.54
Short-Term Liabilities Payments	$0.00	$0.00	$0.00	$0.00	$0.00	$0.00	$0.00	$0.00	$0.00
Long-Term Liability Payments	$316.89	$316.89	$316.89	$316.89	$316.89	$316.89	$316.89	$316.89	$316.89
Investor Dividends or Owners Draw	$1,500.00	$1,500.00	$1,500.00	$1,500.00	$1,500.00	$1,500.00	$1,500.00	$1,500.00	$1,500.00
TOTAL CASH DISBURSEMENTS	$11,104.19	$6,648.22	$5,522.24	$5,221.26	$7,095.27	$7,549.27	$8,683.27	$10,707.25	$15,071.23
Income Taxes	$488.53	$86.66	$0.00	$0.00	$0.00	$0.00	$0.00	$0.00	$0.00
TOTAL CASH DISBURSEMENTS AFTER TAXES	$11,592.72	$6,734.88	$5,522.24	$5,221.26	$7,095.27	$7,549.27	$8,683.27	$10,707.25	$15,071.23
NET CHANGE IN CASH	$907.28	($1,234.88)	($2,022.24)	($2,221.26)	($595.27)	($249.27)	($383.27)	($707.25)	$428.77
ENDING CASH POSITION	$6,907.28	$5,672.40	$3,650.16	$1,428.90	($833.63)	$584.36	$201.09	($506.18)	($77.38)
TOTAL OPERATING PROFIT (BEFORE TAXES)	$1,395.81	$247.59	$0.00	$0.00	$0.00	$0.00	$0.00	$0.00	$0.00

YR 1 Cash Flow Statement

Analyzing the Final Data Contained Within the Cash Flow Statement

The cash flow statement is now complete. The cash flow statement is a very important tool for businesses, as it provides information regarding the actual cash position in any given period of time. This financial tool may not be crucial for a business that operates on a cash and carry basis, because it is easy to determine how much cash is available by looking at its bank statement or the amount of cash secured in the business' safe. However, for start-up businesses and businesses that sell on credit, a cash flow statement is crucial in determining how much money is needed and available to start or operate the business.

Like the completed cash flow statement in this lesson demonstrates, a business can be making a profit and still lack the cash needed to pay its monthly bills. If you look at cell N33, you will note that the Ending Cash Position for the year increased to $14695.28, up from a Starting Cash Position of $6,000.00. This could mean that the business actually made money in its first year, which is unusual for many start-up businesses.

However, if you carefully analyze the cash flow statement, it reveals a very serious problem for months eight (8) and nine (9). If you look at the Ending Cash Position for those months (cells I33 and J33, respectively), they show a negative cash position. This means that if this business were actually operating during those months, they would not have enough money to pay their immediate bills. This could result in the business having to close its doors if additional funds were not available.

If this were a preliminary cash flow statement used for planning a start-up business, the business owner could resolve this potential problem by adding, at minimum, an additional $583.55 to the initial Starting Cash Position in month one (1) to cover the shortfalls for months eight (8) and nine (9). Or, if the business owner was confident that their sales forecast prior to these months would be higher than, then the increased sales could cover for the shortfall.

Moreover, the business owner could decide to open the business in month eight (8) or nine (9) with a starting cash position of $6,000.00. Looking at the completed cash flow statement for this lesson, you will note that the Net Change In Cash for months two (2) through eight (8) were all negative. This means that the business was using more cash to pay its bills than it was receiving in sales. By opening in months eight (8) or nine (9), it would allow the business to open its doors just prior to the big shopping season and increase its cash position significantly before entering the slower sales period of months two (2) through eight (8). This scenario could stabilize the financial position of the business greatly until it could establish itself and make sales and market share gains in the second and third year.

As you have seen, there is rarely one answer to the questions or problems that arise when analyzing a business' financial position. However, by developing the fundamental financial statements with a spreadsheet application such as Calc, a business' management team can identify the potential issues more clearly. By doing so, it can assist in solving problems before they arise.

Additional Resources

U.S. Small Business Administration: Preparing Your Cash Flow Statement
http://www.sba.gov/test/wbc/docs/finance/cashflow.html

Credit Research Foundation: The Trade Creditor's Guide to the Statement of
Cash Flows
http://www.crfonline.org/orc/cro/cro-10.html

Review Questions

1   Font styles can be applied to text within a Calc spreadsheet document by
     utilizing the _____ toolbar or the _____ menu.

2   How would the value 25% be represented within a Calc spreadsheet
     document?

3   What symbol represents multiplication within a spreadsheet formula?

4   (True or False) Toolbars can be made visible or hidden by utilizing the View
     menu.

5   (True or False) Many of the menu and toolbar options that are available for
     formatting text within Writer are the same within Calc as well.

LESSON

8

Creating a Basic Educational Slide Presentation Using Impress

Lesson Objectives

In this lesson, you will learn the following:

1 How to create an educational slide presentation using the OpenOffice.org Impress presentation application.

2 How to create a slide within an Impress document and insert text within textboxes provided.

3 How to format slides within an Impress document, including inserting numbered lists and changing slide background colors.

4 How to insert graphics and clipart within slides.

5 How to save, view and print an Impress slide presentation document.

Overview

The OpenOffice.org office productivity suite contains a slide presentation application called Impress. Impress has all of the fundamental features found in the other major presentation applications, plus features unavailable in any other application similar to it. In this lesson, you will become acquainted with using Impress by creating a basic educational slide presentation related to the topic of experiential learning.   Upon completion of this lesson, you will have learned the fundamentals of creating slides within an Impress document, entering and formatting text within slides, how to insert images within slides, how to view and print an Impress slide document and much more.

Getting Started

Before we do so, we need to open the Lesson Eight file that is available for use with this book. To open the file, follow these steps:

1   If you have not already downloaded the lesson files for this book, use a web browser to go to **http://documentation.openoffice.org/ conceptualguide/OpenOfficeOrg3LessonFiles.zip**. This will provide a direct link for your browser to begin an automatic download of the lesson files. If a dialog window appears asking where you would like to save the file to be downloaded, select your computer workstation's desktop and begin downloading the file.

2   When the file appears on your computer's desktop, double-click the file icon to unzip its contents and access the files associated with each lesson. Double-click the Lesson Files folder icon that contains the available lesson files, locate the Lesson 08 folder and double-click on it to access the file for this lesson. When you have opened the folder, double-click the file named **lesson_08_start.odp** to open the file.

Creating a New Presentation Document

For this lesson, a file has already been created for you to begin working on. However, if you were creating your own presentation project, you would need to start with opening OpenOffice.org and creating a new Impress document. To do so, follow these steps:

1   With an OpenOffice.org document already open, such as this example with the Lesson 08 file, click on the File menu, select New from the menu options that appear and select Presentation from the submenu that appears.

2   When you do so, a Presentation Wizard will appear. Select the appropriate Presentation Type by clicking on the radio buttons provided. Follow the on-screen instruction that the wizard provides in creating a new presentation document.

To remove the new document from the screen, click on the File menu and select Close from the menu options that appear. If a dialogue window appears asking whether you wish to save the document, press the DISCARD button to delete the file without saving it.

For directions regarding creating a new Impress document without OpenOffice.

org already launched and running, refer to Appendix C for directions for creating a new document within Windows and Linux-based operating systems.

Creating a New Slide

The first thing that needs to be done for this presentation is to add a couple of new slides. The lesson_08_start file currently contains thirteen (13) slides, while the completed presentation will contain fifteen (15) slides. To add the additional slides to the presentation, follow these steps:

1 With the lesson_08_start file open, scroll down the list of slides viewable within the Slide Pane located on the left side of the Impress application window. If the Slide Pane is not viewable, simply click on the View menu at the top of the application window and select Slide Pane from the menu options that appear.

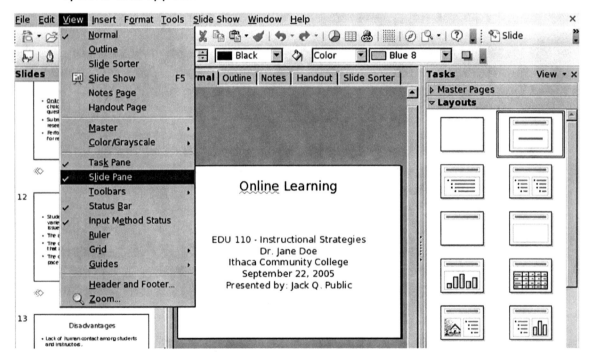

2 Locate slide #13 and select it by clicking on the icon once with your left mouse button.

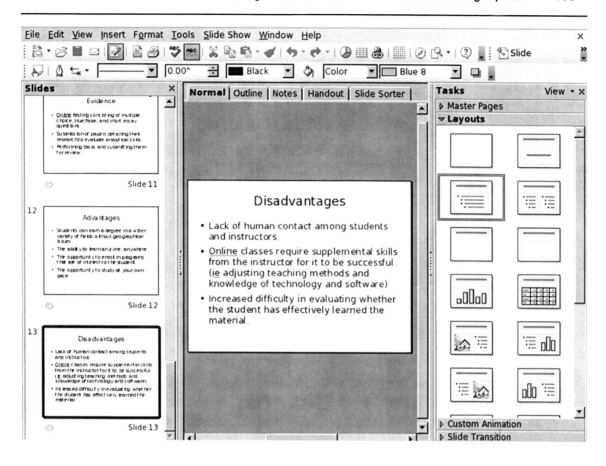

3 Click on the Insert menu and select Slide from the menu options that appear. A new slide is created after slide #13.

4 With slide #14 already selected within the Slide Pane, locate the Task Pane on the right side of the Impress application window. If the Task Pane is not viewable, simply click the View menu at the top of the application window and select Task Pane from the menu options that appear.

5 Within the Task Pane, there are four Page options to choose from: Master Pages, Layouts, Custom Animation and Slide Transition. Select the Layouts page by clicking on the label Layouts with your left mouse button. When the Layouts page appears, select the Title Only layout, which is the third layout in the left-hand column. (Note: If you position your mouse pointer over each option within the Layout page, the pointer will indicate which layout option the icon represents.)

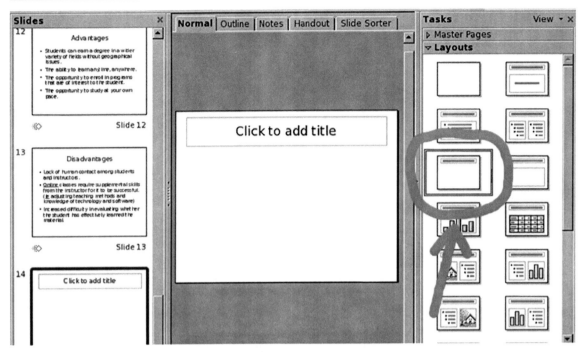

6 Click in the textbox provided with the slide layout. The textbox is the area
    indicated labeled **Click To Add Text**. When you do so, a cursor appears
    indicating that you can begin typing the appropriate text. For this slide
    (slide #14), type ***Demonstration*** within the textbox.

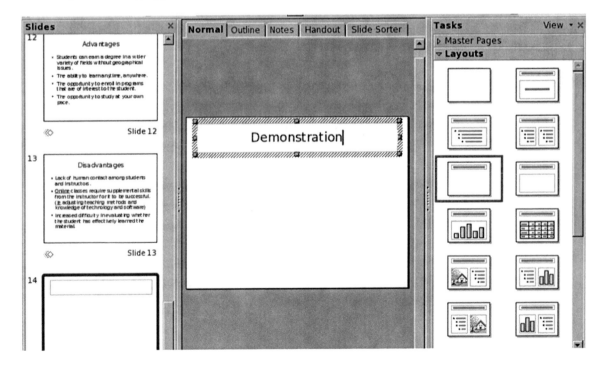

7 Now that the appropriate title has been entered into the textbox, the title needs to be repositioned into the center of the slide. To do so, place the pointer on the border of the textbox, not on the green resizing boxes positioned along the textbox border. When doing so, the pointer transforms itself into a target symbol, indicating that repositioning the textbox can be performed. Holding down the left mouse button, drag the textbox and center it within the slide layout. After doing so, release the left mouse button and click within the blank area of the slide layout to deselect the textbox.

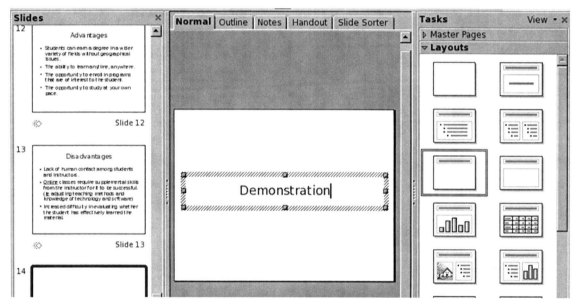

8 Next, we need to add our final slide to the presentation. With slide #14 already selected, click on the Insert menu and select Slide from the menu options that appear. A new slide is created after slide #14.

9 With slide #15 already selected within the Slide Pane, locate the Task Pane on the right side of the Impress application window.

10 In the Layouts page within the Task Pane on the right side of the application window, select the Title Only layout again.

11 Click in the textbox provided with the slide layout. The textbox is the area indicated labeled **Click To Add Text**. When you do so, a cursor appears indicating that you can begin typing the appropriate text. For this slide (slide #15), type ***Questions and Answers*** within the textbox.

12 Like the previous slide created, the title needs to be repositioned into the center of the slide. To do so, place the pointer on the border of the textbox, not on the green resizing boxes positioned along the textbox border. When doing so, the pointer transforms itself into a target symbol, indicating that repositioning the textbox can be performed. Holding down the left mouse button, drag the textbox and center it within the slide layout. After doing so, release the left mouse button and click within the blank area of the slide layout to deselect the textbox.

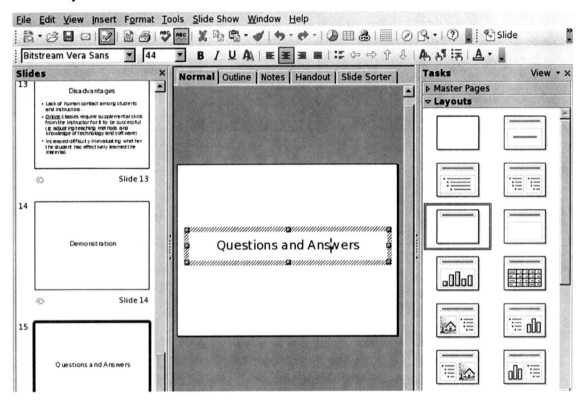

Inserting and Formatting Text

The two additional slides for the presentation have now been created. Next, the text within each slide needs to be formatted to improve the presentation's appearance and readability. As you have learned in the previous section, inserting text within a slide is as simple as clicking within a provided textbox and typing when the cursor appears.

Formatting text within an Impress document is very similar to formatting a Writer word processing document or a Microsoft PowerPoint slide presentation.

Moreover, many of the formatting options available in word processing applications are also available within Impress. For this lesson, we will make several formatting changes to the titles of each slide, as well as add a shadow effect to the text within each slide to improve the readability of the slide when presented on paper or overhead screen.

To properly format the text within each slide in the lesson file, follow these steps:

1 With the presentation file open, select the first slide within the Slide Pane located on the left side of the Impress application window.

2 In the editing window located in the center of the application window, select the title textbox by clicking on it once with your left mouse button. With the textbox selected and the cursor visible, select the text within the textbox by holding down your left mouse button and dragging over the text to highlight it. This is the same method as selecting text within Writer or other word processing applications.

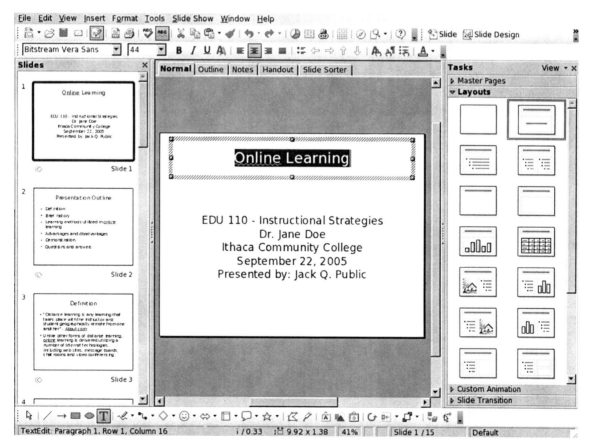

3 For the text contained within the title area of the slide, the following formatting attributes will need to be applied: Bitstream Vera Sans font type, 48 point font size, bold typeface and text shadow effect applied. Click on the Format menu located at the top of the Impress application window and select Character from the menu options that appear.

4 When the Character window appears, click the Font tab located at the top of the window. Select the appropriate font type size and typeface as specified in Step #3.

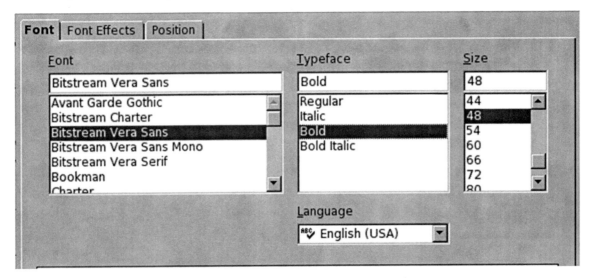

5 Next, click on the Font Effects tab at the top of the Character window. To add a shadow effect to the text selected, click within the Shadow checkbox provided. Then click the OK button to apply the formatting options to the selected text.

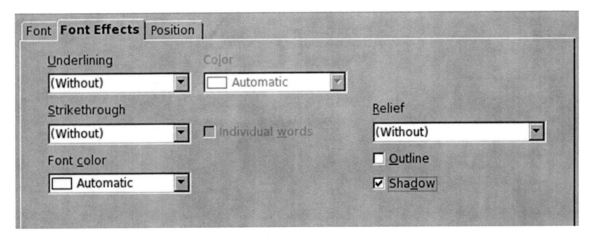

6 To apply the shadow effect to the text within the body text of the slide, select the text within the body textbox. Then click on the Format menu, select the Character menu option that appears and click on the Font Effects tab at the top of the Character window when it appears on the screen. Click within the Shadow checkbox provided to enable text shadowing and click the OK button to apply the formatting option.

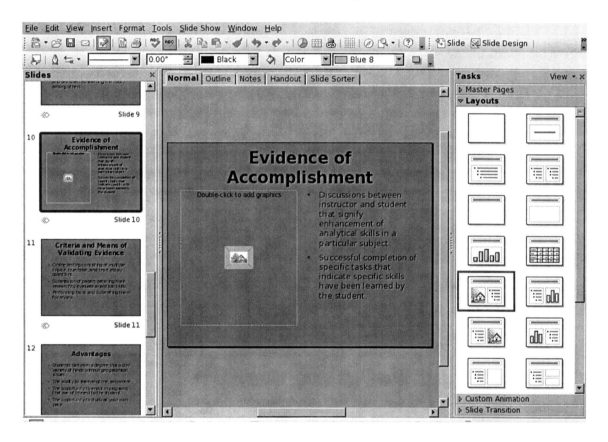

7 Repeat steps one (1) through six (6) for each of the remaining slides within the lesson file. Upon completion, all of the text within the presentation document will be properly formatted.

While selecting the Character menu option provides you with the most comprehensive selection of text formatting options, the most common format options are also available within the Standard toolbar located above the editing area. Do so by simply selecting the text to be formatted within the editing window and click on the appropriate format button or popup menu located in the toolbar.

Inserting Bullet and Numbering Lists

When selecting the appropriate slide layout from the Layouts page within the Task Pane, the text within the Body textbox will automatically bullet the text when typing. Therefore, having to manually select to bullet the text is unnecessary. However, there may be times where you may want to reformat the body text from a bulleted list to a numbered list. While we will want to leave the appropriate body text within the final document of this lesson as bulleted lists, here is an example of how you could transform a bulleted list into a numbered list:

1   With the presentation file open, select the second slide within the Slide Pane located on the left side of the Impress application window.

2   Select the text within the body textbox. Then click on the Format menu, select the Bullets and Numbering menu option that appears and click on the Numbering Type tab at the top of the Bullets and Numbering window when it appears on the screen.

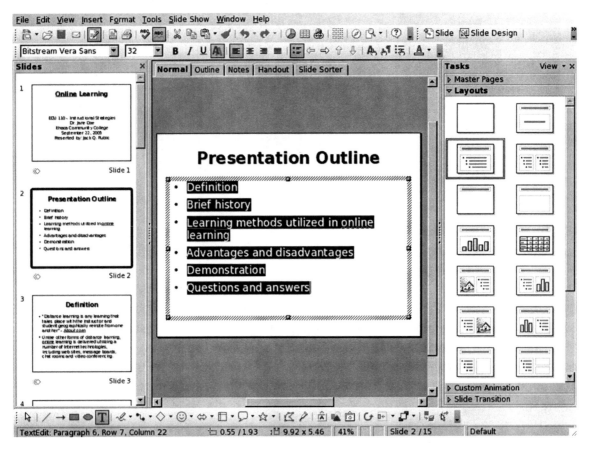

3 Select the appropriate numbering format within the selection area provided. Click the OK button to apply the formatting option.

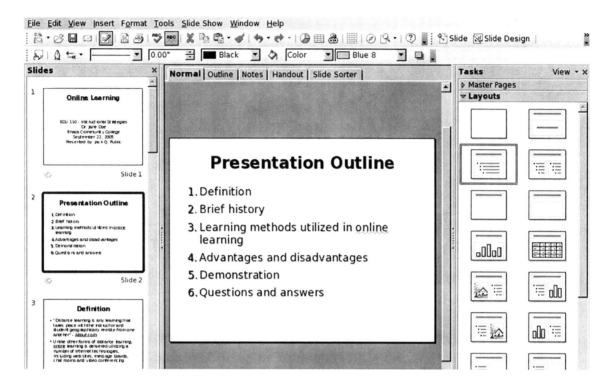

Changing Slide Background Color or Pattern

Now that the text within the slide presentation has been formatted properly, the next thing to do is to change the background color for each slide from white to turquoise to improve the appearance of the presentation. To change the slide background color for this presentation, follow these steps:

1 With the presentation file open, select the first slide within the Slide Pane located on the left side of the Impress application window.

2 Click on the Format menu and select Page from the menu options that appear.

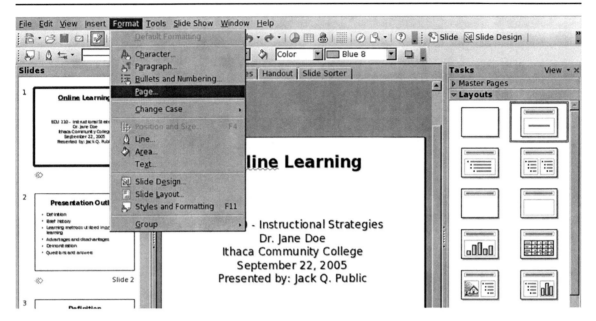

3 When the Page Setup window appears, click on the Background tab located at the top of the window.

4 Impress provides several formats within the popup menu to change the color or pattern of a slide presentation, including applying a solid background color, applying a pre-defined gradient pattern, applying a hatching pattern in combination with a solid background color and applying a bitmap image as a background pattern. For this lesson, select Color from the popup provided and choose Turquoise from the color options provided.

5 Click the OK button to complete the selection. A dialog box will appear asking whether the selection made should be applied to all slides within the Impress document or to apply to the current slide only. Click the YES button to apply the color selection to all slides within the presentation. Each slide within the presentation will now have a Turquoise background.

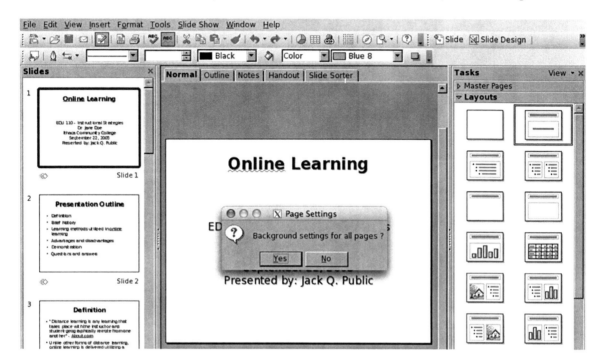

Inserting Graphics and Clip Art

Often, users will add graphics and clip art to help convey the message they are presenting in their presentation. In this lesson, we will add a couple of images to our presentation for such a purpose. To do so, follow these steps:

1 With the presentation file open, select slide #7 within the Slide Pane located on the left side of the Impress application window.

2 To insert an image into the slide, we will need to change the Layout page selected for the slide. With slide #7 selected within the Slide Pane, select the Title, Clipart Left, Text page in the Layouts page within the Tasks Pane. This the fifth layout listed in the left-hand column.

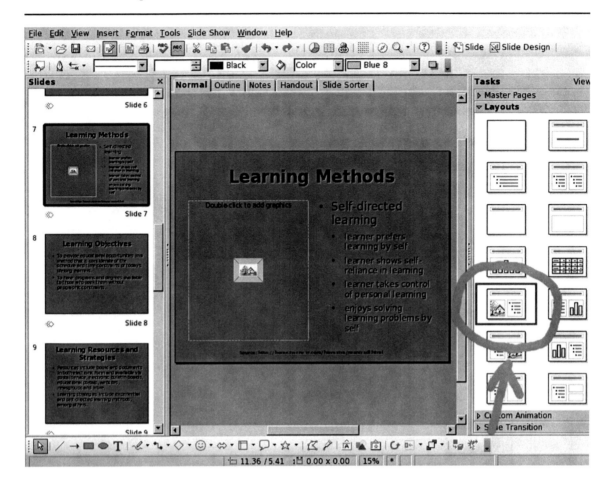

3 Within the editing area located in the center of the Impress application window, double-click on the graphics box that has been placed on the left-hand side of the slide. When doing so, an Insert Picture window will appear.

4 When the Insert Picture window appears, use the navigation buttons located in the upper-right corner of the window to locate the image files associated with this lesson. These photos can be found in the Lesson 08 folder, which is contained within the Lesson Files folder associated with this book. Once you have located the images, use your mouse to click on the image file lesson_08_image01.jpg to select it. If you wish to see a preview of the image within the Insert Picture window, make sure the Preview checkbox is selected by clicking within it. To insert it within the brochure, click the OPEN button.

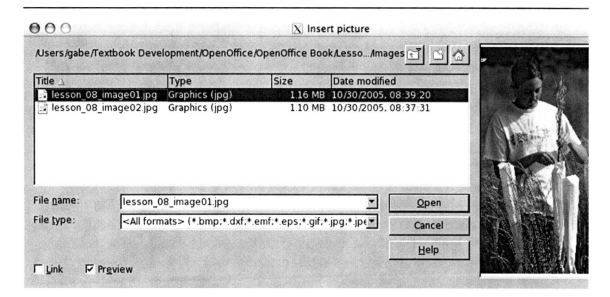

5 Next, we are going to insert an image into slide #10. To do so, select slide #10 within the Slide Pane located on the left side of the Impress application window.

6 Again, to insert an image into the slide, we will need to change the Layout page selected for the slide. With slide #10 selected within the Slide Pane, select the Title, Clipart Left, Text page in the Layouts page within the Tasks Pane. This the fifth layout listed in the left-hand column.

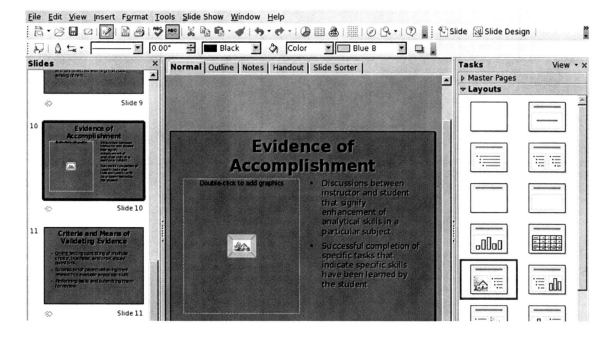

7 Within the editing area located in the center of the Impress application window, double-click on the graphics box that has been placed on the left-hand side of the slide. When doing so, an Insert Picture window will appear.

8 When the Insert Picture window appears, use the navigation buttons located in the upper-right corner of the window to locate the image files associated with this lesson. Again, these photos can be found in the Lesson 08 folder, which is contained within the Lesson Files folder associated with this book. Once you have located the images, use your mouse to click on the image file lesson_08_image02.jpg to select it. If you wish to see a preview of the image within the Insert Picture window, make sure the Preview checkbox is selected by clicking within it. To insert it within the brochure, click the OPEN button. The insertion of graphics within the presentation document is completed.

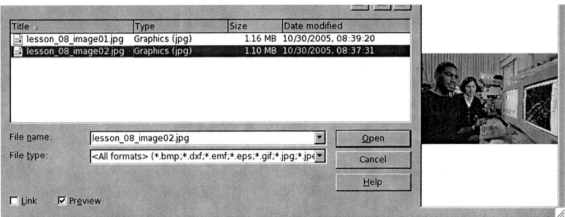

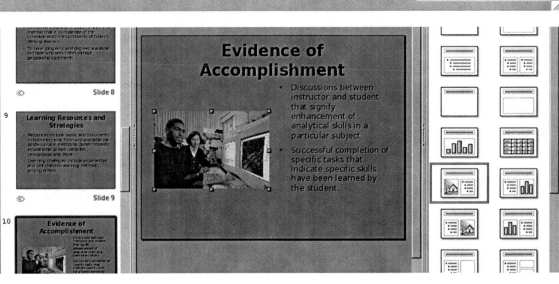

Using Spellcheck

Like a word processing document, you can use the OpenOffice.org spell check tool to check for spelling errors for words contained within an Impress presentation document. Potential spelling errors are indicated where words are underlined in red. To use the OpenOffice.org spell check feature to check for errors within the document for this lesson, follow these steps:

1 In the Slide Pane, select the first slide in the presentation by clicking on the icon with your left mouse button. This will allow the spellcheck tool to begin looking for spelling errors at the beginning of the document rather than in the middle or end of the document.

2 Go to the Tools menu and select Spellcheck from the menu that appears. You may also press the F7 key on your keyboard to begin checking for spelling errors.

3 If any potential spelling errors appear, OpenOffice.org will indicate the potential error and give you a list of possible suggestions to correct the spelling.

4 If you see a spelling suggestion that would correct the error, select it from the Suggestions list and click the CHANGE button.

5 If you believe that the word in question is spelled correctly, you can click the IGNORE ONCE button to proceed to the next potential spelling error. If the word in question is spelled correctly and you use it often when creating documents, you may click the ADD button to add it to the Spellcheck dictionary.

6 When you have completed checking for potential spelling errors, click the CLOSE button to exit and return to the document.

Saving the Document

Now that the slide presentation has been completed, the document file needs to be saved like any other presentation document. OpenOffice.org supports a number of file formats for opening and saving spreadsheet documents, including the native OpenDocument and Microsoft PowerPoint formats. To save the document to your computer's hard drive or removable disk, follow these steps:

1   Click on the File menu and choose Save As from the menu options that appear.

2   A window will appear and prompt you to choose a location to save your document. Choose the location you want to save a document to in the Save In popup field.

3   In the field File Name, type the name you would like to save the file as.

4   In the Save As Type popup menu, select the file format you wish to save the document as, including the OpenDocument Presentation (.odp) or Microsoft PowerPoint (.ppt) file format.

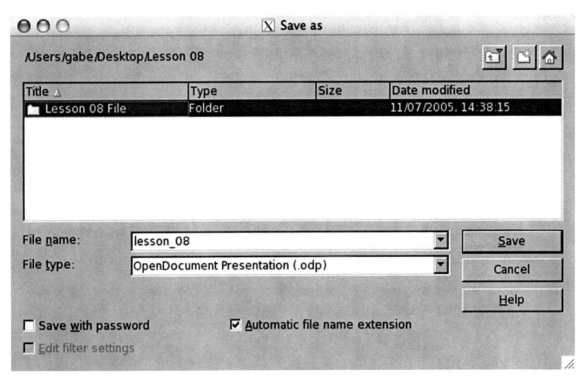

5   Click the button SAVE to complete the operation.

(NOTE: If you are given a window prompt that warns you about saving the document as a Microsoft PowerPoint file, click the YES button. The OpenOffice. org development team has gone to great lengths to help ensure that your document saved in the PowerPoint format will open properly with Microsoft PowerPoint. However, because the programming code utilized to create the PowerPoint file format is proprietary and not available to the OpenOffice.org team to view for ensuring full compatibility with Microsoft PowerPoint, not all of your document's formatting may open up 100% correctly when it is opened using the Microsoft PowerPoint application.)

Exporting a File as a Macromedia Flash Document

If you wish to have a slide presentation embedded within a website, or simply would like to send a slide presentation to someone who doesn't have either OpenOffice.org or Microsoft Office loaded on their computer, you could save the presentation as a Macromedia Flash document. Macromedia Flash is used extensively for multimedia in website development and most web browsers already have the plug-ins preloaded to display Flash content. Even if you didn't want to embed your presentation within a website, you could export a slide presentation as a Macromedia Flash document and anyone could view the presentation by simply opening it using the free Macromedia Flash Player. However, OpenOffice.org cannot edit a document that has been saved as a Macromedia Flash file. Therefore, if you wish to save a document for editing at a later date, save the document in its Native OpenDocument file format.

To save a document in the Macromedia Flash format, follow these steps:

1 Click on the File menu and choose Export from the menu options that appear.

2 A window will appear and prompt you to choose a location to save your document. Choose the location you want to save a document to in the Save In popup field.

3 In the field File Name, type the name you would like to save the file as.

4 In the Save As Type popup menu, select the Macromedia Flash (*.swf) file format.

5 Click the button SAVE to complete the operation.

Viewing Slide Show

To view a slide show within the Impress application, click on the Slide Show menu and select Slide Show from the menu options that appear or simply press the F5 key on the keyboard. To exit a slideshow, press the ESC key on the keyboard to return to the Impress editing window.

Printing a Slide Presentation

Impress provides a number of options for users to print their slide presentations. For most educational and business presentations where slides need to be printed, users either wish to print their slides for a specific page size or need to print the slide presentation in a standard handout format. To print the Lesson 09 Impress slide presentation for a specific page size, follow these steps:

1 If it isn't already, open the completed Lesson 08 Impress presentation.

2 Click on the Format menu, select Page from the menu options that appear and then select Page from the submenu options that appear.

3 In the Layout Settings selection area, click the Fit Object To Paper Format checkbox.

4 In the Paper Format selection area, select one of the format options provided.

5 Click the OK button to complete the operation. Each slide selected is scaled to fit the printed page.

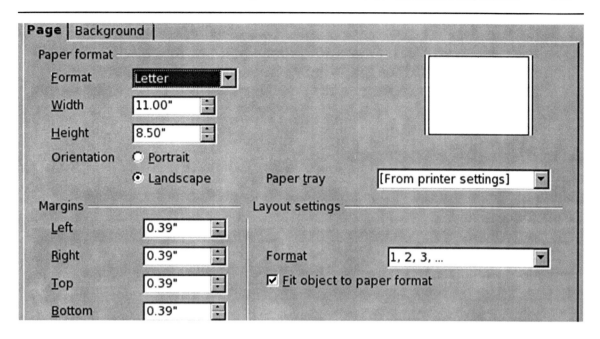

To print the Lesson 08 Impress slide presentation in the standard handout format, follow these steps:

6   If it isn't already, open the completed Lesson 08 Impress presentation.

7   Click on the View menu and select Handout Page from the menu list that appears.

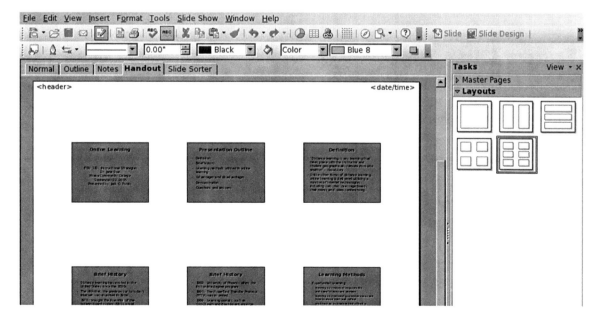

8 Click on the Print button located within the Standard menu bar at the top of the Impress application window. You may also hold down the COMMAND (⌘) key and press P on the keyboard to prompt for the Print window, or click on the File menu and select Print from the menu options that appear.

Additional Resources

Martha C. Sammons: Using Computer Slide Presentations in the College Classroom
http://horizon.unc.edu/projects/monograph/CD/Language_Music/Sammons.asp

Ten Slide Design Tips for Producing Powerful and Effective Presentations
http://articles.techrepublic.com.com/5100-22_11-6117178.html

Presentation-Pointers.com
http://www.presentation-pointers.com/index.asp

OpenOffice.org: How to Create a New Impress Document Using a Template
http://documentation.openoffice.org/HOW_TO/impress/
NewImpressUsingTemplate_revised.pdf

OpenOffice.org: How to Insert Notes in a Presentation
http://documentation.openoffice.org/HOW_TO/impress/HowToInsertNotes.pdf

Review Questions

1 What are two methods in which you can format text within an Impress presentation document?

2 What menu option would you select to change the color or background of a slide?

3 What would you need to do to view an Impress document as a slide show?

4 (True or False) Spellcheck is a feature that is not available within the Impress application.

5 (True or False) Bulleted lists can be converted to numbered lists within a slide, if desired.

LESSON

9

Creating a Bulk Mailing List Using
Base and Writer

Lesson Objectives

In this lesson, you will learn the following:

1 How to create and save a database using the new OpenOffice.org Base database application.

2 How to add, edit and delete records within a database table.

3 How to sort data within a table.

4 How to register a database within OpenOffice.org for use by other applications within the suite.

5 How to use Writer to create mailing labels from records within a Base database document.

Overview

In previous versions of OpenOffice.org, database files created with other applications could be accessed, edited and utilized for document creation within Writer and Calc. Moreover, a Calc spreadsheet document could be utilized as a spreadsheet table for use within Writer. However, prior to version two, OpenOffice.org did not have an application with a Graphic User Interface (GUI) similar to Microsoft Access or FileMaker Pro to easily create database files.

One of the major new features that can be found in version two of OpenOffice.org is a database application called Base. While the current version of Base may not have all of the features of a mature database application such as Microsoft Access or FileMaker Pro, Base has all of the fundamental features to create common business database documents, including the ability to create tables, forms, reports and queries. In this lesson, you will become acquainted with using Base by creating a bulk mail mailing list.   Upon completion of this lesson, you will have learned the fundamentals of creating tables within a Base document, adding and deleting records within tables, how to sort records within a table and much more.

Getting Started

Before we do so, we need to open the Lesson Nine file that is available for use with this book. To open the file, follow these steps:

1 If you have not already downloaded the lesson files for this book, use a web browser to go to **http://documentation.openoffice.org/ conceptualguide/OpenOfficeOrg3LessonFiles.zip**. This will provide a direct link for your browser to begin an automatic download of the lesson files. If a dialog window appears asking where you would like to save the file to be downloaded, select your computer workstation's desktop and begin downloading the file.

2 When the file appears on your computer's desktop, double-click the file icon to unzip its contents and access the files associated with each lesson. Double-click the Lesson Files folder icon that contains the available lesson files, locate the Lesson 09 folder and double-click on it to access the file for this lesson. When you have opened the folder, double-click the file named **lesson_09_start.odb** to open the file.

3 For this exercise, you need to save this file to your computer's hard drive, a network storage drive or a readable/writable removable storage device, such as a floppy disk. To do so, click on the File menu and select Save As from the menu options that appear. Select the location where the database should be saved. In this example, use lesson_09_work as the filename for the saved document. Moreover, select the file type OpenDocument Database. Then click the SAVE button.

Creating a New Database

For this lesson, a file has already been created for you to begin working on. However, if you were creating your own database project, you would need to start with opening OpenOffice.org and creating a new Base document. To do so, follow these steps:

1 Start the Base application from the Start Menu. Or within OpenOffice.org, go to the File menu, select New from the menu options that appear and select Database from the submenu options that appear.

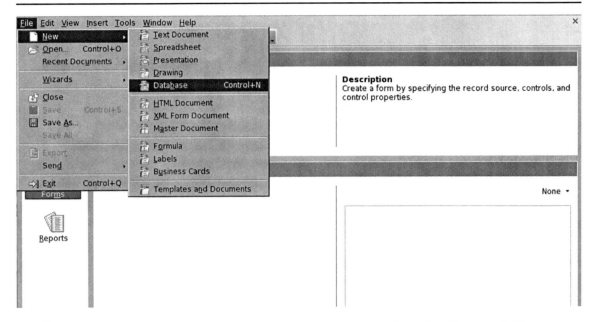

2 When the Database Wizard window appears, select the Create A New Database radio button and click the NEXT button located at the bottom of the window.

3 In the next window, select to have the database registered by clicking on the YES radio button. Within the same window, click both checkboxes available to have the software open the database for editing and have the table wizard assist with creating the necessary tables for the new database. Then click the FINISH button located at the bottom of the window.

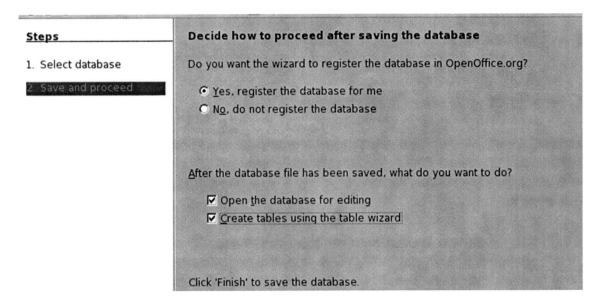

4 When the Save As window appears, select the location where the database should be saved. In this example, use my_sample_database as the filename for the saved document. Moreover, select the file type OpenDocument Database. Then click the SAVE button.

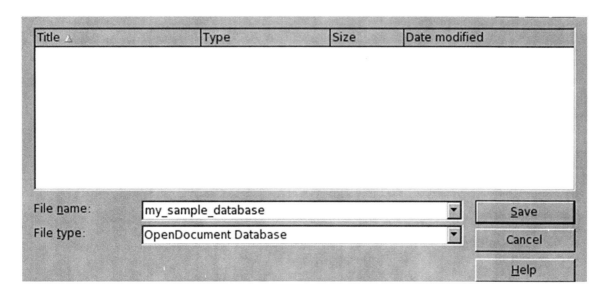

5 After the application has saved the database, the Table Wizard window will appear. In the Category selection area, select whether the database will be used for business or personal purposes by clicking on one of the radio buttons provided. Depending on the category selected, the Sample Table popup menu will provide a list of possible databases to create. For this example, choose the Business category and select MailingList from the Sample Tables popup menu.

6 When a sample table has been selected, a list of available fields associated with the type of table will appear in lower half of the window. In the Available Fields selection area, click on a field to add to the table and click the SINGLE RIGHT ARROW button. The field will then appear in the Selected Fields selection area. Repeat the process for each field to be added to the table. For this example, select the following fields from the Available Fields selection area: Prefix, FirstName, LastName, Address, City, StateorProvince and PostalCode. When all appropriate fields have been selected to appear in the table, use the UP and DOWN arrow buttons to change the order in which the fields will appear within the table. Then click the NEXT button located at the bottom of the window.

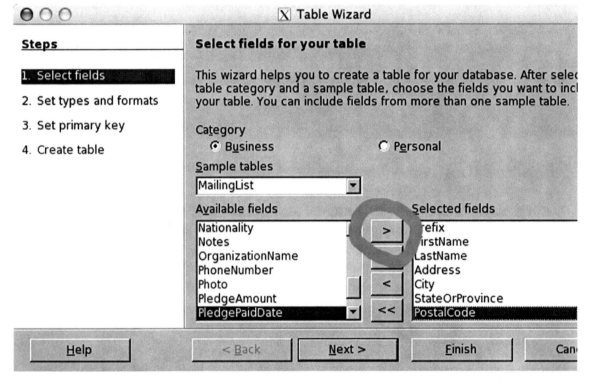

7 In the next window to appear in the Table Wizard, click on a field within the Selected Fields selection area. In the Field Information selection area, various formatting selections can be assigned to each field. Make the appropriate format options for the selected field. Then repeat the process for each field available in the Selected Fields selection area. For this example, all field information selections can remain at their default configurations. Then click the NEXT button.

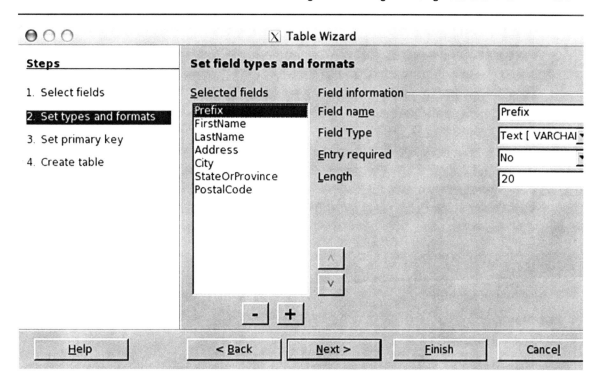

8 In the next window to appear, select the checkbox available to have Base create a primary key for the table and select the Automatically Add A Primary Key radio button. Then click the NEXT button.

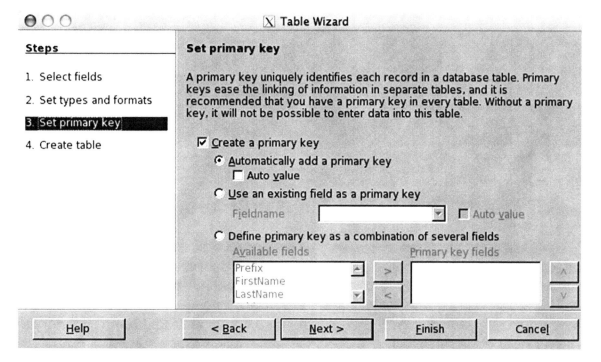

9 In the next window, type a name to identify the table being created using the text field provided. For this example, type the name MailingList if it doesn't already appear within the text field. Moreover, select the Insert Data Immediately radio button. Then click the FINISH button to create the table for the database.

To remove the new table editing window from the screen, click on the File menu and select Close from the menu options that appear. Repeat the same process for the main window for the document my_sample_database. You may then delete the my_sample_database file from your computer and return to the lesson_09_work file.

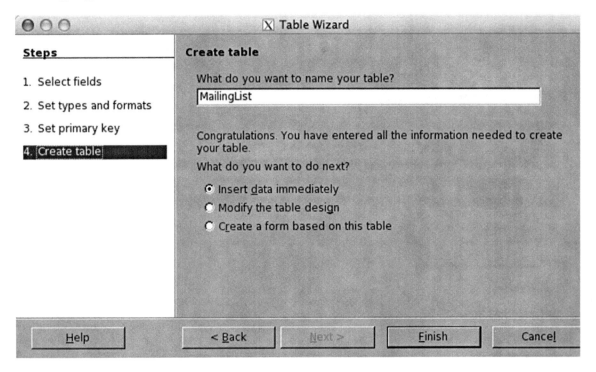

Adding and Deleting a Field within a Table

When creating a new Base document, as performed previously, you had an opportunity to create a table and add fields to the table while completing the document creation process. However, users can add and delete fields after the table creation process has taken place. In the following exercise, you will create a new field to an existing table and then remove it from the table when completed. To add and delete a field within a database table, follow these steps:

1   With the lesson_09_work file open, click on the Tables icon located on the left side of the document window within the Database Pane.

2   In the Tables pane located at the bottom-right of the window, select the MailingList Table to be edited by single-clicking on the icon.

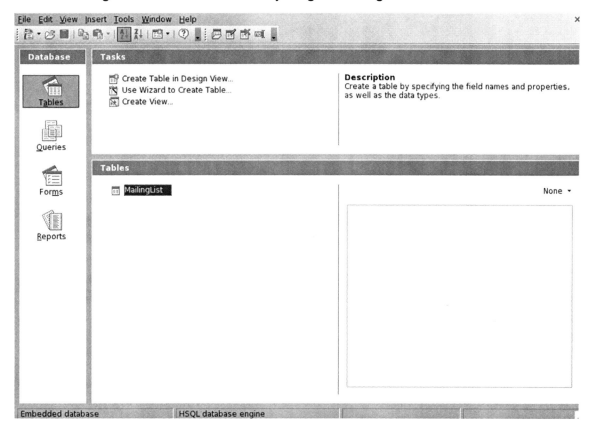

3   Click on the Edit menu at the top of the application window and select Edit from the menu options that appear.

4   When the Table Design window appears, click within the first available field underneath the Field Name column. Type a field name that best describes the information that will be entered into the field. When creating field names, be sure they do not contain any spaces. For example, a field name labeled Date Acquired should be typed as DateAcquired. In this example, type *Organization* for the new field name. When completing the Field Name, press the Tab key on the keyboard to proceed to format the Field Type.

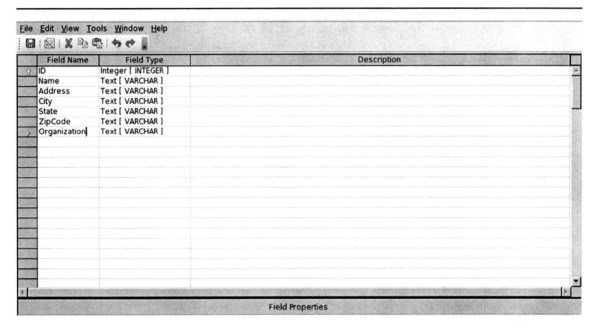

5 When tabbing to the Field Type column, a popup menu will appear to enable selection of the type of data the new field will contain. Select the appropriate field type, and make any additional configurations needed associated with the field within the Field Properties selection area located at the bottom of the Table Design window. In this example, the Field Type will remain Text [VARCHAR], which means variable character text, and the Field Properties will remain at their default configurations. Then press the Tab key on the keyboard to proceed to the Description column.

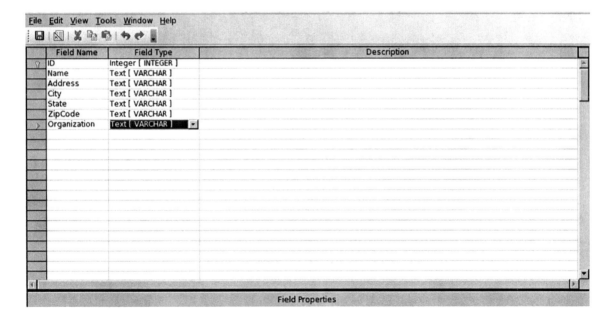

6 In the Description column, type a description for the new field being created (optional).

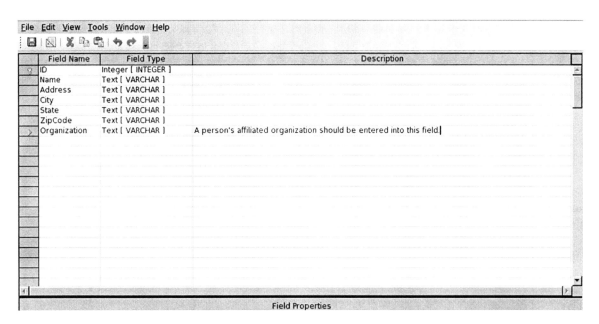

7 To save the changes made to the table, click the File menu and select Save from the menu options that appear. The process for adding the field Organization to the table has been completed. To double-check to make sure the field has been added to the table, minimize the Table Design window you are currently working in, return to the main document window, and double-click on the MailingList table. The table should contain the Organization field.

8 To remove the organization field from the table, return to the Table Design window that you minimized in step #7. If you mistakenly closed the Table Design window, simply repeat steps #1 through #3 in this exercise to return to it. Once you have returned to the Table Design window, select the field by clicking in the grey cell located to the left of the field you wish to delete. In this example, click in the grey cell located just to the left of the field name Organization. When doing so, the entire row for the Organization field will be selected and a green arrow will appear within the grey cell to the immediate left of the field selected.

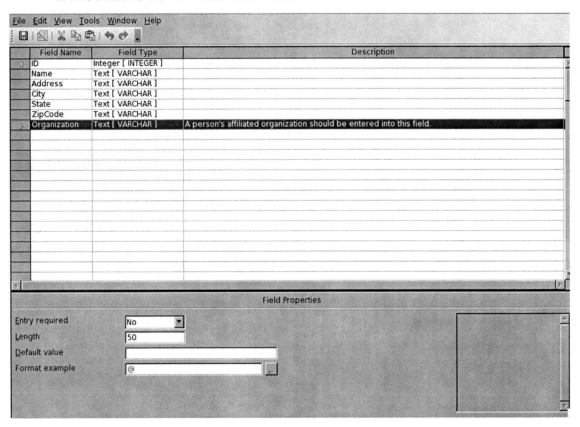

9 Once the organization field has been selected within the Table Design window, click on the Edit menu and select Cut from the menu options that appear. The Organization field will disappear from the table. For this change to take place permanently, click on the File menu and select Save from the menu options that appear.

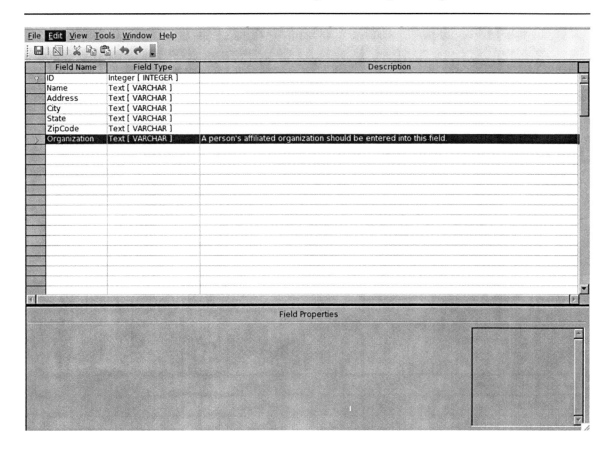

Add, Edit and Delete Records Within a Table

Once a table has been created, records can be entered into it. A record is simply data that is entered and saved within a table. Data entered within a record is associated with each other. For example, if you create a Base document to build a mailing list, the data you enter for a person's name, address, city, state and zip code are associated with each other and, therefore, are entered within the same record.

In this exercise, we will open the table that has been created within the lesson_09_work file and add additional records to the fictitious mailing list. Once those records have been added, you will also learn how to edit and delete records within a table. To add, edit and delete records within a table, follow these steps:

1 With the lesson_09_work file already open, click on the Tables icon located on the left side of the document window within the Database Pane.

2 In the Tables pane located at the bottom-right of the window, open the MailingList Table to enter records by double-clicking on the icon.

3 When the MailingList table window appears, you will notice there are already ten (10) records entered into the table. An empty record exists below the tenth to allow you to begin entering a new record. Within the empty record, place your mouse button on the ID field and click your left mouse button. This will allow you to select the ID field for entering text and numbers, much like selecting a cell within a Calc spreadsheet to enter data. When the empty ID field has been selected, type the number eleven (11) to uniquely identify the new record being entered. For each new record entered into the table, give it a unique identity by consecutively numbering each one. To advance to a new field within the record for entering data, simply press the TAB key on your keyboard like you would for advancing to the next column's cell within a spreadsheet. Beginning with record eleven (11), enter the following addresses:

Ms. Latasha Hutchinson	14778 Sunset Ave.	Clinton	NC	28328
Mr. Raymond Bavaria	15654 Cayuga St.	Ithaca	NY	14850
Mr. Johnny Hillandale	P.O. Box 124457	Starkville	MS	39759
Ms. Maria Cozumel	204 Hwy. 24 W.	Kenansville	NC	28349
Mr. Thomas Shippman	24547 Pacifica Ave.	Berkeley	CA	94701
Ms. Kyle Montague	27440 Franklin St.	Chapel Hill	NC	27514
Mr. Adrian Macon	P.O. Box 61445	Cherokee	NC	28719
Ms. Elizabeth Yorkshire	P.O. Box 9115	Kingston, Ontario	CN	K7L4W
Ms. Kelli Harrels	81157 Lumina Ave.	Wrightsville Beach	NC	28480
Mr. Marcos Jameson	81559 Rt. 12 E	Cape Vincent	NY	13618
Mr. John Doe	123 Main St.	Anytown	NC	12345

4 Once you have entered the additional records, the table should contain a total of twenty-one (21) records. To save the records entered, click the SAVE CURRENT RECORD button located directly beneath the File menu within the MailingList table window.

File Edit View Tools Window Help

ID	Name	Address	City	State	ZipCode
1	Mr. Maurice Sealy	6 Blue Ridge Rd.	Raleigh	NC	27612
2	Ms. Sheri Hon	84478 Stockton St.	San Francisco	CA	94108
3	Ms. Kayla Hauffman	300 N. Main St.	Dryden	NY	13053
4	Mr. Eric Van Buren	P.O. Box 97728	Mt. Airy	NC	27030
5	Ms. Anna Panella	P.O. Box 84448	Burgaw	NC	28425
6	Mr. Sean Concord	101 S. Maple St.	Burlington	VT	05406
7	Ms. Suzanne Paisley	12455 Bay St.	Savannah	GA	31401
8	Ms. Tara Hennesey	P.O. Box 97745	Asheville	NC	28816
9	Ms. Victoria Lychak	12554 Main St.	Niagra Falls, Ontario	CN	L2E 1T6
10	Mr. Michael Ponoma	P.O. Box 10002	Greece	NY	14515
11	Ms. Latasha Hutchenson	14778 Sunset Ave.	Clinton	NC	28328
12	Mr. Raymond Bavaria	15654 Cayuga St.	Ithaca	NY	14850
13	Mr. Johnny Hillandale	P.O. Box 124457	Starkville	MS	39759
14	Ms. Maria Cozumel	204 Hwy. 24 W.	Kenansville	NC	28349
15	Mr. Thomas Shippman	24547 Pacifica Ave.	Berkeley	CA	94701
16	Ms. Kyle Montague	27440 Franklin St.	Chapel Hill	NC	27514
17	Mr. Adrian Macon	P.O. Box 61445	Cherokee	NC	28719
18	Ms. Elizabeth Yorkshire	P.O. Box 9115	Kingston, Ontario	CN	K7L 4W
19	Ms. Kelli Harrels	81157 Lumina Ave.	Wrightsville Beach	NC	28480
20	Mr. Marcos Jameson	81559 Rt. 12E	Cape Vincent	NY	13618
21	Mr. John Doe	123 Main St.	Anytown	NC	12345

5 Once a record has been added to a table, the data within it can be edited later if needed. Selecting data within a database record for editing is the same as selecting a cell within a spreadsheet. Simply click within the field that you wish to edit the data for. For example, place your mouse pointer on top of the City field for record number twenty-one (21) and click your left mouse button. The data "Anytown" is selected, and you can now begin typing "Charlotte" to change the name of the city. Remember to click the SAVE CURRENT RECORD button located directly beneath the File menu to permanently save the changes.

File Edit View Tools Window Help

ID	Name	Address	City	State	ZipCode
1	Mr. Maurice Sealy	6 Blue Ridge Rd.	Raleigh	NC	27612
2	Ms. Sheri Hon	84478 Stockton St.	San Francisco	CA	94108
3	Ms. Kayla Hauffman	300 N. Main St.	Dryden	NY	13053
4	Mr. Eric Van Buren	P.O. Box 97728	Mt. Airy	NC	27030
5	Ms. Anna Panella	P.O. Box 84448	Burgaw	NC	28425
6	Mr. Sean Concord	101 S. Maple St	Burlington	VT	05406
7	Ms. Suzanne Paisley	12455 Bay St.	Savannah	GA	31401
8	Ms. Tara Hennesey	P.O. Box 97745	Asheville	NC	28816
9	Ms. Victoria Lychak	12554 Main St	Niagra Falls, Ontario	CN	L2E 1T6
10	Mr. Michael Ponoma	P.O. Box 10002	Greece	NY	14515
11	Ms. Latasha Hutchenson	14778 Sunset Ave.	Clinton	NC	28328
12	Mr. Raymond Bavaria	15654 Cayuga St.	Ithaca	NY	14850
13	Mr. Johnny Hillandale	P.O. Box 124457	Starkville	MS	39759
14	Ms. Maria Cozumel	204 Hwy. 24 W.	Kenansville	NC	28349
15	Mr. Thomas Shippman	24547 Pacifica Ave.	Berkeley	CA	94701
16	Ms. Kyle Montague	27440 Franklin St.	Chapel Hill	NC	27514
17	Mr. Adrian Macon	P.O. Box 61445	Cherokee	NC	28719
18	Ms. Elizabeth Yorkshire	P.O. Box 9115	Kingston, Ontario	CN	K7L 4W
19	Ms. Kelli Harrels	81157 Lumina Ave.	Wrightsville Beach	NC	28480
20	Mr. Marcos Jameson	81559 Rt. 12E	Cape Vincent	NY	13618
21	Mr. John Doe	123 Main St.	Charlotte	NC	12345

6   To delete a record that has been entered into a table, right-click within the grey cell located to the left of the record you wish to delete and select Delete Rows from the contextual menu that appears. To delete record number twenty-one (21), right-click your mouse in the grey cell to the left of ID number twenty-one (21) and select Delete Rows from the contextual menu that appears. When the dialogue window appears to ask whether you want to delete the selected data, click the YES button. Then click the SAVE CURRENT RECORD button located directly beneath the File menu to permanently save the changes.

File   Edit   View   Tools   Window   Help

ID	Name	Address	City	State	ZipCode
1	Mr. Maurice Sealy	6 Blue Ridge Rd.	Raleigh	NC	27612
2	Ms. Sheri Hon	84478 Stockton St.	San Francisco	CA	94108
3	Ms. Kayla Hauffman	300 N. Main St.	Dryden	NY	13053
4	Mr. Eric Van Buren	P.O. Box 97728	Mt. Airy	NC	27030
5	Ms. Anna Panella	P.O. Box 84448	Burgaw	NC	28425
6	Mr. Sean Concord	101 S. Maple St.	Burlington	VT	05406
7	Ms. Suzanne Paisley	12455 Bay St.	Savannah	GA	31401
8	Ms. Tara Hennesey	P.O. Box 97745	Asheville	NC	28816
9	Ms. Victoria Lychak	12554 Main St.	Niagra Falls, Ontario	CN	L2E 1T6
10	Mr. Michael Ponoma	P.O. Box 10002	Greece	NY	14515
11	Ms. Latasha Hutchenson	14778 Sunset Ave.	Clinton	NC	28328
12	Mr. Raymond Bavaria	15654 Cayuga St.	Ithaca	NY	14850
13	Mr. Johnny Hillandale	P.O. Box 124457	Starkville	MS	39759
14	Ms. Maria Cozumel	204 Hwy. 24 W.	Kenansville	NC	28349
15	Mr. Thomas Shippman	24547 Pacifica Ave.	Berkeley	CA	94701
16	Ms. Kyle Montague	27440 Franklin St.	Chapel Hill	NC	27514
17	Mr. Adrian Macon	P.O. Box 61445	Cherokee	NC	28719
18	Ms. Elizabeth Yorkshire	P.O. Box 9115	Kingston, Ontario	CN	K7L 4W
19	Ms. Kelli Harrels	81157 Lumina Ave.	Wrightsville Beach	NC	28480
20	Mr. Marcos Jameson	81559 Rt. 12E	Cape Vincent	NY	13618
21	Mr. John Doe	123 Main St.	Charlotte	NC	12345

Table Format...
Row Height...
Delete Rows
Save Record

Sorting Data Within a Table

If this were an actual mailing list to be used to send mail, it would be a small enough list to simply print on one sheet of adhesive labels, apply the labels to envelopes and drop the envelopes in the mail. But if a mailing list database table contained five hundred (500) records, then it would take as much as twenty-five (25) sheets of standard-sized adhesive labels to print all of them. Moreover, sending a five hundred (500) person mailing might require doing so via bulk mailing, which in turn would require sorting the envelopes by zip code.

Rather than applying the labels onto envelopes and then sorting them by hand, the process could be simplified significantly by sorting the records via zip code within the Base application before printing the labels. Therefore, the mailing addresses would already be sorted in the correct order when printed onto the labels. The labels could be applied onto envelopes in the order in which they appear on the label sheets, eliminating the need to sort the envelopes afterwards.

To sort the records within the MailingList table by zip code, follow these steps:

1 With the lesson_09_work file already open, click on the Tables icon located on the left side of the document window within the Database Pane.

2 In the Tables pane located at the bottom-right of the window, open the MailingList Table to enter records by double-clicking on the icon.

3 Using your left mouse button, single-click on the ZipCode field label located at the top of the MailingList table window. When doing so, the entire column of zip codes for each record will be selected.

File Edit View Tools Window Help

ID	Name	Address	City	State	ZipCode
1	Mr. Maurice Sealy	6 Blue Ridge Rd.	Raleigh	NC	27612
2	Ms. Sheri Hon	84478 Stockton St.	San Francisco	CA	94108
3	Ms. Kayla Hauffman	300 N. Main St.	Dryden	NY	13053
4	Mr. Eric Van Buren	P.O. Box 97728	Mt. Airy	NC	27030
5	Ms. Anna Panella	P.O. Box 84448	Burgaw	NC	28425
6	Mr. Sean Concord	101 S. Maple St.	Burlington	VT	05406
7	Ms. Suzanne Paisley	12455 Bay St.	Savannah	GA	31401
8	Ms. Tara Hennesey	P.O. Box 97745	Asheville	NC	28816
9	Ms. Victoria Lychak	12554 Main St.	Niagra Falls, Ontario	CN	L2E 1T6
10	Mr. Michael Ponoma	P.O. Box 10002	Greece	NY	14515
11	Ms. Latasha Hutchenso	14778 Sunset Ave.	Clinton	NC	28328
12	Mr. Raymond Bavaria	15654 Cayuga St.	Ithaca	NY	14850
13	Mr. Johnny Hillandale	P.O. Box 124457	Starkville	MS	39759
14	Ms. Maria Cozumel	204 Hwy. 24 W.	Kenansville	NC	28349
15	Mr. Thomas Shippman	24547 Pacifica Ave.	Berkeley	CA	94701
16	Ms. Kyle Montague	27440 Franklin St.	Chapel Hill	NC	27514
17	Mr. Adrian Macon	P.O. Box 61445	Cherokee	NC	28719
18	Ms. Elizabeth Yorkshire	P.O. Box 9115	Kingston, Ontario	CN	K7L 4W
19	Ms. Kelli Harrels	81157 Lumina Ave.	Wrightsville Beach	NC	28480
20	Mr. Marcos Jameson	81559 Rt. 12E	Cape Vincent	NY	13618

4 To sort the records by zip code, click the SORT ASCENDING button located within the Table Data View toolbar at the top of the window. When doing so, the records are sorted by zip code in numerical order and then by alphabetical order. When the labels are printed, the addresses will print in the order in which they appear on the screen.

ID	Name	Address	City	State	ZipCode
1	Mr. Maurice Sealy	6 Blue Ridge Rd.	Raleigh	NC	27612
2	Ms. Sheri Hon	84478 Stockton St.	San Francisco	CA	94108
3	Ms. Kayla Hauffman	300 N. Main St.	Dryden	NY	13053
4	Mr. Eric Van Buren	P.O. Box 97728	Mt. Airy	NC	27030
5	Ms. Anna Panella	P.O. Box 84448	Burgaw	NC	28425
6	Mr. Sean Concord	101 S. Maple St.	Burlington	VT	05406
7	Ms. Suzanne Paisley	12455 Bay St.	Savannah	GA	31401
8	Ms. Tara Hennesey	P.O. Box 97745	Asheville	NC	28816
9	Ms. Victoria Lychak	12554 Main St.	Niagra Falls, Ontario	CN	L2E 1T6
10	Mr. Michael Ponoma	P.O. Box 10002	Greece	NY	14515
11	Ms. Latasha Hutchenso	14778 Sunset Ave.	Clinton	NC	28328
12	Mr. Raymond Bavaria	15654 Cayuga St.	Ithaca	NY	14850
13	Mr. Johnny Hillandale	P.O. Box 124457	Starkville	MS	39759
14	Ms. Maria Cozumel	204 Hwy. 24 W.	Kenansville	NC	28349
15	Mr. Thomas Shippman	24547 Pacifica Ave.	Berkeley	CA	94701
16	Ms. Kyle Montague	27440 Franklin St.	Chapel Hill	NC	27514
17	Mr. Adrian Macon	P.O. Box 61445	Cherokee	NC	28719
18	Ms. Elizabeth Yorkshire	P.O. Box 9115	Kingston, Ontario	CN	K7L 4W
19	Ms. Kelli Harrels	81157 Lumina Ave.	Wrightsville Beach	NC	28480
20	Mr. Marcos Jameson	81559 Rt. 12E	Cape Vincent	NY	13618

At this time, the records within the table should remain sorted. However, if you ever wanted the records to reappear in their original order, you could do so by sorting the ID records in ascending order the same way you sorted the records by zip code.

Registering a Database Within OpenOffice.org

Before we can use Writer to create mailing labels from the database records, the database document we are working in must be registered within OpenOffice.org. If a database document is not registered within OpenOffice.org, then the Label Wizard will not be able to identify the correct database to extract the records from. If you had created the original database yourself using the Database Wizard, you could have specified to have the database automatically registered. Because you didn't create the original file, however, you must perform the simple task of registering the database manually.

To manually register the database within OpenOffice.org, follow these steps:

1 With the lesson_09_work file already open, click on the Tools menu and select Options from the menu options that appear.

2 When the OpenOffice.org User Data window appears, click on the plus "+" icon located next to the OpenOffice.org Base option located on the left side. When doing so, a list of options will appear related to the Base application.

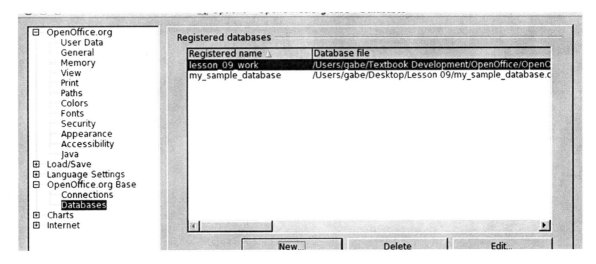

3 Select Databases from the OpenOffice.org Base options that appear by clicking on the label. When doing so, the list of databases that are already registered within OpenOffice.org will appear in the Registered Databases selection area on the right side of the window. To register the lesson_09_ work database document, click the NEW button, then click the BROWSE button in the Create Database Link dialogue window and locate the lesson file. After locating the file, select it and press the OPEN button. You will then be reverted back to Create Database Link dialogue window, where you can press the OK button to register the database.

4 To complete the registration, click the OK button within the OpenOffice.org User Data window.

Using Writer to Create Mailing Labels from Database Records

Now that the address records have been entered into the database table and the document registered within OpenOffice.org, we are ready for creating the mailing labels. Unlike Microsoft Access, OpenOffice.org Base doesn't have a Form Wizard for creating mailing labels. Instead, OpenOffice.org relies on a wizard within Writer to complete the process of creating mailing labels, which ultimately produces the same result. To create mailing labels from address records within a Base document, follow these steps:

1 From any application within OpenOffice.org, including Base or Writer, click on the File menu, select New from the menu options that appear and select Labels from the submenu options that appear.

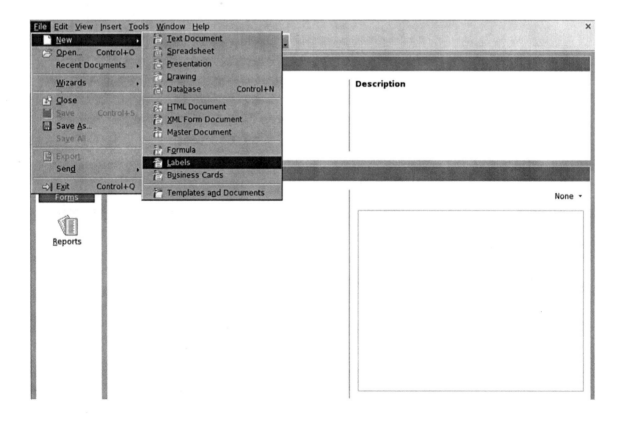

2 A Labels window should now appear on the screen. At the top of the Labels window, there should be three tabs present: Labels, Format and Options. If it isn't already selected, click on the Labels tab. Within the selection areas provided, select the following Label configurations:

- Place a check within the Addresses checkbox
- Select the **lesson_09_work** document within the Databases popup menu
- Select **MailingList** within the Tables popup menu
- Select the SHEET radio button
- Select Avery Letter Size within the Brand popup menu
- For this sample exercise, select 5261 Address within the Type popup menu. If this were an actual mailing list you were utilizing to prepare a mailing, you would select the type of labels you or your office have purchased.

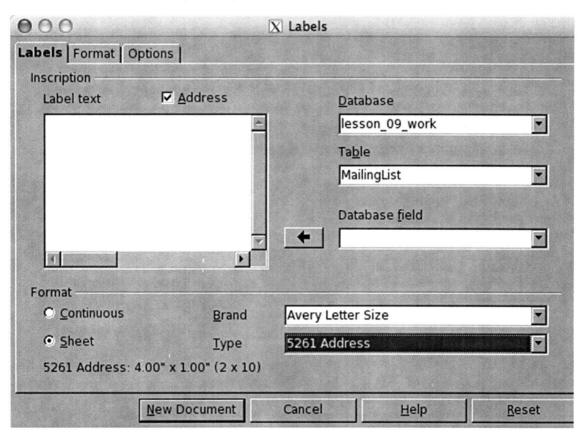

3 Continuing within the Labels tab window, select Name from the Database Field popup menu and press the LEFT ARROW button to place the field within the Inscription window. Then press the ENTER or RETURN key on your keyboard to move the cursor to the next line within the window.

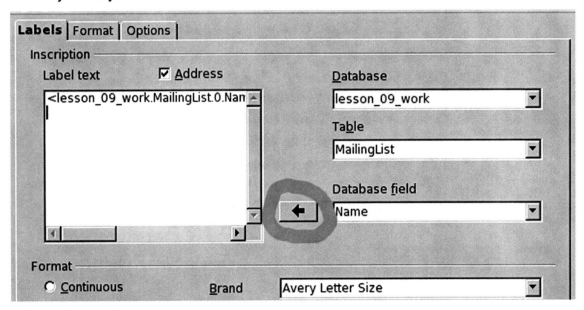

4 Next, select Address from the Database Field popup menu and press the LEFT ARROW button to place the field on the second line within the Inscription window. Then press the ENTER or RETURN key on your keyboard to move the cursor to the next line within the window.

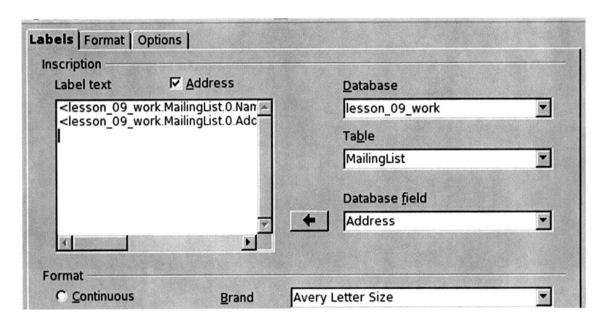

5 Select City from the Database Field popup menu and press the LEFT ARROW button to place the field on the third line within the Inscription window. Type a comma (,) immediately following the City field and press the SPACE BAR key once on the keyboard. Then select State from the Database Field popup menu and press the LEFT ARROW button to place the field behind the City field. Press the SPACE BAR key twice on the keyboard. Finally, select ZipCode from the Database Field popup menu and press the LEFT ARROW button to place the field behind the State field. Then press the ENTER or RETURN key on your keyboard to move the cursor to the next line within the window. The format displayed within the Inscription window indicates how the address information will be printed on the labels.

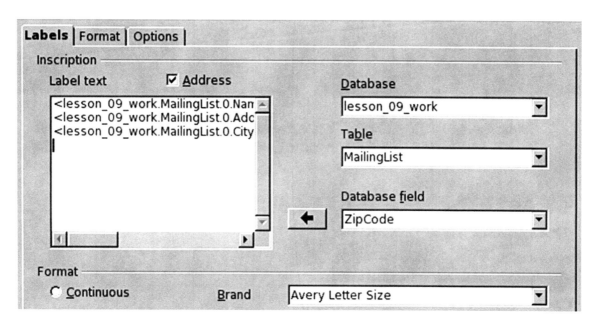

6 Click on the Options tab at the top of the Labels window. When the selection areas appear within the Options tab, select the ENTIRE PAGE radio button and place a check within the Synchronize Contents checkbox. This will format the labels to print on an entire sheet of labels, as you would purchase from an office supply store. Moreover, the Synchronize Contents option means that the data will automatically sync with the data contained within the MailingList table. Finally, if you wish to setup the labels to print on a printer other than what is specified in the window, click the SETUP button and configure accordingly.

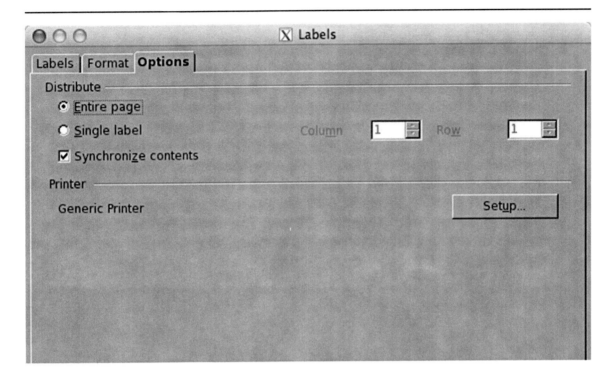

7 Press the NEW DOCUMENT button within the Labels window. Writer will then create a template that will format a sheet of labels as specified in the previous selections.

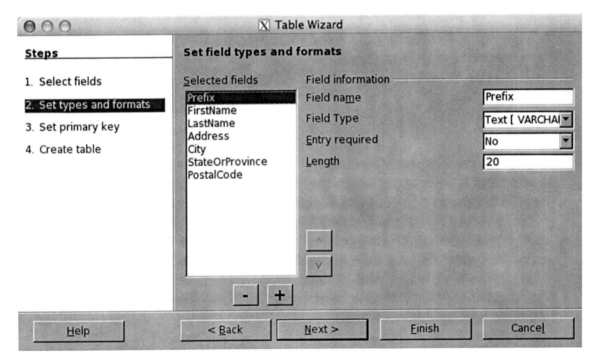

8 Within the Writer label template window, click the File menu and select Print from the menu options that appear. A dialogue window will appear stating that the document contains address data fields and asks whether you wish to print a form letter. Click the YES button.

9 When the Mail Merge window appears, you should notice some of the addresses within the database document are viewable. Make sure the ALL radio button is selected to print all of the addresses within the database. Also, make sure the PRINTER radio button is selected.

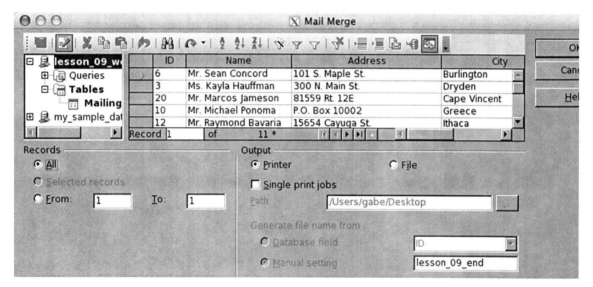

10 If you wish to print the addresses on actual mailing labels, make sure that your printer is loaded with the correct type of sheet labels, as selected in Step #2. In this case, the labels we chose for this exercise were Avery 5261 labels. Otherwise, click the OK button and the addresses will print on the regular paper presently loaded in the printer. The addresses should then print in the format presented in the Writer template. You will notice that when the addresses are printed, they are done so in ascending order by zip code, making it easier to prepare for bulk mailing.

Additional Resources

OpenOffice.org: Base Discussion Forum
http://www.oooforum.org/

General Information Regarding Databases via Wikipedia
http://en.wikipedia.org/wiki/Database

Review Questions

1 For changes to tables and records to remain permanent within Base, what do you need to do prior to closing the document or application?

2 What is a database record?

3 What does a computer user have to do before they can utilize the data contained within a Base database document for use in a Writer document?

4 (True or False) Unlike Microsoft Access, OpenOffice.org Base doesn't have a Form Wizard for creating mailing labels.

5 (True or False) Users cannot add and delete fields after the table creation process has taken place.

LESSON

10

Analyzing North Atlantic Hurricane Data Using Base

Lesson Objectives

In this lesson, you will learn the following:

1 How to create, run and save a query using Base.

2 How to perform comparisons among records using queries.

3 How to sort query data results.

4 How to specify field properties within table records.

5 How to create and print reports.

Overview

In the previous lesson, you learned how to use Base in conjunction with Writer to create labels for a bulk mailing list. Base has the capability to do much more than create basic tables and produce mailing labels. Base also has the capability to create queries, perform comparisons among records, create forms and reports, and more. Moreover, Base can also import from and export to other database applications, including Microsoft Access and FileMaker Pro.

In this lesson, you will become acquainted with additional features and capabilities within Base. Using a Base file containing tables and records related to North Atlantic hurricanes, you will learn about the strongest and costliest hurricanes to strike the United States / North Atlantic region by using Base as a way to analyze and compare available data. Upon completion of this lesson, you will have learned how to use Base to create and run queries, perform record comparisons, how to create and print reports, how to specify field properties within table records and more.

Getting Started

Before we do so, we need to open the Lesson Ten file that is available for use with this book. To open the file, follow these steps:

1   If you have not already downloaded the lesson files for this book, use a web browser to go to **http://documentation.openoffice.org/conceptualguide/OpenOfficeOrg3LessonFiles.zip**. This will provide a direct link for your browser to begin an automatic download of the lesson files. If a dialog window appears asking where you would like to save the file to be downloaded, select your computer workstation's desktop and begin downloading the file.

2   When the file appears on your computer's desktop, double-click the file icon to unzip its contents and access the files associated with each lesson. Double-click the Lesson Files folder icon that contains the available lesson files, locate the Lesson 10 folder and double-click on it to access the file for this lesson. When you have opened the folder, double-click the file named **lesson_10_start.odb** to open the file.

3   For this exercise, you need to save this file to your computer's hard drive, a network storage drive or a readable/writable removable storage device, such as a floppy disk. To do so, click on the File menu and select Save As from the menu options that appear. Select the location where the database should be saved. In this example, use lesson_10_work as the filename for the saved document. Moreover, select the file type OpenDocument Database. Then click the SAVE button.

How to Create and Run a Query Using the Query Design View

In our previous lesson, we created mailing labels utilizing a table that contained twenty records. When working with databases at school or in the workplace, you may often be entering and analyzing hundreds, even thousands, of records. However, searching or analyzing data by glancing through a table can be a time consuming and cumbersome task when that many records are involved. A much better method of searching and analyzing the data contained within table records is by utilizing queries. A query can be thought of as simply a subset, or filtered set, of records from a table that was created by specifying certain criteria to obtain a desired result.

Before a query can be performed, a new database document must be created and contain at least one table with records entered into it. For this lesson, a file has already been created for you to begin working on which contains two tables: Costliest Ranking and Intensity Ranking. We will use these tables to learn to create a simple query. To do so, follow these steps:

1 With the lesson_10_work.odb file open, click on the Queries icon located on the left side of the document window within the Database Pane.

2 In the Tasks pane located at the top of the window, single-click Create Query in Design View to launch the Design View window.

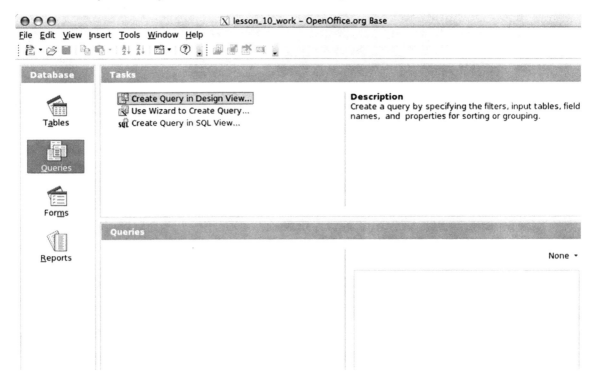

3 When the Query Design View window appears, the Add Table or Query window will also appear. Using the radio buttons available within the window, tables or queries that have been created within the database file are listed for availability to perform a query. For this example, select the Intensity Ranking table by single-clicking its icon among the list and click the ADD button. Once the Intensity Ranking table appears within the Query Design View window, click the CLOSE button within the Add Table or Query window.

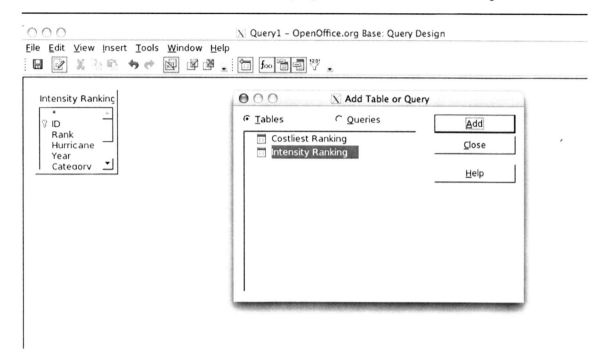

4   The next step in creating a query is to select which fields to utilize to run the query. To do so, utilize the first Field popup menu provided within the lower pane of the window to select the appropriate field name. This can be accomplished by simply using the mouse pointer to click within the field. In this example, select the **Intensity Ranking.Hurricane** field.

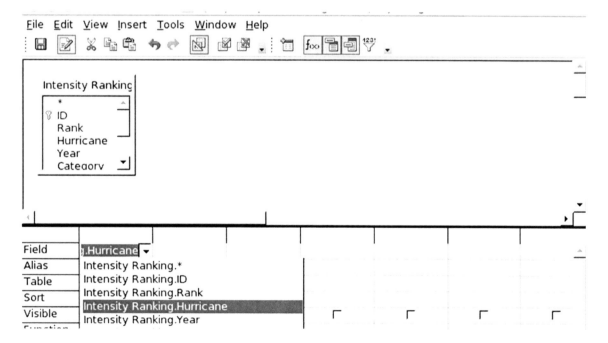

5 After selecting the Intensity Ranking.Hurricane field, select the table that is associated with the field from Step #5 by using the Table popup menu provided within the same column. In this case, the table selected should be the **Intensity Ranking** table.

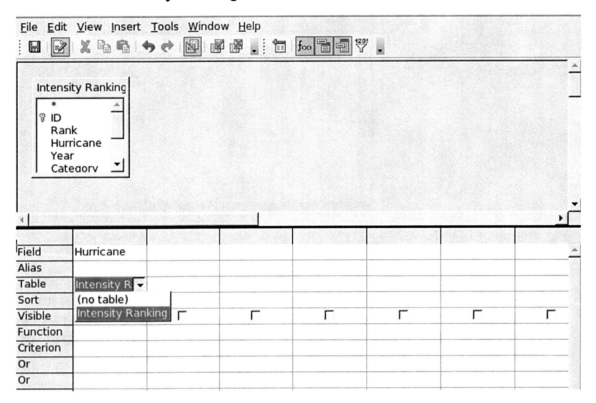

At this point, we could execute the run command to create a basic query. However, the results would not be meaningful, as the query would only contain a list of hurricanes. Therefore, to make this query produce some useful results, we will continue with the creation of the query by selecting the Year field to display the year the hurricane struck the Unites States coast. Moreover, we will enter a criterion to have the query only display hurricanes that reached an intensity of Category 4 strength or greater based upon the Saffir-Simpson scale. To complete this query, continue with the following steps:

6 To achieve the desired query results listed above, we will need to select a second field and third field for our query. Under the second column within the lower pane of the Query Design View window, select the **Intensity Ranking.Year** field within the available Field popup menu. Under the third column, select the **Intensity Ranking.Category** field.

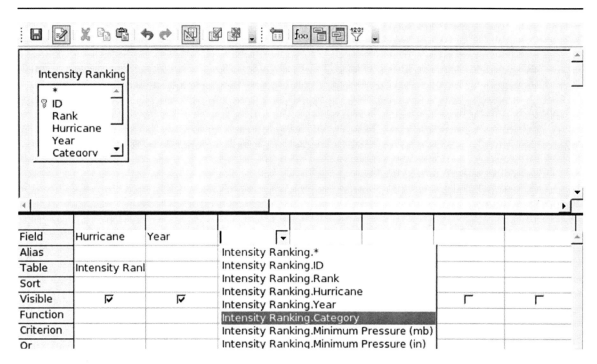

7 Next, select the tables associated with each field by using the Table popup menu provided under the respective columns. In this case, the **Intensity Ranking** table should be selected for both the second and third column Table fields.

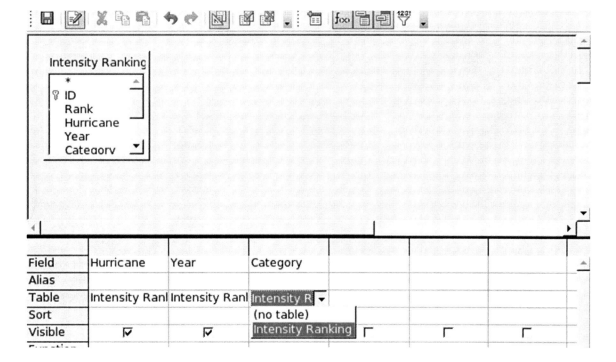

8 For this query, we want all of the fields that have been selected to be visible when the query results appear. To make sure this occurs, each column should have a checkmark within the Visible field. This signifies that we are selecting to have the field within the respective column to appear in the results when we execute the Run Query command. If any of the Visible fields do not have a checkmark, use your left mouse button to click within the appropriate checkboxes provided to have a checkbox appear.

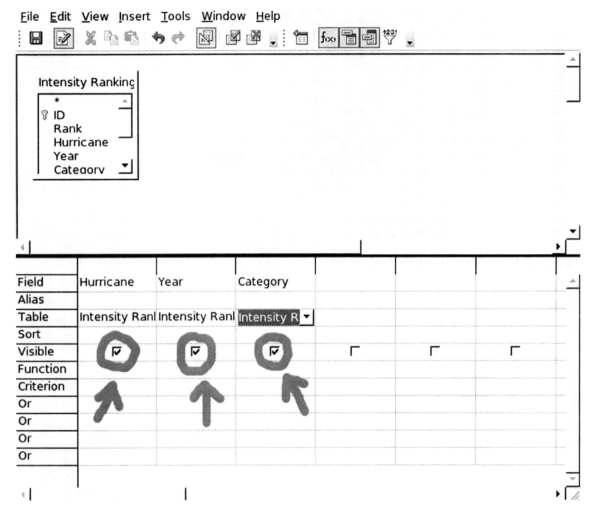

9 When the query results appear, we want the results to be sorted by a hurricane's intensity and in descending order. This will result in Category 5 storms appearing at the top of the list, followed by Category 4 storms. To sort the results of the query in this manner, select **Descending** from the Sort field popup menu in the third column provided.

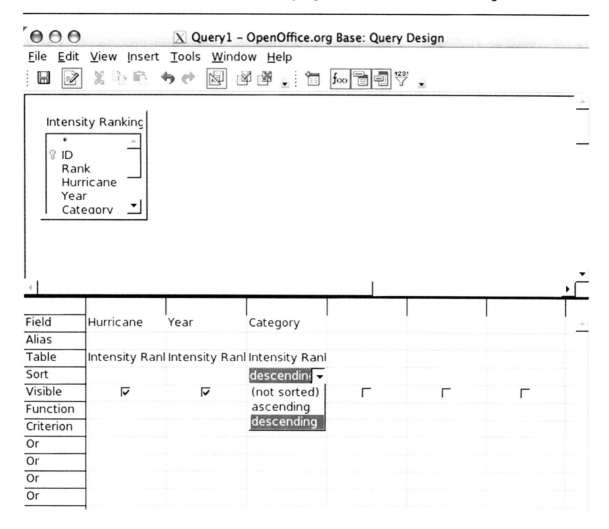

10 Finally, we need to enter criteria regarding ~~of~~ ^the^ data to display for the
query results. Specifically, we need only Category 4 and 5 storms to
appear within the query results. To make sure this occurs, we will utilize
comparison operators within the query. Comparison operators that are
supported within Base include > (greater than), < (less than), >= (greater
than or equal to), <= (less than or equal to) and NOT (not equal to).

To do so, take your left mouse button and single-click within the Criterion
field located within the third column. When the cursor appears, type **>=4**
within the field. This comparison operator specifies that only hurricanes
with an intensity of greater than or equal to Category 4 will appear within
the query results.

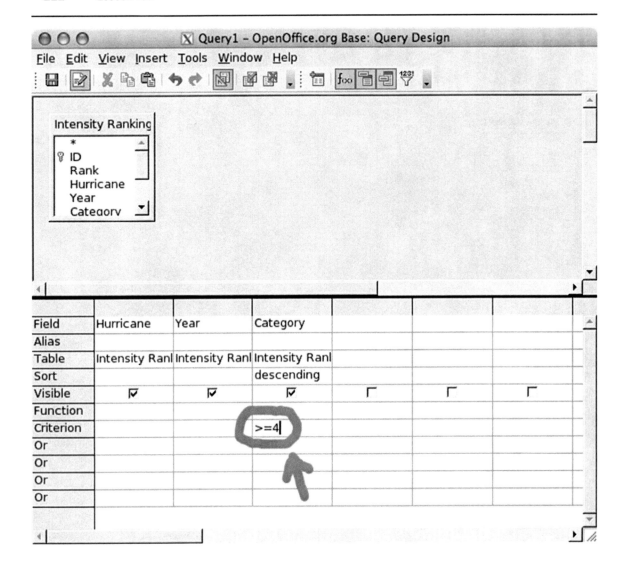

How to Run a Query

Prior to running a query, you may wish to execute the Distinct Values command to omit any duplicate entries that may appear within the query results as a result of the criteria selected. To execute the Distinct Values command, simply click the Edit menu and select Distinct Values from the menu options that appear.

Once criteria have been selected to perform a query, the RUN command must be executed to produce its results. To do so, click on the Edit menu and select Run Query from the menu options that appear. Queries can also be ran by clicking on the Run Query button located within the Query Design toolbar at the top of the application window. If the toolbar is not visible, it can be made to appear by clicking on the View menu, select Toolbars from the menu options and selecting Query Design from the submenu options that appear.

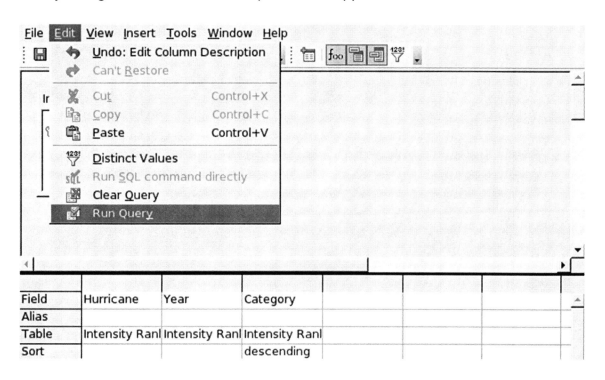

Field	Hurricane	Year	Category		
Alias					
Table	Intensity Ranl	Intensity Ranl	Intensity Ranl		
Sort			descending		

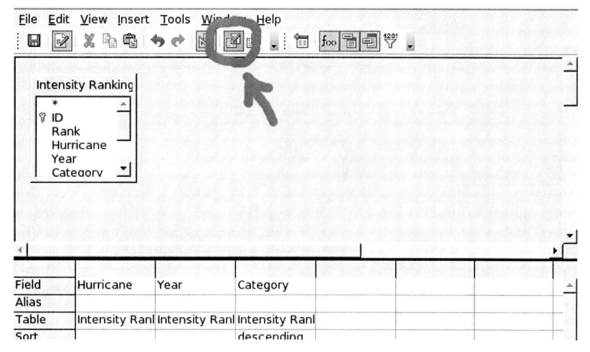

Field	Hurricane	Year	Category		
Alias					
Table	Intensity Ranl	Intensity Ranl	Intensity Ranl		
Sort			descending		

Changing the Format of Data Appearing Within a Query Result

When the query results appear, you will notice that only records where a hurricane had an intensity equal to or greater than Category 4 strength appear within the results. You will also notice that the dates that appear within the Year column contain decimal values. We can change the format of the date to exclude decimal values and present the year in its proper form. To do so, follow these steps:

1   Within the upper pane of the Query Design View window where the query results appeared, right-click on the column label **Year** and select Column Format from the contextual menu options that appear.

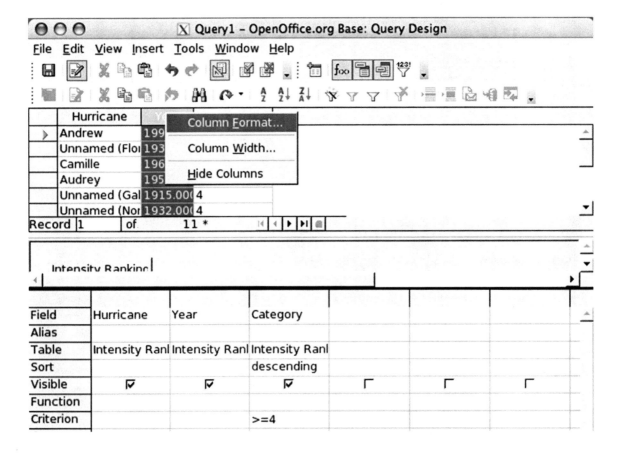

2   When the Field Format window appears, enter **0** within the Decimal Places located under the Options selection area.

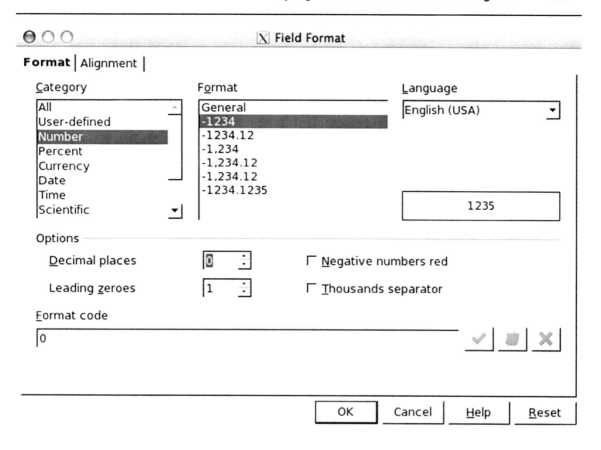

3 Click the OK button. When the Query Design View window returns, the year for each query result should now be in their correct format.

How to Save a Query

Once a query has been ran, a query can be saved so that the results can be accessed later. To save a new query within a database file, follow these steps:

1 To save the query performed, click the File menu and select Save As from the menu options that appear.

2 When selecting the Save As menu option, a window will appear prompting a Query Name to be entered. Enter **Lesson Ten 01** for the query name and click the OK button. The query has now been saved. (NOTE: For the purposes of this lesson, do not close the query results window at this time. We will utilize this query for our next exercise associated with this lesson.)

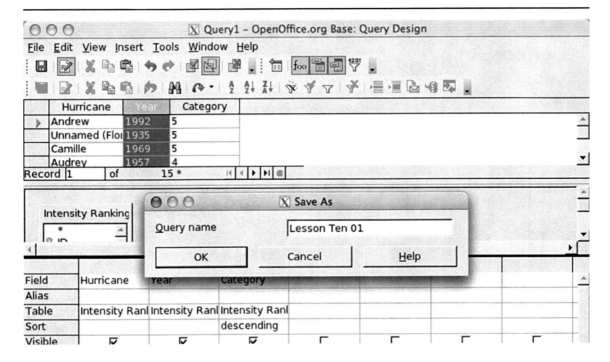

3   When returning to the main database file window, click on the Queries icon located on the left side of the window within the Database pane. When doing so, the query that was saved should appear within the Queries pane in the lower portion of the window. The query can be viewed by double-clicking its icon within the window.

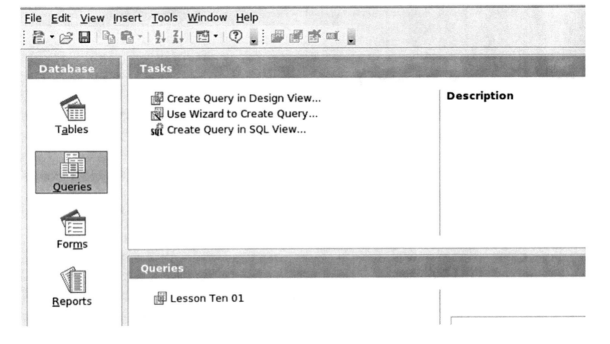

Making Changes to a Query

Once a query has been ran, you can make corrections or changes to the query if you do so before closing the Query Design window, which displays the query results. This makes it a much more efficient way to make corrections or changes, as opposed to closing the Query Design window and starting over with a new query. In our next exercise, we will make changes to our existing query by entering new query criteria and using compound criteria to produce query results. Afterward, we will save the query results for this exercise and learn how to clear the query design without closing the entire Query Design View window.

Entering Query Criteria

To begin this next exercise, we will begin making changes to the existing query results by entering new query criteria. To do so, we will need to add a new table, as well as change the tables and fields selected for the query. To perform these tasks, follow these steps:

1 Within the Lesson Ten 01 Query Design View results window, click on the Insert menu and select Add Table or Query from the menu options that appear.

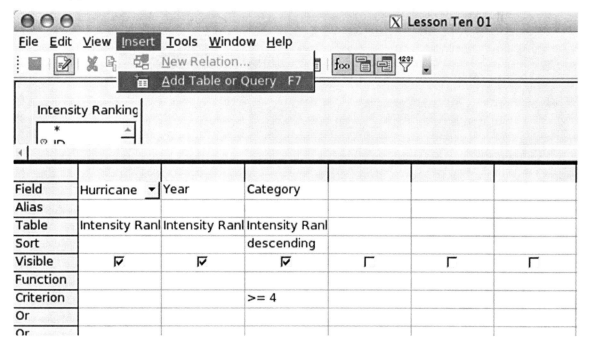

2   When the Add Table or Query window appears, use the radio buttons available within the window to select the Costliest Ranking table. To do so, single-click its icon among the list and click the ADD button. Once the Costliest Ranking table appears within the Query Design View window, click the CLOSE button within the Add Table or Query window.

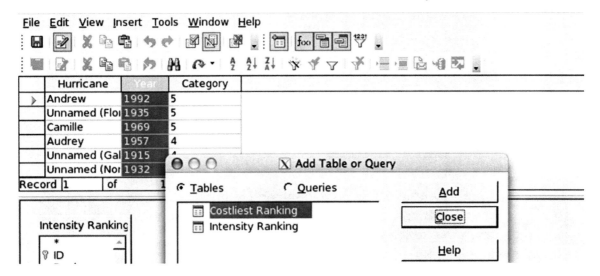

3   The next step is to select different tables to utilize for the new query. To do so, utilize the first Table popup menu provided within the lower pane of the window to select the appropriate table. This can be accomplished by simply using the mouse pointer to click within the field. In this example, select the **Costliest Ranking** table.

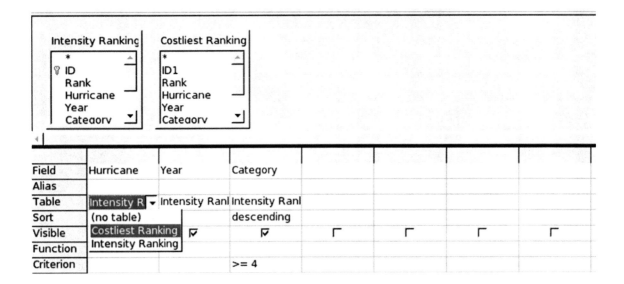

4 After selecting the Costliest Ranking table, select the appropriate field that is associated with the table from Step #3 by using the Field popup menu provided within the same column. In this case, the field selected should be the **Hurricane** field.

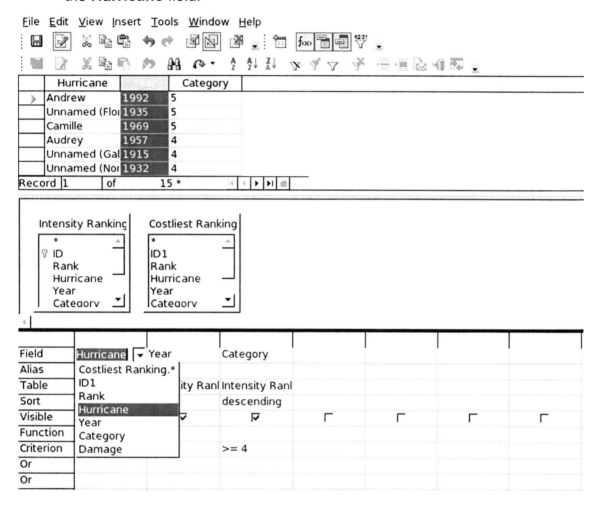

5 Next, we will need to change the tables associated with the second and third columns within our query. Under the second and third columns within the lower pane of the Query Design View window, select the **Costliest Ranking** table within the available Table popup menus.

6 Select the appropriate field associated with each table by using the Table popup menu provided under the respective columns. In this case, the **Year** field should be selected from the second column Field popup menu while **Category** should be selected for the third column Field popup menu.

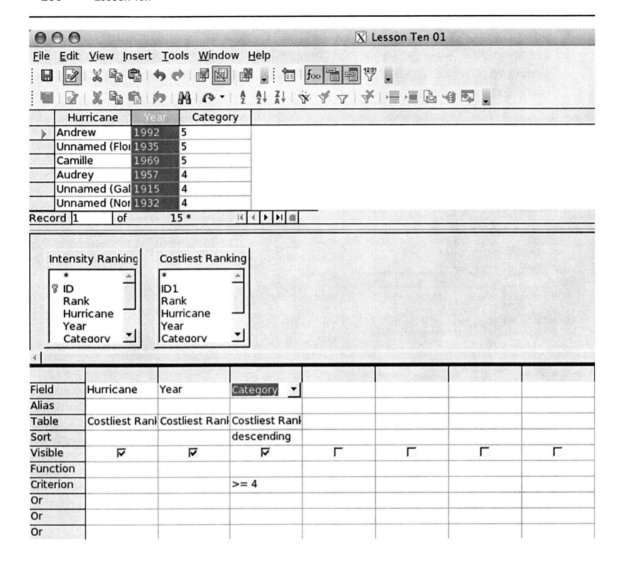

7 For this query, we will not have the query results sorted by category. Therefore, using your left mouse button, click on the Sort field located within the third column and select **(not sorted)** from the popup menu provided. This will disable sorting the query by category.

8 Now that the fields and tables associated with the query have been changed, we will add an additional field to be included within the query. In the fourth column provided, select the **field Costliest Ranking.Damage** from the Field popup menu provided. Underneath the same column, select **Costliest Ranking** from the Table popup menu. Finally, choose **Descending** from the Sort popup menu within the same column to specify that the query results be sorted by damage estimated in descending order.

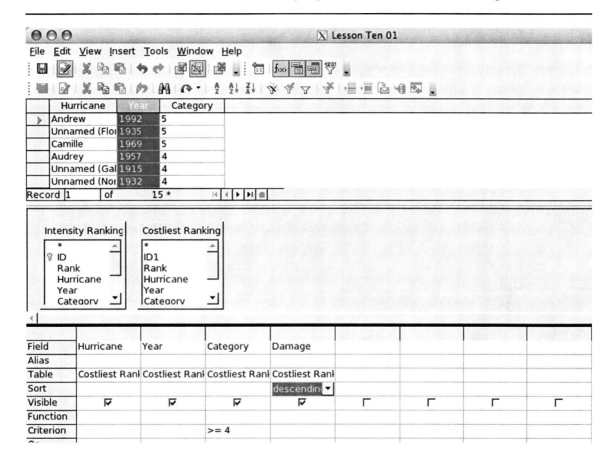

9   Like the first query we created earlier, we want all of the fields that have
    been selected to be visible when the query results appear. To make sure
    this occurs, each column should have a checkmark within the Visible field.
    This signifies that we are selecting to have the field within the respective
    column to appear in the results when we execute the Run Query command.
    If any of the Visible fields do not have a checkmark, use your left mouse
    button to click within the appropriate checkboxes provided to have a
    checkbox appear.

Using Compound Criteria Within Queries

Base, as with many database applications, support the use of compound criteria
within queries. Compound criterion typically involves two types: AND criterion and
OR criterion. With AND criterion, each criterion selected for their respected fields
must be true for the results to appear within the completed compound criteria
query. With OR criterion, any true result for each individual criterion will appear

within the completed compound criteria query.

Now that the tables and fields for the query have been changed, we now need to specify new criteria for the query prior to running it again. For this query, we will actually utilize AND criterion to produce our desired results. Afterward, we will run the query we designed again to view its results. To do so, follow these steps:

1 First, we need to change the query criteria for the Category field. Specifically, we want all storms with an intensity of Category 1 strength or greater to appear within the query results. To do so, take your left mouse button and single-click within the Criterion field located within the third column. When the cursor appears, type **>=1** within the field. This comparison operator specifies that only hurricanes with an intensity of greater than or equal to Category 1 (minimal hurricane strength) will appear within the query results.

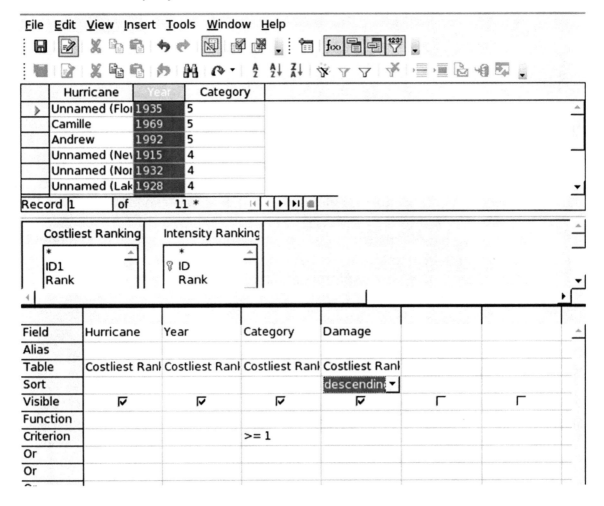

2 Next, we need to specify that our query results produce a list of hurricanes that are at least a Category 1 in intensity <u>and</u> caused at least U.S. $3 billion ($3,000,000,000) in property damage. To do this, single-click within the Criterion field located within the fourth column. When the cursor appears, type **>=3000000000** within the field. This comparison operator specifies that only hurricanes with an intensity of greater than or equal to Category 1 (minimal hurricane strength) will appear within the query results. (NOTE: When entering numerical values, be sure to type the numbers without any additional characters included. For example, if the criterion to query includes $2,000, then the numerical value should be typed as 2000 within the Criterion field.)

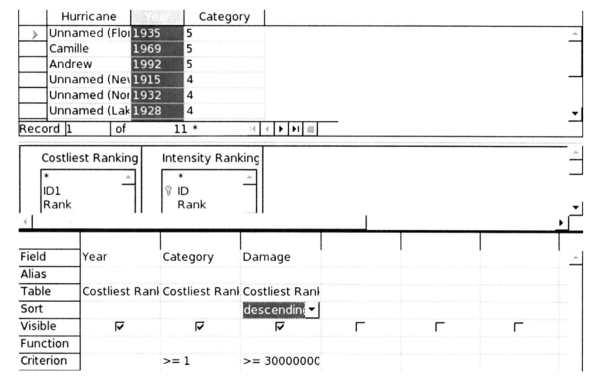

3 Prior to running a query, you may wish to execute the Distinct Values command to omit any duplicate entries that may appear within the query results as a result of the criteria selected. To execute the Distinct Values command, simply click the Edit menu and select Distinct Values from the menu options that appear.

4 Once criteria have been selected to perform a query, the RUN command must be executed to produce its results. To do so, click on the Edit menu and select Run Query from the menu options that appear. Queries can also be ran by clicking on the Run Query button located within the Query Design toolbar at the top of the application window. If the toolbar is not visible, it can be made to appear by clicking on the View menu, select Toolbars from the menu options and selecting Query Design from the submenu options that appear.

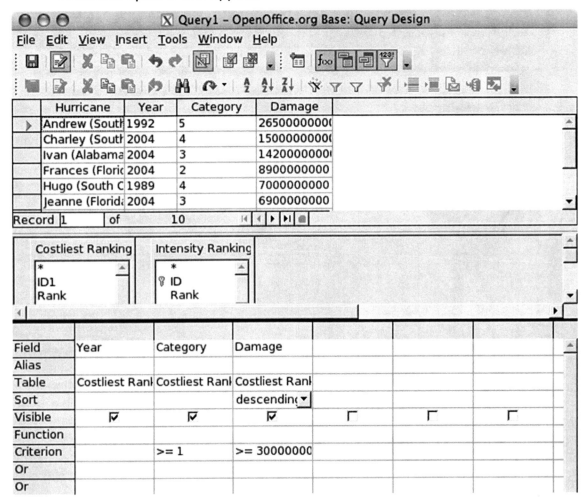

Saving the Second Query

Once the second query has been ran, it can be saved so that the results can be accessed later. To save the second query within the database file, follow these steps:

1 To save the query performed, click the File menu and select Save As from the menu options that appear.

2 When selecting the Save As menu option, a window will appear prompting a Query Name to be entered. Enter **Lesson Ten 02** for the query name and click the OK button. The query has now been saved. (NOTE: For the purposes of this lesson, do not close the query results window at this time.)

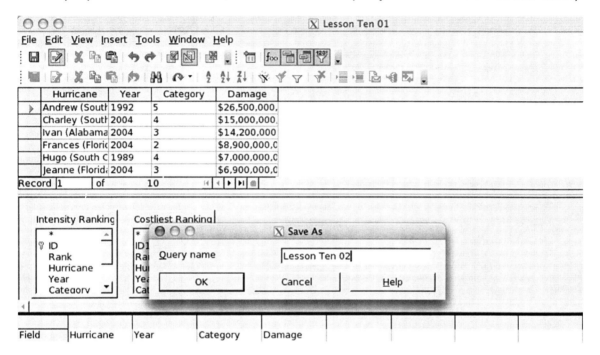

3 When returning to the main database file window, click on the Queries icon located on the left side of the window within the Database pane. When doing so, the query that was saved should appear within the Queries pane in the lower portion of the window. The query can be viewed by double-clicking its icon within the window.

Clearing the Query Design

If a user wishes to make corrections or changes to criteria selected prior to or after running a query, they can clear the Query Design View window as opposed to closing it and restarting. To clear the Query Design View window, follow these steps:

1   Click the Edit menu and select Clear Query from the menu options that appear. All tables and criteria selected will be cleared from the Query Design View window. However, the window will not be closed to allow the user to add new tables or queries and select new criteria.

2   The Query Design View window can also be cleared by clicking on the Clear Query button located within the Query Design toolbar at the top of the application window. If the toolbar is not visible, it can be made to appear by clicking on the View menu, select Toolbars from the menu options and selecting Query Design from the submenu options that appear.

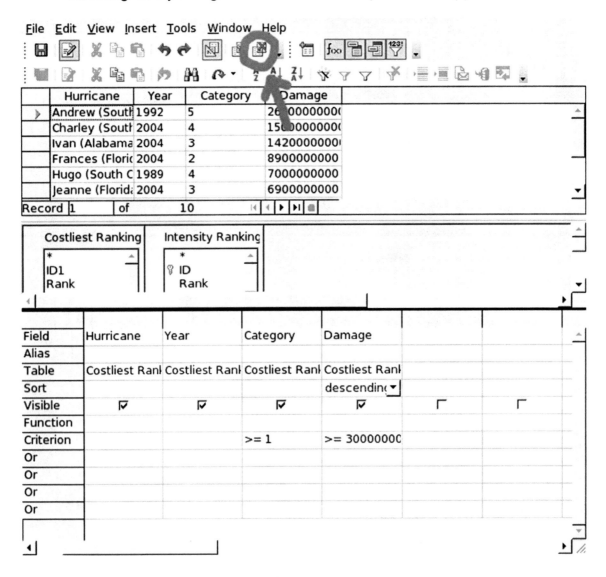

3 To close the Query Design View window for this exercise, click the File menu and select Close from the menu options that appear.

Examining the Results of the Queries

As mentioned at the beginning of this lesson, a query provides a simpler way of analyzing data contained within database records by allowing users to specify certain criteria to obtain a subset, or filtered set, of desired results. To provide an example of using databases for real-world use, you will utilize the queries just created to answer the following questions regarding the hurricane statistics found within this lesson's database file. When answering these questions, you might also find it useful to create new queries to further assist in answering the questions.

1) From 1851 to 2004, how many Category 5 hurricanes have made landfall in the United States?

2) Of those Category 5 hurricanes that made landfall in the United States, which years did they make landfall and how many years apart were there between storms?

3) Of the Top 10 costliest storms in the United States, as identified in the Lesson Ten 02 query results, how many are considered to be strong or intense hurricanes? (Strong or intense hurricanes are those classified as Category 3,4 or 5 based upon the Saffir-Simpson scale.)

4) Of the Top 10 costliest storms in the United States, as identified in the Lesson Ten 02 query results, how many made landfall between 1990 and 2004?

5) Based upon the query results performed, do you think there may be a correlation between the rise of the Industrial Revolution, global warming and the number of catastrophic hurricanes (Category 5) to form in the Atlantic Ocean and strike the United States? Why? (HINT: You may want to refer to the Additional Resources section for web links to documents that can help you answer this question. However, there is not a specific answer to this question.)

6) The records within this lesson's database table(s) contain intensity data regarding hurricanes that made landfall in the United States from 1851 to 2004. Are there other intense hurricanes that made a significant impact to the United States after 2004? If so, what was the name of the hurricane, where did it make landfall, and what impact did it have to the area affected by the storm and the United States as a whole? (HINT: You may want to refer to the Additional Resources section for web links to documents that can help you answer this question.)

7) In October 1998, Hurricane Mitch made landfall in the Central American country of Honduras. Mitch became one of the deadliest hurricanes to strike the Western Hemisphere in over two centuries, with an estimated death toll of 11,000 people. At landfall in Honduras, Mitch was a Category 2 storm with sustained winds of 100 miles per hour (85 knots) and a minimum central pressure of approximately 987 millibars (mb). How does the storm's category and minimum central pressure compare to strong hurricanes that have made landfall in the United States? If the wind speed of the storm was not the primary cause of loss of life, what was? (HINT: Refer to the following webpage to help answer the question - http://www. nhc.noaa.gov/1998mitch.html.)

How to Specify Field Properties Within Tables

Earlier when we ran the queries we created, you noticed the dates that appear within the Year column contained decimal values. We were able change the format of the date to exclude decimal values and present the year in its proper form within the Query Design View window. However, we could have also changed the format prior to running the query by opening the table associated with the query and entering field property specifications. That way, the data would have appeared in its correct format immediately after running the query. To specify field properties within a Base, follow these steps:

1 In the Database pane located on the left side of the window, click on the Tables icon.

2 In the Tables pane located at the bottom-right of the window, select the Intensity Ranking table by single-clicking on the icon.

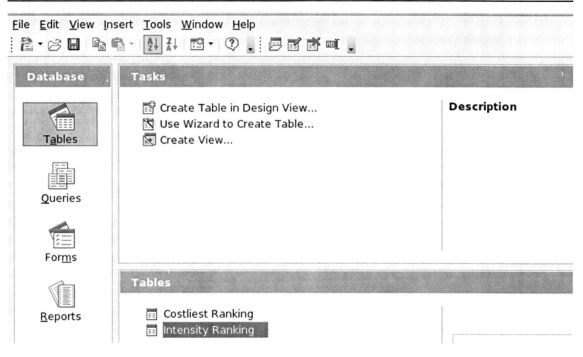

3 Click on the Edit menu at the top of the application window and select Edit from the menu options that appear. You can also select the edit command by right-clicking on the table icon and select Edit from the contextual menu that appears.

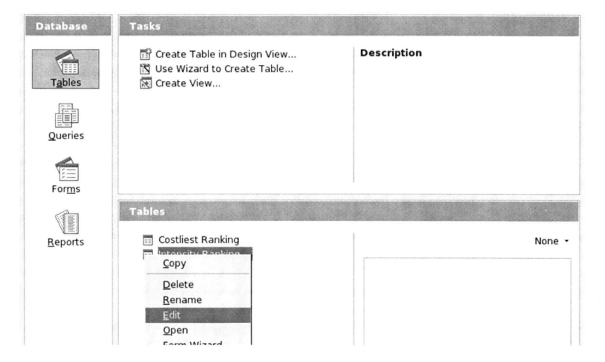

4 When the Table Design window appears, left-click within the gray area to the left of the field name **Year** to select the entire row.

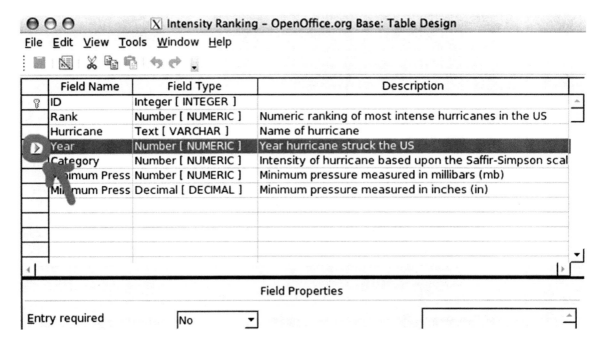

5 In the Field Properties selection area located at the bottom of the Table Design window, change the Decimal Places field properties to **0** and the Length field properties to **4** utilizing the selection fields provided.

Field Name	Field Type	Description
ID	Integer [INTEGER]	
Rank	Number [NUMERIC]	Numeric ranking of most intense hurricanes in the US
Hurricane	Text [VARCHAR]	Name of hurricane
Year	Number [NUMERIC]	Year hurricane struck the US
Category	Number [NUMERIC]	Intensity of hurricane based upon the Saffir-Simpson scal
Minimum Press	Number [NUMERIC]	Minimum pressure measured in millibars (mb)
Minimum Press	Decimal [DECIMAL]	Minimum pressure measured in inches (in)

Field Properties

Entry required   No

Length   4

Decimal places   0

Default value

Specify the number of decimal places permitted in this field.

6 To exit the Table Design window, click on the Window menu at the top of the window and select Close Window from the menu options that appear or simply press CTRL+W on the keyboard to return to the main Base application window. When closing the window, a prompt window may appear asking whether to save the changes being made to the table. Click the YES button to do so and the window will close.

How to Create and Print a Report

Like many other database applications, Base has the ability to create and print reports. A report can be thought of as simply a text document that presents the current data within the database, or the data selected at the time of printing. Base provides a wizard that walks users step-by-step through the process of creating a report. For this exercise, we will utilize the records within our database to create a basic report. To create a new report using the Report Wizard, follow these steps:

1 In the Database pane located on the left side of the window, click on the Reports icon.

2 In the Tasks pane located at the top of the window, left-click Use Wizard To Create Report to launch the Report Wizard.

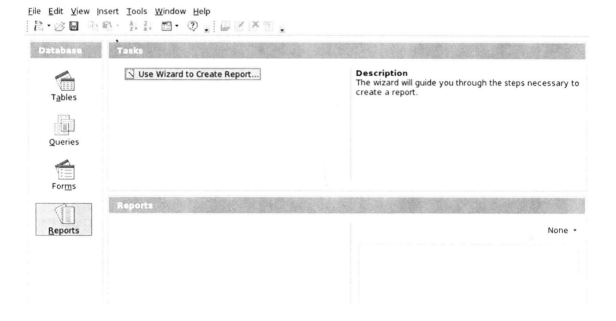

3 When the Report Wizard window appears, the first step will be to select the fields from an existing table to include in the report. In the Tables or Queries popup menu, select the **Intensity Ranking** table from the popup menu provided.

4 After the table has been selected, fields that contain records to be presented in the report need to also be selected. Using the selection area provided, single-click the **Hurricane** field and click the right arrow button in the middle of the window to specify that the field be included in the report creation process. After doing so, also select the **Year** and **Minimum Pressure (mb)** fields to be included in the report creation process. Then click the NEXT button.

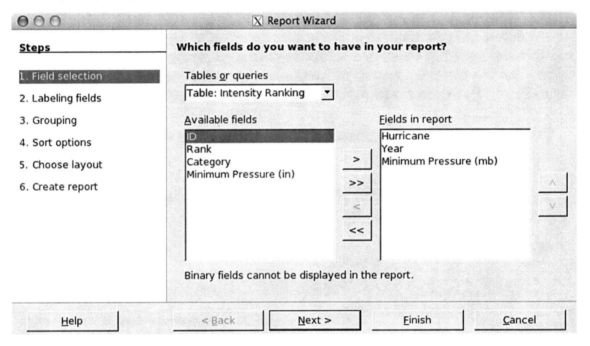

5 In the next step of the Report Wizard, you can customize the field labels by entering the labels into the text fields provided (optional). For this example, we will leave the field labels as they are. Then click the NEXT button.

6 In this step of the Report Wizard, you can customize the group levels using the selection area provided (optional). Records are grouped based upon the values in the selected fields. Up to four fields can be grouped in a report. For this example, we will leave the group levels as they are. Then click the NEXT button.

7 Next, you can customize the sort order of the fields using the selection area provided (optional). For this example, we will select to sort the data by Minimum Pressure (mb) and in ascending order. Using the popup menu and radio buttons provided, make the appropriate selection. Then click the NEXT button.

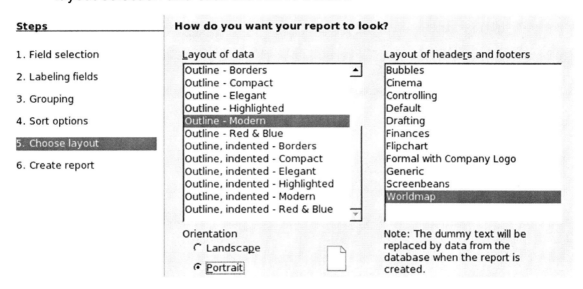

8 In this step of the Report Wizard, you can select the layout in which the report data will be presented. If the report should not possess a custom layout, you would make sure Default is selected for the header and footer layout, as well as the data layout. For this example, we will choose **Modern** for the data layout and **Worldmap** for the header / footer layout. We will also select **Portrait** for the page orientation. Make the appropriate layout selection and click the NEXT button.

Steps

1. Field selection

2. Labeling fields

3. Grouping

4. Sort options

5. Choose layout

6. Create report

How do you want your report to look?

Layout of data

| Outline - Borders |
| Outline - Compact |
| Outline - Elegant |
| Outline - Highlighted |
| Outline - Modern |
| Outline - Red & Blue |
| Outline, indented - Borders |
| Outline, indented - Compact |
| Outline, indented - Elegant |
| Outline, indented - Highlighted |
| Outline, indented - Modern |
| Outline, indented - Red & Blue |

Layout of headers and footers

| Bubbles |
| Cinema |
| Controlling |
| Default |
| Drafting |
| Finances |
| Flipchart |
| Formal with Company Logo |
| Generic |
| Screenbeans |
| Worldmap |

Orientation
  ○ Landscape
  ● Portrait

Note: The dummy text will be replaced by data from the database when the report is created.

9 In the final step of the Report Wizard, select a title to save a report as by entering a title into the text field provided. For this example, we will title the report as **Intensity Ranking 1851-2004**. Also, select to create a static report or a dynamic report by clicking the appropriate radio button provided. A static report is where the data in the report will not change, and a dynamic report is where the data in the report may change periodically based upon the data entered into the corresponding table. For this example, we will select **Static Report**. Then click the FINISH button to complete the process of creating a report.

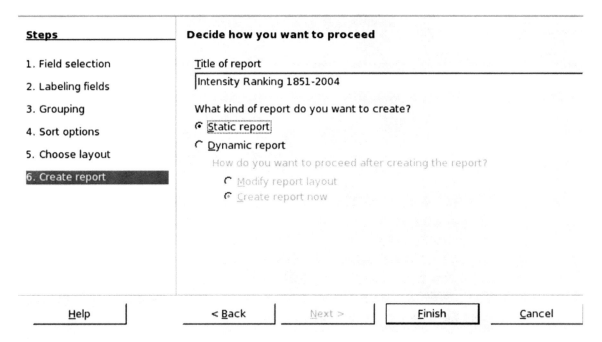

10 To print a copy of the report generated, click on the File menu and select Print from the menu options that appear. To print one copy of the entire report, simply press the OK button and the report will begin to print. Otherwise, use the Page Range and Copies selection area to customize the print configuration before clicking the OK button.

Additional Resources

Drew Jensen – OpenOffice.org Base Discussion Forum: Beginners Base Tutorial
http://www.oooforum.org/forum/viewtopic.phtml?t=25060

The OpenOffice.org Documentation Project
http://ooodocs.sourceforge.net/

National Oceanic and Atmospheric Administration (NOAA) – National Hurricane
Center
http://www.nhc.noaa.gov/

JetStream – An Online School for Weather: Introduction to Tropical Weather
http://www.srh.noaa.gov/srh/jetstream/tropics/tropics_intro.htm

The Deadliest Atlantic Tropical Cyclones, 1492-1996
http://www.nhc.noaa.gov/pastdeadly.shtml
National Hurricane Center Monthly Weather Reviews, 1872-2002
http://www.aoml.noaa.gov/general/lib/lib1/nhclib/mwreviews/mwreviews.html

National Hurricane / Tropical Prediction Center Library
http://www.aoml.noaa.gov/general/lib/lib1/nhclib/index.htm

Summary of Hurricane Katrina
http://lwf.ncdc.noaa.gov/oa/climate/research/2005/katrina.html#impacts

Links to Reference Material Regarding Hurricane Katrina
http://www.srh.noaa.gov/lix/Katrina_overview.html

Review Questions

1 What are two methods to change the format of data presented within query
results?

2 Within Base, which command should a computer user execute prior to
running a query to eliminate duplicate entries?

3 What is a query?

4 (True or False) If a user wishes to make corrections or changes to criteria
selected prior to or after running a query, they must close the Query Design
View window it and start over by creating a new query.

5 (True or False) Within Base, a user can create a report either using the Report Wizard or by utilizing the Report Design View window.

APPENDIX

 Quick Guide to Creating and Editing Writer Documents

Appendix A
Quick Guide to Creating and Editing Writer Documents

Section One: Overview of Writer

Starting Writer

To launch the Writer application within the Microsoft Windows operating system, follow these steps:
1. Beginning at the desktop, click on the Start button located in the lower-left corner of the screen, and select Programs or All Program from the menu list that appears.
2. Select the OpenOffice.org 3.0 application folder that appears, and select Writer from the applications options that appear.

To launch the Writer application within a Linux-based operating system, follow these steps:
1. Beginning at the desktop, click on the Start button located in the lower-left corner of the screen, and select Office Productivity from the menu list that appears.
2. Select the OpenOffice.org 3.0 Writer application icon from the list that appears, and the Writer application will launch and present a blank document.

Displaying Toolbars

Writer contains many toolbars to assist in formatting and editing your documents. Sometimes you may need to view certain toolbars to assist you with creating your documents, while other toolbars may need to hidden from view to prevent from getting in your way and free up screen space for other tools. To view or hide a toolbar within Writer, follow these steps:
1. Click the View menu and select Toolbars from the menu list. A list of available toolbars will appear.
2. Select a toolbar to appear within Writer by simply clicking on the appropriate toolbar within the list. If a toolbar within the list has a checkmark beside it, this means that the toolbar is already visible within the

Writer application.
3. If you wish to hide a toolbar from view within Writer, simply click on it from the list. Toolbars listed that do not have a checkmark beside them indicates that the toolbar is hidden from view within Writer.

Adjusting Page View

To adjust the view of the document you are working in, click on the View menu and select Zoom from the menu list. You may also select to Zoom by clicking on the magnifying glass icon within the Standard toolbar located just beneath the main application menu.

Using the Navigator

The Navigator allows a user to quickly view objects that are within a document. The Navigator displays "categories", or the various contents within the Navigator window. Within each category contains the objects that are present in the document.

To view and utilize the Navigator while creating and editing Writer documents, follow these steps:
1. To open the Navigator window, click on the Edit menu and select Navigator from the menu list. You may also view the Navigator window by pressing the F5 key at the top of your keyboard.
2. If you see a "+" icon located next to a category within the Navigator, that indicates that there is at least one object within the document related to that particular category. Click the "+" sign to expand the list to view the objects related to the category. To quickly jump to the location in your document where the object is placed, double-click on the object listed in the Navigator window.

Viewing Nonprinting Characters

To view nonprinting characters, such as line spacing or paragraph indentation indicators, click on the View menu and select Nonprinting Characters from the menu list. You may also view nonprinting characters by pressing the CTRL+F10 keys simultaneously on your keyboard.

Viewing and Editing the Styles and Formatting Organizer

The Styles and Formatting Organizer allows you to quickly select pre-defined formatting options to include in your documents simply by double-clicking on a style option listed within the Organizer. To view and edit the Openoffice.org Formatting Styles Organizer, follow these steps:

1. To view the organizer, click the Format menu and select Styles and Formatting or simply press the F11 key at the top of your keyboard. A window will appear displaying by default the various paragraph styles available.
2. When the Organizer window is open, you will notice a small palette within the window. You can view other formatting styles as well by clicking on the appropriate button. From left-to-right, the style options you may view include Paragraph, Character, Frame, Page and List styles. In the popup menu located at the bottom of the Styles Organizer window, be sure the menu has the option All Styles selected to view all of your available options for each style.
3. You can also create or modify formatting styles based upon existing styles by right-clicking on a style listed within the Organizer and select the appropriate command from the contextual menu that appears. You may also delete custom styles you created from the Organizer by right-clicking on it within the list.

How to Set OpenOffice.org to Automatically Open Microsoft Office Generated Files Using Windows

If you did not choose during the installation of OpenOffice.org to have the software automatically open Microsoft Office formatted documents, you may select to do so by following these steps:

1. Close all OpenOffice.org applications and return to your desktop.
2. Click on the Windows operating system Start button and select Control Panel from the list that appears. Then choose Add or Remove Programs from the submenu that appears, followed by the OpenOffice.org 3.0 list option, then click Install/Uninstall.
3. In the window that appears, click the NEXT button, select the Modify option and click NEXT until the wizard prompts you to select the file types you wish OpenOffice.org to automatically open for you.
4. Select or deselect the file types you wish OpenOffice.org to automatically open for you. Click NEXT until it prompts you to click Install to complete the setup. Clicking the Install button will make the necessary changes

to automatically open the file types you selected. You should not need to have the installation CD inserted into your computer's CD-ROM to complete this process.

Installing OpenOffice.org Extensions

To install extensions using the OpenOffice.org Extensions Manager, whether they are intended for an individual user or for shared use among multiple users, follow these steps:

1. Go to the OpenOffice.org Online Extension Repository at **http:// extensions.services.openoffice.org/** and select the extension you wish to install. You may also install an extension from any webpage where a hyperlink is provided with a direct link to a hosted extension file (*.oxt). Once you have selected the extension you wish to install, click the GET IT button located on the repository's Extension product page to initiate the downloading process for the extension. You may also download an extension by clicking your computer's right mouse button on a hyperlink and selecting Download File from the contextual menu that appears. Macintosh users who have a one-button mouse can initiate the same process by holding down the CONTROL button on the keyboard and click their mouse button on a webpage's hyperlink. (HINT: If your operating system provides you with an option for selecting where you wish the file to be downloaded and stored on your computer, select the Desktop for easiest access later in the installation process.)
2. Within the OpenOffice.org application, click on the Tools menu and select the Extensions Manager menu option that appears.
3. When the Extensions Manager window appears, select to perform a User Extension installation or a Shared Extension installation by single-clicking the appropriate directory. Remember, you would select the 'OpenOffice.org Extension' directory to perform a Shared Extension installation and the 'My Extensions' directory to perform an installation of an extension for use by only the user who initiates the installation process.
4. Once you have selected the appropriate directory to perform a specific installation type, click the ADD button located within the Extensions Manager window.
5. When the Add Extensions window appears, use the file browser navigation buttons located in the upper-right corner of the window to locate the extension file (*.oxt) you downloaded. Once you have located the extension file, single-click it within the window. Then click the OPEN button to begin the installation.

6. When the installation is complete, you should be automatically returned to the Extension Manager window. To double-check to make sure the installation successfully completed, double-click the directory you selected for installation in Step #3. When the directory list collapses, the extension should appear in the directory's content list. If the ENABLE button located on the right side of the window is greyed out, this signifies that the installation is successful and is ready for use.

7. In some instances, you may need to shut down the OpenOffice.org application and relaunch it for an extension to become available for use. If you have problems accessing the functionality of an extension that has been installed, perform this operation. You can double-check to see if an extension is enabled at this point simply by returning to the Extension Manager and see if the ENABLE button is greyed out within its window. Many extensions also install a guide within the OpenOffice.org Help menu that can assist you with the use of the extension as well.

Section Two: Formatting Text and Paragraphs

Selecting and Moving Text

There are a number of ways you can select text for editing or relocating to another area of your document. Below are a few tips for doing so:

1. To select text for formatting or relocating to another area of your document, hold down your left mouse button while dragging the I-bar over the text you wish to select.

2. To select text that exists in locations not adjacent to one another, hold down the left mouse button while dragging the I-bar over the first selection of text. Afterward, hold down the Command key (the key located next to your spacebar key that has the Microsoft Windows icon on it) and select the next set of text. Only the text that was highlighted with the I-bar will be included with your selection.

3. To move the text you selected to another location, press your left mouse button on the text you selected, drag the mouse to the location you wish to move the text to, and release the mouse button.

4. To copy the text you selected to another location (leaving the selected text in its present location), hold down the Control (CTRL) key while pressing the left mouse button on the text you selected, drag the mouse to the location you wish to copy the text to, and release the mouse button.

Changing the Font Type

To change the font type of the text within your document, follow these steps:
1. Select the text you wish to change the font type. If you starting with a blank document, proceed with Step #2.
2. Click on the Format menu and select Character from the menu list.
3. If it is not already selected, click the Font tab within the window that appears. Select the Font within the window list. Click the OK button to complete the selection.

You may also change the font type by using the Font Name popup menu located within the Formatting toolbar.

Changing the Font Size

To change the font size of the text within your document, follow these steps:
1. Select the text you wish to change the font size. If you starting with a blank document, proceed with Step #2.
2. Click on the Format menu and select Character from the menu list.
3. If it is not already selected, click the Font tab within the window that appears. Select the font size within the window list. Click the OK button to complete the selection.

You may also change the font size by using the Font Size popup menu located within the Formatting toolbar.

Changing the Font Style (including Bold, Italicize, and Underline)

To change the font style of the text within your document, follow these steps:
1. Select the text you wish to change the font style. If you starting with a blank document, proceed with Step #2.
2. Click on the Format menu and select Character from the menu list.
3. If it is not already selected, click the Font tab within the window that appears. Select the font style within the window list. Click the OK button to complete the selection.

You may also change the font style by using the appropriate Font Style buttons located within the Formatting toolbar.

Changing the Font Color

To change the font color of the text within your document, follow these steps:
1. Select the text you wish to change the font color. If you starting with a blank document, proceed with Step #2.
2. Click on the Format menu and select Character from the menu list.
3. Click the Font Effects tab within the window that appears. Select the font color within the Font color popup menu. Click the OK button to complete the selection.

You may also change the font color by using the Font Color popup menu located within the Formatting toolbar.

Changing and Rotating Text Position

There are a couple of different ways you can change or rotate the position of text within a document. To change and rotate test utilizing your standard menu options, follow these steps:
1. Select the text you wish to change the font position. If you starting with a blank document, proceed with Step #2.
2. Click on the Format menu and select Character from the menu list.
3. Click the Position tab within the window that appears. Select the font rotation and scaling options within the window list. Click the OK button to complete the selection.

You can also rotate text by creating a text object using the Drawing toolbar options within Writer. To use this method of rotating text, follow these steps:
1. Click on the View menu and select Toolbars from the menu list. Select Drawing from the list that appears to have the Drawing toolbar become visible.
2. Within the Drawing toolbar, click the icon represented by a bold "T" to select the Text tool. When you move your pointer inside the page area of your document, your pointer will transform into a target sight. Hold down the left mouse button and drag to create a text box to enter text into. Release the left mouse button once you have created the appropriate sized text box.
3. Inside the text box, a cursor will be flashing. Begin typing the text you wish to rotate. When you have completed move your pointer inside the text box until it transforms into a bold target sign. Then click your left mouse button. The text box will be surrounded by small boxes around its border.

4. Select the Rotate button within the Drawing Objects toolbar that appears above your document's ruler. The small boxes that surrounded the border of your text box will transform into red oval icons. Place your pointer on one of the oval located on the corner of the textbox. The pointer will transform into the rotation icon. Hold down the left mouse button and drag the text box into the direction you wish to rotate. When you have rotated the text to the position desired, release the left mouse button. Click your pointer outside of the text box to deselect it.

Wrapping Text Around Objects

To wrap text around objects, follow these steps:
1. Select the object you wish to wrap text around.
2. Click on the Format menu and select Wrap from the menu list. Select the wrap type from the list that appears. The current wrapping style is indicated with a checkmark.
3. To specify wrapping properties you wish to have, select the object, click on the Format menu and select Object from the menu list, and click on Text Attributes option that appears. Select the properties you wish to have, and then click the OK button.
4. To change the wrapping contour of a graphic, right-click on the graphic, choose Wrap from the contextual menu that appears, then select the Edit option. Use the tools available to change the contour and click the OK button.

Paragraph Alignment

To change the paragraph alignment within your document, follow these steps:
1. Select the text or paragraph you wish to change the alignment. If you are starting off with a blank document or a new paragraph, proceed with Step #2.
2. Click on the Format menu and select Paragraph from the menu list.
3. Click on the Alignment tab in the window that appears. Select the alignment style (left, right, center or justified) by clicking on the radio button next to your desired selection.
4. Click the OK button to complete the selection.

You may also change the paragraph alignment by using the appropriate alignment buttons located within the Formatting toolbar.

Creating Paragraph Indents

To create first-line paragraph indents within your document, follow these steps:
1. Select the paragraph you wish to change the first line paragraph indent. If you are starting off with a blank document or a new paragraph, proceed with Step #2.
2. Click on the Format menu and select Paragraph from the menu list.
3. Click on the Indents and Spacing tab in the window that appears.
4. Under your indents option, you will find a popup menu that will allow you to select the appropriate indention spacing. To select the spacing, click on the little arrows to the right of the popup menu. You may also click in the checkbox next to Automatic to set your first line indent to 0.20" by default.
5. Click the OK button to complete the selection.

You may also change the paragraph indent by utilizing the ruler located between the toolbar and the document area. Simply drag the top-left triangle within the ruler to the new indent location. If the ruler is not visible, go to the View menu and select Ruler from the menu list. Furthermore, you may create a first-line paragraph indent by utilizing the Styles and Formatting Organizer. To view the Styles and Formatting Organizer, click on the Format menu and select Styles and Formatting from the menu list or simply press the F11 key on your keyboard.

Creating Hanging Indents

To create hanging paragraph indents within your document (where the second and subsequent lines of a paragraph are indented), follow these steps:
1. Select the paragraph you wish to change the hanging paragraph indent. If you are starting off with a blank document or a new paragraph, proceed with Step #2.
2. Click on the Format menu and select Styles and Formatting from the menu list, or simply press the F11 key on your keyboard to view the Styles and Formatting Organizer.
3. Click on the Paragraph styles button (the first button in the upper-left corner of the organizer window) to view your paragraph formatting options. Double-click Hanging Indent from the list within the window to automatically create a hanging indent in your document.
4. You may close the Styles and Formatting Organizer window by clicking the Close button in the upper-right corner of the Organizer window (the button marked with an "X").

You may also change the hanging paragraph indent by utilizing the ruler located between the toolbar and the document area. Simply drag the bottom-left triangle within the ruler to the new hanging indent location. Adjust your first-line paragraph indent by dragging the top-left triangle within the ruler. If the ruler is not visible, go to the View menu and select Ruler from the menu list.

Sorting Paragraphs

To sort paragraphs within your document, follow these steps:
1. Select the paragraphs you wish to sort in your document. If you would like to sort all paragraphs within the document, go to the Edit menu and choose Select All from the menu list that appears.
2. Click on the Tools menu and select Sort from the menu list that appears.
3. Select the sort criteria utilizing the options that appear in the Sort window. In the Separator area, select whether Tabs or Characters will be utilized in the paragraph sorting criteria.
4. Click the OK button to complete the selection.

Inserting Tables

To insert a table within your document, follow these steps:
1. Place your cursor at the location in your document you wish to insert a table by clicking your left mouse button once at the location.
2. Click on the Table menu, select the Insert menu option and select Table from the submenu that appears. You may also hold down the Control (CTRL) key and press F12 to have the menu selection appear.
3. In the window that appears, select the number of columns and rows you wish the table to contain utilizing the popup menus presented. Select any other formatting options you wish the table to have utilizing the selections presented to you within the window.
4. Click the OK button to complete the selection.

Inserting Frames

To create a frame (or border) around a paragraph within your document, follow these steps:
1. Place your cursor within the paragraph you wish to create a frame around by clicking your left mouse button once within the paragraph.
2. Click on the Format menu and select Paragraph from the menu list.

3. Click on the Borders tab in the window that appears.
4. Within your Line Arrangements selection area, choose the appropriate border arrangement to be placed around your paragraph. (Note: The first selection within Line Arrangements does not set a border around your paragraph.)
5. Within the Line selection area, choose the appropriate style (thickness) of the line that will appear as your border frame. You also may select a color by using the Color popup menu available.
6. Continue to make any other appropriate border formatting selections using the options presented to you, including border position, shadow style and more.
7. Click the OK button to complete the selection.

Inserting Bullet and Numbering Lists

To insert bullet or numbered lists within your document, follow these steps:
1. Select the paragraph you wish transform into a bulleted or numbered list. If you are starting off with a blank document or a new paragraph, proceed with Step #2.
2. Click on the Format menu and select Bullets and Numbering from the menu that appears.
3. Within the window that appears, you have numerous bullet and numbering format options available to you that are sorted within tabs that are presented along the top. Click on the tab that presents the bulleted or numbered format you wish to select to view your options.
4. Click on the bulleted or numbered list option within the Selection area to specify your desired format type.
5. Click the OK button to complete the selection.

You may also create a bulleted or numbered list by utilizing the Styles and Formatting Organizer. To view the Styles and Formatting Organizer, click on the Format menu and select Styles and Formatting from the menu list or simply press the F11 key on your keyboard. Then click on the Character Styles button (the second icon from the left at the top of the Organizer) to view your bulleted or numbered list format option.

Section Three: Formatting Pages

Selecting Page Size

To select the appropriate page size for your document, follow these steps:
1. Click on the Format menu and select Page from the menu that appears.
2. When the Page Style window appears, click on the Page tab at the top of the window (if it isn't already selected).
3. Using the Format popup menu, select the predefined paper size you will print your document on. When you select an option, the width and height will automatically change to format itself to the predefined paper format. If you wish to select a custom paper size, utilize the Width and Height menus to enter the appropriate page size.
4. In the Margins selection area, specify your page margins for your document by entering the appropriate measurements.
5. In the Layout selection area, you have the option to select the register-true feature format feature. When you select this feature, it can make pages easier to read by preventing gray shadows from appearing between the lines of text. This could be a useful feature if your document will be printed on the front and back of pages, such as a book or newsletter. To select this feature, click inside the checkbox. When a checkmark appears within the box, the feature is enabled.
6. Once you have selected your page style formatting options, click the OK button to complete the selection.

Inserting Headers

Headers are areas located within the top page margins that are added to your page style and allow you to add text and/or graphics within the area. Typical uses for headers include chapter titles and page numbers. To insert a header into your document, simply click on the Insert menu, select Header from the menu that appears, and select the header type from the submenu that appears.

You may also create a header by utilizing the Styles and Formatting Organizer. To view the Styles and Formatting Organizer, click on the Format menu and select Styles and Formatting from the menu list or simply press the F11 key on your keyboard. Then click on the Paragraph Styles button (the first icon from the left at the top of the Organizer) and double-click on Header within the list available.

Inserting Footers

Footers are areas located within the bottom page margins that are added to your page style and allow you to add text and/or graphics within the area. Typical uses for headers include chapter titles, page numbers and endnotes. To insert a footer into your document, simply click on the Insert menu, select Footer from the menu that appears, and select the footer type from the submenu that appears.

You may also create a footer by utilizing the Styles and Formatting Organizer. To view the Styles and Formatting Organizer, click on the Format menu and select Styles and Formatting from the menu list or simply press the F11 key on your keyboard. Then click on the Paragraph Styles button (the first icon from the left at the top of the Organizer) and double-click on Footer within the list available.

Adjusting Page Margins

To adjust the page margins for your document, follow these steps:
1. Click on the Format menu and select Page from the menu that appears.
2. When the Page Style window appears, click on the Page tab at the top of the window (if it isn't already selected).
3. In the Margins selection area, specify your page margins for your document by entering the appropriate measurements.
4. Once you have selected your page style formatting options, click the OK button to complete the selection.

Adding Page Columns

If you are creating a manuscript or a newsletter, you may wish to have your text formatted within multiple columns on your page layout. OpenOffice.org allows for great flexibility in creating multiple columns within your document. To create columns, follow these steps:
1. Click on the Format menu and select Page from the menu that appears.
2. When the Page Style window appears, click on the Columns tab at the top of the window.
3. Within the Settings selection area, you may click on one of the predefined column formats available to you or enter the number of columns you wish your document to have.
4. If you want to customize the width and spacing of the columns within your document or add a separator line, utilize the fields available within the appropriate selection areas.

5. Click the OK button to complete the selection.

Using the Organizer to Format Pages

The Styles and Formatting Organizer allows you to quickly select pre-defined formatting options to include in your documents simply by double-clicking on a style option listed within the Organizer. To view and edit the Openoffice.org Formatting Styles Organizer, follow these steps:

1. To view the organizer, click the Format menu and select Styles and Formatting or simply press the F11 key at the top of your keyboard. A window will appear displaying by default the various paragraph styles available.
2. When the Organizer window is open, you will notice a small toolbar within the window. You can view other formatting styles as well by clicking on the appropriate button. Click on the Page Styles button (the fourth button in the upper-left corner of the organizer window) to view your page formatting options. Double-click on the appropriate style to make your format selection.
3. You can also create or modify formatting styles based upon existing styles by right-clicking on a style listed within the Organizer and select the appropriate command from the contextual menu that appears. You may also delete custom styles you created from the Organizer by right-clicking on it within the list.

Section Four: Inserting Clip Art and Graphics

Supported Graphic File Types

OpenOffice.org supports a wide array of file types for graphics files to be imported into Writer. If you have a graphic file you wish to import into your Writer document, chances are OpenOffice.org supports it. Supported graphic file types for importing into a Writer document include:

- Windows Bitmap (*.bmp)
- AutoCAD Interchange Format (*.dxf)
- Enhanced Metafile (*.emf)
- Encapsulated PostScript (*.eps)
- Graphics Interchange Format (*.gif)
- Joint Photographic Experts Group (*.jpg or *jpeg)

- OS/2 Metafile (*.met)
- Portable Bitmap (*.pbm)
- Kodak Photo CD (*.pcd)
- Macintosh Picture Format (*.pct or *.pict)
- Zsoft Paintbrush (*.pcx)
- Portable Graymap (*.pgm)
- Portable Network Graphic (*.png)
- Portable Pixelmap (*.ppm)
- Adobe Photoshop (*.psd)
- Sun Raster Image (*.ras)
- StarWriter Graphics Format (*.sgf)
- StarDraw 2.0 (*.sgv)
- StarView Metafile (*.svm)
- Truevision Targa (*.tga)
- Tagged Image File Format (*.tif or *.tiff)
- Windows Metafile (*.wmf)
- X Bitmap (*.xbm)
- X PixMap (*.xpm)

Inserting a Graphic or Clip Art

To insert a graphic or clip art image into your Writer document, follow these steps:
1. Click on the Insert menu and select the Picture menu option that appears.
2. When you select the Picture menu option, a submenu will appear allowing you to choose an image file or retrieve a picture from a scanner. Select the appropriate option.
3. If you selected to insert a picture from an image file, locate the file using Insert Picture window that appears. Click once on the file displayed to select the appropriate image to insert.
4. At the bottom of the Insert Picture window, OpenOffice.org gives you the option to link the file rather than embedding the image into the document. If you have an image that is being used in a number of places throughout the document, you can choose to link the image to reduce the file size of your document. If you ever move the image to another location, however, you will need to re-link the image for it to appear in the document. If you wish to link the image, click within the checkbox located next to the Link selection.
5. Click OK to complete your selection.

Adjusting a Graphic Image Location

If you wish to adjust the location of your graphic image, follow these steps:
1. Click once within the graphic image with your left mouse button. Small boxes will appear around the edge of the image when it has been properly selected.
2. Move your pointer within the graphic area. The pointer will transform into a black target icon. Holding down your left mouse button on the image, drag the image. Once you have the image in your desired location, release the mouse button.
3. If you wish to center the graphic within the page, select the image as detailed in Step #1. Then click the Center Horizontal tool within the Formatting toolbar located above your document's ruler. The image should then center itself within the page.

Resizing a Graphic Image

If you wish to resize an image or graphic within your document, follow these steps:
1. Click once within the graphic image with your left mouse button. Small boxes will appear around the edge of the image when it has been properly selected.
2. To proportionally resize the graphic, place your pointer on one of the small boxes located one the corner of the image. Your pointer will transform into a black bar with arrows on each end of it. Hold down the left mouse button and begin to drag either outward or inward to make your graphic larger or smaller, respectively. When you have resized it to the desired width and height, release the left mouse button.
3. If you know the exact width and height you wish your graphic to be, you may also resize an image by right-clicking on the image and select Graphics from the contextual menu that appears.

Section Five: Saving and Printing a Document

Supported File Types for Saving

OpenOffice.org can open and save documents formatted in a wide array of file types. Although it might not be their primary office suite, many users have found OpenOffice.org to be a useful tool for opening and saving files not supported through their primary applications. Writer supports the following file formats:

- Hypertext Markup Language Documents (*.htm or *.html)
- OpenOffice.org 3.0 Native OpenDocument Text (*.odt)
- OpenOffice.org 3.0 Native OpenDocument Text Template (*.ott)
- OpenOffice.org 1.0 Text Document (*.sxw)
- Microsoft Word 6.0/95/97/2000/XP/2007 Documents (*.doc, *.docx)
- Microsoft Word 2003 XML Documents (*.xml)
- Palm AportisDoc Documents (*.pdb)
- Pocket Word Documents (*.psw)
- Portable Document Format Documents (*.pdf)
- Rich Text Format (*.rtf)
- StarWriter 3.0/4.0/5.0 Text Documents (*.sdw)
- StarWriter 3.0/4.0/5.0 Text Templates (*.vor)
- Text Files (*.txt)

Saving a File as a Native Writer Document

To save a document in the native Writer 3.0 OpenDocument format, follow these steps:
1. Click on the File menu and choose Save As from the menu list.
2. A window will appear and prompt you to choose a location to save your document. Choose the location you want to save a document to in the Save In popup field.
3. In the field File Name, type the name you would like to save the file as.
4. In the Save As Type popup menu, select the OpenDocument Text (.odt) file format.
5. Click the button SAVE to complete the operation.

Saving a File as a Microsoft Word Document

To save a document in the Microsoft Word format, follow these steps:
1. Click on the File menu and choose Save As from the menu list.
2. A window will appear and prompt you to choose a location to save your document. Choose the location you want to save a document to in the Save In popup field.
3. In the field File Name, type the name you would like to save the file as.
4. In the Save As Type popup menu, select the appropriate Microsoft Word (*.doc) file format.
5. Click the button SAVE to complete the operation.

Exporting a File as a Portable Document Format (PDF) Document

One of the many useful features OpenOffice.org has built-in to the office suite is the ability to export documents as a Portable Document Format (PDF) file. To save a document as a read-only PDF file, follow these steps:
1. Click on the File menu and choose Export As PDF from the menu list.
2. A window will appear and prompt you to choose a location to save your document. Choose the location you want to save a document to in the Save In popup field.
3. In the field File Name, type the name you would like to save the file as.
4. In the File Format popup menu, make sure Portable Document Format (PDF) is selected.
5. Click the button SAVE to complete the operation.

(NOTE: OpenOffice.org documents saved as a PDF file is a convenient way to share read-only documents to other users that have a PDF reader application installed on their computer. However, OpenOffice.org cannot edit a document that has been saved as a PDF file. To save a document for editing at a later date, save the document in its Native OpenDocument file format.)

Exporting a File as a Web Page (HTML) Document

To save a document in the Hypertext Markup Language (HTML) format, follow these steps:
1. Click on the File menu and choose Save As from the menu list.
2. A window will appear and prompt you to choose a location to save your document. Choose the location you want to save a document to in the Save In popup field.
3. In the field File Name, type the name you would like to save the file as.
4. In the Save As Type popup menu, select the HTML (*.htm or *.html) file format.
5. Click the button SAVE to complete the operation.

Printing A Document

To print a document within any OpenOffice.org application, follow these steps:
1. Click on the File menu and select Print from the menu that appears. You may also hold down the Control (CTRL) key and press P on the keyboard to prompt for the Print window.
2. If you have more than one printer that your computer can send print jobs to,

select the printer you wish to send the document to in the Printer selection area.

3. In the Print Range selection area, use the radio buttons to select which pages you wish to print. If you choose the Pages option, enter the page range you wish to print (example: 1-5 will print pages one through 5; 1,2,5 will print pages one, two and five). If you choose the Selection option, OpenOffice.org will only print the text you have selected (highlighted) within your document.

4. In the Copies selection area, enter the number of copies you wish to print of the document.

5. If you wish to customize the print job, click on the OPTIONS button and select or deselect the print options you wish to choose. If you do not want to customize any print settings, skip to Step #6.

6. Once you have completed specifying your print settings, click the OK button to begin printing.

Section Six: Correcting Document Errors

Using Cut, Copy and Paste

Using Cut, Copy and Paste is one of the most fundamental operations you will perform to correct document errors. You may also use these commands to transfer text or graphics from one document into another. If you are unfamiliar with using these operations, use these steps to assist in determining which to use when correcting document errors:

1. Highlight the text you want to cut or copy.
2. To eliminate text to reinsert in another location in the document, click the Edit menu and choose the Cut menu option.
3. To duplicate text in another part of the document, click the Edit menu and choose the Copy menu option.
4. Place the cursor at the location you want the text to appear.
5. In the Edit menu, choose the Paste menu option.

Deleting Text

To permanently delete text from your document, follow these steps:

1. Highlight the text you want to permanently delete.
2. Press the Delete key on your keyboard to permanently remove the text

from your document.

Using Undo

If you make the mistake of deleting something you didn't wish to do or make a formatting error, immediately go to the Edit menu and choose Undo from the menu list that appears to go back to the document's previous state before the error was made. You can continue to select the Undo menu command multiple times to continue to go back to each previous step.

Using Spelling and Grammar Check

With the latest version of OpenOffice.org, not only does Writer have the ability to spellcheck documents but can also check for grammatical errors as well when an appropriate extension is installed.

To download and install the grammar checker extension for your appropriate language, go to the official Openoffice.org Extension site at **http://extensions. services.openoffice.org/** and search for "grammar check". For step-by-step instructions for downloading and installing an extension, see the section *Installing OpenOffice.org Extensions* within Lesson One in this book or *Section One: Overview of Writer* within this appendix.

When spell and grammar check is enabled (which it is by default when you install the application), possible spelling errors within a document are underlined in red, while possible grammatical errors are underlined in blue.

To use the OpenOffice.org spell and grammar check feature, follow these steps:
1. If you wish to spell check a specific word or sentence, select the text you wish to spell check. Otherwise, proceed to Step #2.
2. Go to the Tools menu and select Spelling and Grammar from the menu that appears. You may also press the F7 key on your keyboard to begin checking for spelling errors.
3. If any potential spelling or grammatical errors appear, OpenOffice.org will indicate the potential error and give you a list of possible suggestions to correct it.
4. If you see a spelling or grammatical suggestion that would correct the error, select it from the Suggestions list and click the CHANGE button.
5. If you believe that the word or sentence in question is correct, you can click the IGNORE ONCE button to proceed to the next potential spelling error. If

the word in question is spelled correctly and you use it often when creating documents, you may click the ADD button to add it to the Spellcheck dictionary.

6. When you have completed checking for potential errors, click the CLOSE button to exit and return to the document.

Using the Thesaurus

To use the OpenOffice.org thesaurus feature, follow these steps:

1. Select the text you wish to look up using the thesaurus.
2. Go to the Tools menu, select Language from the menu that appears and choose Thesaurus from the submenu. You may also hold down the Control (CTRL) key on your keyboard and press F7 to launch the thesaurus.
3. The thesaurus window will appear and will provide you with the meaning and a list of synonyms for the word you selected. If you wish to replace the word with a synonym, select the word from the list of synonyms and click the OK button.

Using AutoCorrect

AutoCorrect is enabled by default. However, AutoCorrect can be enabled or disabled at any time. To enable or disable a specific AutoCorrect feature, go to the Tools menu and select AutoCorrect from the menu that appears. Once the AutoCorrect window appears, click on the tab related to the specific feature you wish to enable or disable and select the appropriate options.

Using AutoFormat

Like AutoCorrect, the AutoFormat features are enabled by default. However, AutoFormat may also be enabled or disabled at any time. To enable or disable the AutoFormat feature, click on the Format menu, select AutoFormat from the menu that appears, and select While Typing from the submenu that appears. A checkmark will appear next to the submenu option when the feature is enabled.

Section Seven: Beyond The Basics

Inserting Notes

To insert a note within a Writer document, follow these steps:
1. Place the cursor where you wish the note to be positioned within the document.
2. Go to the Insert menu and select Note from the menu that appears.
3. When the Note window appears, type the note you wish to insert into the document utilizing the textbox provided.
4. Click the OK button to complete the operation.

When you have completed preparing the note, a yellow rectangle will appear where your cursor was placed within the document. To read the note, double-click on the yellow box.

Creating Footnotes

To insert a footnote within a Writer document, follow these steps:
1. Place your cursor within the page you wish the footnote to appear.
2. Go to the Insert menu and select Footnote from the menu that appears.
3. In the Insert Footnote window that appears, select Automatic within the Numbering selection area for the footnotes to be listed numerically at the bottom of the page.
4. Select Footnote within the Type selection area.
5. Click the OK button to complete the operation. The footnote will appear at the bottom of the current page.

Creating Endnotes

To insert an endnote within a Writer document, follow these steps:
1. Place your cursor within the document you wish the endnote to appear.
2. Go to the Insert menu and select Footnote from the menu that appears.
3. In the Insert Footnote window that appears, select Automatic within the Numbering selection area for the endnote to be listed with roman numerals at the bottom of the page.
4. Select Endnote within the Type selection area.
5. Click the OK button to complete the operation. The endnote will appear at the end of the document.

Insert Bibliography Entries

To store bibliography within the OpenOffice.org Bibliography Database, follow these steps:

1. Go to the Tools menu and select Bibliography Database from the menu that appears.
2. When the Bibliography Database window appears, go to the Insert menu and select Record from the menu that appears.
3. In the Short Name field provided in the lower half of the window, enter a short name that best describes the bibliography entry you are entering. This will be entered as the Identifier within the database.
4. After entering the Short Name, complete the remaining data fields in the lower half of the window that is appropriate for your bibliography entry.
5. After you have completed entering data into the remaining data fields, close the Bibliography Database window. Your data will automatically be saved into the database.

To insert a bibliography entry into your Writer document, follow these steps:

1. Place your cursor within the document you wish the bibliography entry to appear.
2. Go to the Insert menu, select Indexes and Tables from the menu that appears and then select Bibliography Entry from the submenu that appears.
3. In the Insert Bibliography Entry window that appears, click the radio button next to the Entry selection From Bibliography Database.
4. In the Short Name popup menu, select the Bibliography entry you wish to insert into the document.
5. Click the INSERT button for the bibliography entry to appear within the document. Then click the CLOSE button to close out the Insert Bibliography Entry window.

Indexes and Entries

To create a user-defined index and add entries to it, follow these steps:

1. Select a word or multiple words within your Writer document that you want to add into your index.
2. Go to the Insert menu, select Indexes and Tables from the menu that appears and select Entry from the submenu that appears.
3. Click the button located next to the Index popup menu to create a new user-defined index.

4. Type a name to identify the new user-defined index and click the OK button.
5. When you are returned to the Insert Index Entry window, click the INSERT button to add the word(s) to the new user-defined index. Click the CLOSE button to return to the Writer document.

To insert a user-defined index into a Writer document, follow these steps:
1. Place your cursor within the document you wish the index to appear.
2. Go to the Insert menu, select Indexes and Tables from the menu that appears and then select Index and Tables from the submenu that appears.
3. When the Insert Index/Table window appears, click on the Index/Table tab at the top of the window if it is not already selected.
4. Click on the Type popup menu and select the user-defined index you created.
5. Select any additional formatting options you wish your index to have by utilizing the options available within the tabs located at the top of the window.
6. When you have selected the formatting options you wish the new index to have, click the OK button to complete the operation.

Line Numbering

To enable line numbering within a document, follow these steps:
1. Go to the Tools menu and select Line Numbering from the menu that appears.
2. Click within the Show Numbering checkbox to enable line numbering.
3. Select any view styles you wish line numbering to have.
4. Once you have selected the viewing options you wish your line numbering to have, click the OK button to complete the operation.

Outline Numbering

To create a specific numbering format for outlines you are creating, follow these steps:
1. Go to the Tools menu and select Outline Numbering from the menu that appears.
2. When the Outline Numbering window appears, click on the Numbering tab at the top of the window if it isn't already selected.
3. Within the Numbering selection area, click on the Paragraph Style popup menu and select the style you wish the outline to have. If you wish to

create a standard outline, select Default within the popup menu.
4. Click on the Number popup menu and select the numbering style you wish the outline to have.
5. Select any additional formatting styles you wish the outline to have.
6. When you have selected the formatting option you wish the outline to have, click the FORMAT button and select Save As.
7. In the Format selection area within the Save As window that appears, type a name that best describes the outline format you are creating and click the OK button.

When you want to use a custom Outline Numbering style, go to the Tools menu, select Outline Numbering from the menu that appears and select the style from the Paragraph Style popup menu.

Creating a Page Break

To create a new, basic page within a Writer document, follow these steps:
1. Place the cursor in the document where you wish the new section to begin.
2. Go to the Insert menu and select Manual Break from the menu that appears.
3. When the Manual Break window appears, click on the Page Break radio button within the Type selection area.
4. If you are creating the page break for a specific purpose, you may select one of the formatting options from the Style popup menu. If you wish to have a standard page break, leave the popup menu selected None.
5. When you have selected the formatting options you wish the new page to have, click the OK button to complete the operation.

You can also create a new page break by holding down the Control (CTRL) key and press the Enter key on the keyboard.

Creating a Section Break

To create a new, basic section within a Writer document, follow these steps:
1. Place the cursor in the document where you wish the new section to begin.
2. Go to the Insert menu and select Section from the menu that appears.
3. When the Section window appears, go to the New Section selection area and type a name in the field that best describes the contents of the new section.
4. Select any formatting options you wish the section to have by clicking on

the appropriate tabs that are displayed at the top of the window.
5. When you have selected the formatting options you wish the new section to have, click the INSERT button to complete the operation.

Creating Bookmarks and Hyperlinks

OpenOffice.org provides great flexibility in embedding hyperlinks for web pages or to target other sections of a Writer document. If you wish to embed a hyperlink to target a specific section of your document, you must first create a bookmark within the document for the hyperlink to target and then create the hyperlink.

To create a bookmark within a Writer document, follow these steps:
1. Place your cursor in your document where you wish the hidden bookmark to be placed.
2. Go to the Insert menu and select Bookmark from the menu that appears.
3. When the Insert Bookmark window appears, type a name in the first text field that best describes the contents or position of the bookmark. (NOTE: the bookmark name must not contain any spaces.)
4. Click the OK button to complete the insertion of the hidden bookmark within the document.

To create a hyperlink to send a reader to a bookmarked section within a Writer document, follow these steps:
1. Select the text you wish to embed the hyperlink into.
2. Go to the Insert menu and select Hyperlink from the menu that appears.
3. When the Hyperlink window appears, click on the Document button located on the left side of the window.
4. In the Target In Document selection area, click the Target button located to the right of the Target text field.
5. When the Target In Document window appears, click the "+" icon located next to the item Bookmarks. The bookmarks you have embedded within your Writer document will appear in a list.
6. Select the bookmark you wish to link to and click the APPLY button. Click the CLOSE button to close the Target In Document window.
7. The Hyperlink window will now indicate the bookmark you selected as the target. Click the APPLY button within the Hyperlink window to complete the hyperlink operation. The click the CLOSE button to close the Hyperlink window. If the hyperlink was successfully created, the text you selected in Step #1 should be blue in color and underlined.

To create a hyperlink to send a reader to an Internet destination, such as a webpage or FTP address, follow these steps:

1. Select the text you wish to embed the hyperlink into.
2. Go to the Insert menu and select Hyperlink from the menu that appears.
3. When the Hyperlink window appears, click on the Internet button located on the left side of the window.
4. In the Hyperlink Type selection area, choose the appropriate hyperlink type by clicking the radio button next to the selection. For example, if you are going to create a hyperlink to link your readers to a website, select Web.
5. In the Target text field, type the full address of the webpage you wish to link to. (NOTE: To ensure that the hyperlink will refer readers to a webpage properly, begin all addresses with the referrer http://)
6. Click the APPLY button within the Hyperlink window to complete the hyperlink operation. The click the CLOSE button to close the Hyperlink window. If the hyperlink was successfully created, the text you selected in Step #1 should be blue in color and underlined.

Creating a Mail Merge

With OpenOffice.org 3.0, creating a mail merge is much simpler than with the older version. OpenOffice.org 3.0 now includes a Mail Merge Wizard that walks users through step-by-step in creating a mail merge. To create a mail merge, go to the Tools menu and select Mail Merge Wizard from the menu that appears. Follow the on-screen instructions to complete the mail merge.

Importing a Calc Spreadsheet as an OLE Object

Importing a Calc spreadsheet as an OLE Object into a Writer document not only allows you to place the spreadsheet contents within a text document, but also allows you to edit the spreadsheet directly within the text document as well. To import a Calc spreadsheet as an OLE object, follow these steps:

1. Open both the Writer document you wish to import a spreadsheet into and the Calc spreadsheet you will be exporting data from.
2. Within the Calc spreadsheet, select the spreadsheet area to want to place within the Writer document.
3. Place your pointer within the selected area of the Calc Spreadsheet, hold down the left mouse button and drag the selected spreadsheet area into the Writer text document. Once the cursor appears at the location you wish to place the spreadsheet, release the mouse button. The spreadsheet in now inserted as an OLE object into the Writer document.

4. To edit the Calc spreadsheet directly within the Writer document, double-click the spreadsheet. If you need to have the menu commands available to edit the spreadsheet, right-click on the spreadsheet and choose Edit from the contextual menu that appears.

About Macros

OpenOffice.org Writer cannot run the same macro code that Microsoft Office utilizes. This is because OpenOffice.org Writer uses Basic code for its macros, while Microsoft Office uses Visual Basic for Applications (VBA) for its macros. While OpenOffice.org Basic and VBA share many similarities, objects and methods within each scripting language are different. In addition to Basic, OpenOffice.org also supports JavaScript and BeanShell for scripting macros.

To utilize the macros created in one application within another, you must edit the macros. OpenOffice.org can load macros that are contained within Microsoft Office documents. You can then view and edit the macro code within the OpenOffice.org Basic editor.

B

Quick Guide to Creating and Editing Calc Documents

Appendix B
Quick Guide to Creating and Editing
Calc Documents

Section One: Overview of Calc

Starting Calc

To launch the Calc application within the Microsoft Windows operating system, follow these steps:

1. Beginning at the desktop, click on the Start button located in the lower-left corner of the screen, and select Programs or All Program from the menu list that appears.
2. Select the OpenOffice.org 3.0 application folder that appears, and select Calc from the applications options that appear.

To launch the Calc application within a Linux-based operating system, follow these steps:

1. Beginning at the desktop, click on the Start button located in the lower-left corner of the screen, and select Office Productivity from the menu list that appears.
2. Select the OpenOffice.org 3.0 Calc application icon from the list that appears, and the Calc application will launch and present a blank spreadsheet.

Displaying Toolbars

Calc contains many toolbars to assist in formatting and editing your spreadsheets. Sometimes you may need to view certain toolbars to assist you with creating your spreadsheets, while other toolbars may need to hidden from view to prevent from getting in your way and free up screen space for other tools. To view or hide a toolbar within Calc, follow these steps:

1. Click the View menu and select Toolbars from the menu list. A list of available toolbars will appear.
2. Select a toolbar to appear within Calc by simply clicking on the appropriate toolbar within the list. If a toolbar within the list has a checkmark beside it, this means that the toolbar is already visible within the Calc application.

3. If you wish to hide a toolbar from view within Calc, simply click on it from the list. Toolbars listed that do not have a checkmark beside them indicates that the toolbar is hidden from view within Calc.

Formula Bar

If the Calc formula bar is not visible when you open a Calc document, you may make it so by going to the View menu and select Formula Bar from the menu that appears. A checkmark should appear next to the menu option when the formula bar is visible. If you wish to hide the formula bar from view within Calc, simply click on it from the list. When the menu option does not have a checkmark beside it, this indicates that the formula bar is hidden from view within Calc.

Status Bar

If the Calc status bar, located at the bottom of the Calc application window, is not visible when you open a Calc document, you may make it so by going to the View menu and select Status Bar from the menu that appears. A checkmark should appear next to the menu option when the status bar is visible. If you wish to hide the status bar from view within Calc, simply click on it from the list. When the menu option does not have a checkmark beside it, this indicates that the status bar is hidden from view within Calc.

Adjusting Page View

To adjust the view of the document you are working in, click on the View menu and select Zoom from the menu list. You may also select to Zoom by clicking on the magnifying glass icon within the Standard toolbar located just beneath the main application menu.

Value Highlighting

Whenever you create a formula for a cell to calculate, Calc can automatically highlight the value within the spreadsheet for easier viewing. To utilize this feature, go to the View menu and select Value Highlighting from the menu that appears. A checkmark should appear next to the menu option when value highlighting is enabled. If you wish to disable this feature within Calc, simply click on it from the list. When the menu option does not have a checkmark beside it, this indicates that value highlighting is disabled within Calc.

Using the Navigator

The Navigator allows a user to quickly view objects that are within a document. The Navigator displays "categories", or the various contents within the Navigator window. Within each category contains the objects that are present in the document.

To view and utilize the Navigator while creating and editing Calc spreadsheets, follow these steps:

1. To open the Navigator window, click on the Edit menu and select Navigator from the menu list. You may also view the Navigator window by pressing the F5 key at the top of your keyboard.
2. If you see a "+" icon located next to a category within the Navigator, that indicates that there is at least one object within the document related to that particular category. Click the "+" sign to expand the list to view the objects related to the category. To quickly jump to the location in your document where the object is placed, double-click on the object listed in the Navigator window.

Viewing and Editing the Styles and Formatting Organizer

The Styles and Formatting Organizer allows you to quickly select pre-defined formatting options to include in your documents simply by double-clicking on a style option listed within the Organizer. To view and edit the Openoffice.org Formatting Styles Organizer, follow these steps:

1. To view the organizer, click the Format menu and select Styles and Formatting or simply press the F11 key at the top of your keyboard. A window will appear displaying by default the various paragraph styles available.
2. When the Organizer window is open, you will notice a small palette within the window. You can view other formatting styles as well by clicking on the appropriate button. From left-to-right, the style options you may view include Cells and Page styles. In the popup menu located at the bottom of the Styles Organizer window, be sure the menu has the option All Styles selected to view all of your available options for each style.
3. You can also create or modify formatting styles based upon existing styles by right-clicking on a style listed within the Organizer and select the appropriate command from the contextual menu that appears. You may also delete custom styles you created from the Organizer by right-clicking on it within the list.

How to Set OpenOffice.org to Automatically Open Microsoft Office Generated Files Using Windows

If you did not choose during the installation of OpenOffice.org to have the software automatically open Microsoft Office formatted documents, you may select to do so by following these steps:

1. Close all OpenOffice.org applications and return to your desktop.
2. Click on the Windows operating system Start button and select Control Panel from the list that appears. Then choose Add or Remove Programs from the submenu that appears, followed by the OpenOffice.org 3.0 list option, then click Install/Uninstall.
3. In the window that appears, click the NEXT button, select the Modify option and click NEXT until the wizard prompts you to select the file types you wish OpenOffice.org to automatically open for you.
4. Select or deselect the file types you wish OpenOffice.org to automatically open for you. Click NEXT until it prompts you to click Install to complete the setup. Clicking the Install button will make the necessary changes to automatically open the file types you selected. You should not need to have the installation CD inserted into your computer's CD-ROM to complete this process.

Section Two: Calc Basics

Selecting a Worksheet

The worksheets are available for viewing at the bottom of the spreadsheet layout window, just above the Status Bar. To select a specific worksheet for viewing or editing, simply click the tab labeled with appropriate worksheet name with the left mouse button.

Creating a New Worksheet

When opening a new Calc spreadsheet, OpenOffice.org automatically displays three worksheets. These worksheets are labeled Sheet1, Sheet2 and Sheet3. However, additional worksheets can be created within the Calc spreadsheet document. To create a new worksheet within a Calc spreadsheet document, follow these steps:

1. Click the Insert menu and select Sheet from the menu list that appears.
2. In the Position selection area, choose whether the new worksheet should be positioned before or after the current worksheet by selecting the appropriate radio button.
3. In the Sheet selection area, select the number of worksheets to be added by using the selection field provided. If only one new worksheet is to be created, type the name the new worksheet should be labeled as using the Name text field provided.
4. Click OK to complete the operation. The new worksheet should appear within the worksheet list located just above the Status Bar at the bottom of the spreadsheet window.

Renaming a Worksheet

To rename a worksheet from the default name to another, follow these steps:
1. Select the worksheet that is to be renamed by clicking on the worksheet tab located just above the Status Bar.
2. Click the Format menu, select Sheet from the menu options and select Rename from the submenu that appears.
3. When the Rename Sheet window appears, type the name the worksheet should be renamed as.
4. Click the OK to complete the operation.

Selecting a Cell

Spreadsheet document layouts are organized by columns (labeled alphabetically) and rows (labeled numerically). The intersection of a row and column within the spreadsheet creates a cell. Cells are identified by their column and row location within the spreadsheet. For example, cell A1 is located within the spreadsheet where column A intersects with row 1.

Before any formatting or calculations are performed within a spreadsheet, often you must first select the cells associated with the operation you are trying to perform. To select an individual cell, simply click on the cell location with the left mouse button. To select multiple cells, hold down the left mouse button while selecting the range of cells.

Entering Text and Numbers

To enter text and numbers within spreadsheet cells, simply select a cell and begin typing. The text and numbers will appear within the Formula Bar located just above the spreadsheet layout. Press the Enter key and the text and numbers are entered into the appropriate cell.

Sorting Data

To perform a basic data sort within a Calc worksheet, follow these steps:
1. Select the column or row of cells that contain the data to be sorted.
2. Click the Data menu and select Sort from the menu options that appear.
3. If it is not already selected, click the Sort Criteria tab within the Sort window that appears.
4. Select the criteria the data should be sorted as using the available popup menus and radio buttons.
5. Click the Options tab at the top of the Sort menu and select any appropriate sort options (optional).
6. Click the OK button to complete the operation.

Section Three: Formatting Text

Changing the Font Type

To change the font type of the text within the cells of your Calc spreadsheet document, follow these steps:
1. Select the text you wish to change the font position by clicking within the cell that contains the text you wish to format and selecting the appropriate text within the formula bar.
2. Click on the Format menu and select Cells from the menu list.
3. If it is not already selected, click the Font tab within the window that appears. Select the Font within the window list. Click the OK button to complete the selection.

You may also change the font type by using the Font Name popup menu located within the Formatting toolbar.

Changing the Font Size

To change the font size of the text within the cells of your Calc spreadsheet document, follow these steps:
1. Select the text you wish to change the font position by clicking within the cell that contains the text you wish to format and selecting the appropriate text within the formula bar.
2. Click on the Format menu and select Cells from the menu list.
3. If it is not already selected, click the Font tab within the window that appears. Select the font size within the window list. Click the OK button to complete the selection.

You may also change the font size by using the Font Size popup menu located within the Formatting toolbar.

Changing the Font Style (including Bold, Italicize, and Underline)

To change the font style of the text within the cells of your Calc spreadsheet document, follow these steps:
1. Select the text you wish to change the font position by clicking within the cell that contains the text you wish to format and selecting the appropriate text within the formula bar.
2. Click on the Format menu and select Cells from the menu list.
3. If it is not already selected, click the Font tab within the window that appears. Select the font style within the window list. Click the OK button to complete the selection.

You may also change the font style by using the appropriate Font Style buttons located within the Formatting toolbar.

Changing the Font Color

To change the font color of the text the cells of your Calc spreadsheet document, follow these steps:
1. Select the text you wish to change the font position by clicking within the cell that contains the text you wish to format and selecting the appropriate text within the formula bar.
2. Click on the Format menu and select Cells from the menu list.
3. Click the Font Effects tab within the window that appears. Select the font color within the Font color popup menu. Click the OK button to complete

the selection.

You may also change the font color by using the Font Color popup menu located within the Formatting toolbar.

Changing Text Position

To change the font position of the text within the cells of your Calc spreadsheet document, follow these steps:
1. Select the text you wish to change the font position by clicking within the cell that contains the text you wish to format and selecting the appropriate text within the formula bar.
2. Click on the Format menu and select Cells from the menu list.
3. Click the Font Position tab within the window that appears. Select the font position and scaling options within the window list. Click the OK button to complete the selection.

Section Four: Formatting Cells

Changing the Width of Columns

To change the width of a column within a Calc spreadsheet document, follow these steps:
1. Select the cells that are to be formatted.
2. Click on the Format menu, select Columns from the menu that appears and select Width from the submenu that appears.
3. In the Column Width window that appears, select the value within the window and enter in the new column width using either the numeric keypad on the computer keyboard or by clicking on the arrows to the right of the Width selection field.
4. Click OK to complete the operation.

Changing the Height of Rows

To change the height of a row within a Calc spreadsheet document, follow these steps:
1. Select the cells that are to be formatted.
2. Click on the Format menu, select Row from the menu that appears and select Height from the submenu that appears.

3. In the Row Height window that appears, select the value within the window and enter in the new row height using either the numeric keypad on the computer keyboard or by clicking on the arrows to the right of the Height selection field.
4. Click OK to complete the operation.

Cell Borders

To format borders for cells within a Calc spreadsheet document, follow these steps:
1. Select the cells that are to be formatted.
2. Click on the Format menu and select Cells from the menu that appears.
3. When the Format Cells window appears, click on the Borders tab located at the top of the window.
4. In the Line Arrangement selection area, select the border arrangement by clicking on one of the default arrangements provided. Border arrangements can also be customized by utilizing the User-Defined configuration area provided (optional).
5. In the Line selection area, select the border thickness using the Styles selections and choose the border color using the Color popup menu.
6. In the Spacing To Contents area, select the appropriate border spacing for each side of the selected cells (optional).
7. Once all formatting selections have been made, click the OK button to complete the operation.

Cell Colors

To format cell colors within a Calc spreadsheet document, follow these steps:
1. Select the cells that are to be formatted.
2. Click on the Format menu and select Cells from the menu that appears.
3. When the Format Cells window appears, click on the Background tab located at the top of the window.
4. In the tab window that appears, click on the appropriate color from the selections provided.
5. Click the OK button to complete the operation.

Adding a Drop Shadow to a Cell

To format drop shadows for cells within a Calc spreadsheet document, follow these steps:

1. Select the cells that are to be formatted.
2. Click on the Format menu and select Cells from the menu that appears.
3. When the Format Cells window appears, click on the Borders tab located at the top of the window.
4. In the Shadow Style selection area, select the shadow position by clicking on one of the selections provided.
5. Select the distance the shadow extends from the cell by entering the appropriate measurements within the configuration box located to the right of the shadow position area (optional).
6. Using the Color popup menu located within the Shadow Style selection area, select the shadow color. By default, the color will be gray.
7. Once all drop shadow format selections have been made, click the OK button to complete the operation.

Number Formatting Within Cells

To change the number formatting for cells within a Calc spreadsheet document, follow these steps:
1. Select the cells that are to be formatted.
2. Click on the Format menu and select Cells from the menu that appears.
3. When the Format Cells window appears, click on the Numbers tab located at the top of the window.
4. In the Category selection area, select the type of numbers that are to be presented in the selected cells.
5. Once a category has been selected, select a format type located within the Format selection area.
6. Within the Language selection area, if the numbers to appear within the cells are to be formatted to a language other than the default language when OpenOffice.org was installed, select the language type using the popup menu provided (optional).
7. In the Options selection area, select the decimal places, leading zeros, negative numbering format and thousands separator options provided where appropriate.
8. Once all number formatting selections have been made, click the OK button to complete the operation.

Changing Text Alignment Within Cells

To change the text alignment within Calc spreadsheet cells, follow these steps:
1. Select the cells that are to be formatted.

2. Click on the Format menu and select Cells from the menu that appears.
3. When the Format Cells window appears, click on the Alignment tab located at the top of the window.
4. In the Text Alignment selection area, select the appropriate horizontal and/or vertical text alignment using the popup menus provided.
5. If text within the selected cells needs to be rotated, use the options within the Text Orientation and Properties selection areas to do so (optional).
6. Once all alignment selections have been made, click the OK button to complete the operation.

Text alignment within cells may also be performed utilizing the alignment buttons within the Formatting toolbar located above the Formula Bar.

Section Five: Formatting Spreadsheets

Selecting Page Size

To select the appropriate page size for a Calc spreadsheet document, follow these steps:
1. Click on the Format menu and select Page from the menu that appears.
2. When the Page Style window appears, click on the Page tab at the top of the window (if it isn't already selected).
3. Using the Format popup menu, select the predefined paper size you will print your document on. When you select an option, the width and height will automatically change to format itself to the predefined paper format. If you wish to select a custom paper size, utilize the Width and Height menus to enter the appropriate page size.
4. In the Margins selection area, specify your page margins for your document by entering the appropriate measurements.
5. In the Layout selection area, select the appropriate page layout, format and table alignment for the document.
6. Once you have selected your page style formatting options, click the OK button to complete the selection.

Adjusting Page Margins

To adjust the page margins for a Calc spreadsheet document, follow these steps:
1. Click on the Format menu and select Page from the menu that appears.

2. When the Page Style window appears, click on the Page tab at the top of the window (if it isn't already selected).
3. In the Margins selection area, specify the page margins for the document by entering the appropriate measurements.
4. Once you have selected your page style formatting options, click the OK button to complete the selection.

Using the Organizer to Format Pages

The Styles and Formatting Organizer allows you to quickly select pre-defined formatting options to include in your documents simply by double-clicking on a style option listed within the Organizer. To view and edit the Openoffice.org Formatting Styles Organizer, follow these steps:

1. To view the organizer, click the Format menu and select Styles and Formatting or simply press the F11 key at the top of your keyboard. A palette will appear displaying by default the various cell styles available.
2. When the Organizer palette is open, you will notice a small toolbar within the window. You can view other formatting styles as well by clicking on the appropriate button. Click on the Page Styles button (the second button in the upper-left corner of the organizer window) to view your page formatting options. Double-click on the appropriate style to make your format selection.
3. You can also create or modify formatting styles based upon existing styles by right-clicking on a style listed within the Organizer and select the appropriate command from the contextual menu that appears. You may also delete custom styles you created from the Organizer by right-clicking on it within the list.

Section Six: Inserting Clip Art and Graphics

Supported Graphic File Types

OpenOffice.org supports a wide array of file types for graphics files to be imported into Calc. If you have a graphic file you wish to import into your document, chances are OpenOffice.org supports it. Supported graphic file types for importing into a Calc document include:

- Windows Bitmap (*.bmp)
- AutoCAD Interchange Format (*.dxf)

- Enhanced Metafile (*.emf)
- Encapsulated PostScript (*.eps)
- Graphics Interchange Format (*.gif)
- Joint Photographic Experts Group (*.jpg or *jpeg)
- OS/2 Metafile (*.met)
- Portable Bitmap (*.pbm)
- Kodak Photo CD (*.pcd)
- Macintosh Picture Format (*.pct or *.pict)
- Zsoft Paintbrush (*.pcx)
- Portable Graymap (*.pgm)
- Portable Network Graphic (*.png)
- Portable Pixelmap (*.ppm)
- Adobe Photoshop (*.psd)
- Sun Raster Image (*.ras)
- StarWriter Graphics Format (*.sgf)
- StarDraw 2.0 (*.sgv)
- StarView Metafile (*.svm)
- Truevision Targa (*.tga)
- Tagged Image File Format (*.tif or *.tiff)
- Windows Metafile (*.wmf)
- X Bitmap (*.xbm)
- X PixMap (*.xpm)

Inserting a Graphic or Clip Art

To insert a graphic or clip art image into your Calc spreadsheet document, follow these steps:

1. Click on the Insert menu, select the Picture menu option and select From File from the submenu that appears.
2. Locate the file using the Insert Picture window that appears. Click once on the file displayed to select the appropriate image to insert.
3. At the bottom of the Insert Picture window, OpenOffice.org gives you the option to link the file rather than embedding the image into the document. If you have an image that is being used in a number of places throughout the document, you can choose to link the image to reduce the file size of your document. If you ever move the image to another location, however, you will need to re-link the image for it to appear in the document. If you wish to link the image, click within the checkbox located next to the Link selection.
4. Click OK to complete your selection.

Adjusting a Graphic Image Location

If you wish to adjust the location of your graphic image within a Calc spreadsheet document, follow these steps:

1. Click once within the graphic image with your left mouse button. Small boxes will appear around the edge of the image when it has been properly selected.
2. Move your pointer within the graphic area. The pointer will transform into a black target icon. Holding down your left mouse button on the image, drag the image. Once you have the image in your desired location, release the mouse button.

Resizing a Graphic Image

If you wish to resize an image or graphic within your Calc spreadsheet document, follow these steps:

1. Click once within the graphic image with your left mouse button. Small boxes will appear around the edge of the image when it has been properly selected.
2. To proportionally resize the graphic, place your pointer on one of the small boxes located one the corner of the image. Your pointer will transform into a black bar with arrows on each end of it. Hold down the left mouse button and begin to drag either outward or inward to make your graphic larger or smaller, respectively. When you have resized it to the desired width and height, release the left mouse button.

If you know the exact width and height you wish your graphic to be, you may also resize an image by right-clicking on the image and select Position And Size from the contextual menu that appears.

Section Seven: Creating Charts From Calc Spreadsheet Data

Adding a 3-D Pie Chart To A Spreadsheet

To create a 3-D pie chart within a Calc spreadsheet document, follow these steps:

1. Select the text and data that is to appear within the chart.
2. Go to the Insert menu and select Chart from the menu options that appear.
3. When the AutoFormat Chart window appears, the selection made in Step #1 should appear in the range field. If the selection is correct, click the NEXT button at the bottom of the window. If the selection is not correct, click the Shrink button located next to the range field to enter back into the worksheet and select the appropriate cells containing the data to appear within the chart.
4. In the next window to appear, select the appropriate Chart Type. Use the scroll bar located on the right side of the window to view all of the available selections, including the 3-D pie chart. Also select the appropriate Data Series options using the radio buttons below the Chart Type selections, and click the checkbox Show Text Elements In Preview to view how the chart will be labeled. The click the NEXT button.
5. In the Display selection area that appears in the next window, type a Chart Title within the text field provided. Make sure the checkboxes are selected for both the Chart Title and Legend.
6. Click the CREATE button to complete the operation. The completed chart should appear within the worksheet.

Adding A Bar Graph To A Spreadsheet

To create a bar graph within a Calc spreadsheet document, follow these steps:
1. Select the text and data that is to appear within the chart.
2. Go to the Insert menu and select Chart from the menu options that appear.
3. When the AutoFormat Chart window appears, the selection made in Step #1 should appear in the range field. If the selection is correct, click the NEXT button at the bottom of the window. If the selection is not correct, click the Shrink button located next to the range field to enter back into the worksheet and select the appropriate cells containing the data to appear within the chart.
4. In the next window to appear, select the appropriate Chart Type. Use the scroll bar located on the right side of the window to view all of the available selections, including the bar graph. Also select the appropriate Data Series options using the radio buttons below the Chart Type selections, and click the checkbox Show Text Elements In Preview to view how the chart will be labeled. The click the NEXT button.
5. In the Display selection area that appears in the next window, type a Chart Title within the text field provided. Make sure the checkboxes are selected for both the Chart Title and Legend.

6. Click the CREATE button to complete the operation. The completed chart should appear within the worksheet.

Adding a Line Graph To A Spreadsheet

To create a line graph within a Calc spreadsheet document, follow these steps:

1. Select the text and data that is to appear within the chart.
2. Go to the Insert menu and select Chart from the menu options that appear.
3. When the AutoFormat Chart window appears, the selection made in Step #1 should appear in the range field. If the selection is correct, click the NEXT button at the bottom of the window. If the selection is not correct, click the Shrink button located next to the range field to enter back into the worksheet and select the appropriate cells containing the data to appear within the chart.
4. In the next window to appear, select the appropriate Chart Type. Use the scroll bar located on the right side of the window to view all of the available selections, including the line graph. Also select the appropriate Data Series options using the radio buttons below the Chart Type selections, and click the checkbox Show Text Elements In Preview to view how the chart will be labeled. The click the NEXT button.
5. In the Display selection area that appears in the next window, type a Chart Title within the text field provided. Make sure the checkboxes are selected for both the Chart Title and Legend.
6. Click the CREATE button to complete the operation. The completed chart should appear within the worksheet.

Section Eight: Formulas and Performing Calculations

Entering Formulas

Formulas can be created by typing the formula within the cell that will contain the final value, or by typing the formula within the field provided within the Formula Bar located just above the spreadsheet area. Formulas usually begin with an equal (=) sign and selected cells and cell ranges are contained within parentheses. Formulas can be created to perform a wide array of calculations, including adding, subtracting, multiplying, dividing, averaging and much more.

Using The SUM Function

The SUM function within Calc allows you to add the numbers contained within multiple cells selected throughout a worksheet. You can also select a range of cells to allow the SUM function to total the values contained within the range. The following are examples of formulas containing the SUM function:

=sum(A1...A4) This formula calculates the total for cell range A1 through A4.
=sum(A1+B2) This formula calculates the total for cells A1 and B2

Using The AVG (Average) Function

The AVG function within Calc allows you to average values contained within multiple cells selected throughout a worksheet. You can also select a range of cells to allow the AVG function to calculate the average among the values contained within the range.   The following are examples of formulas containing the AVG function:

=avg(A1...A4) This formula calculates the average for the values contained within cell range A1 through A4.
=avg(A1+B2) This formula calculates the average for the values contained within cells A1 and B2

Using The MAX (Maximum) Function

The MAX function within Calc allows you to extract the maximum value contained within multiple cells selected throughout a worksheet. You can also select a range of cells to allow the MAX function to extract the maximum value contained within the range.   The following are examples of formulas containing the MAX function:

=max(A1...A4) This formula displays the largest value contained within cell range A1 through A4.
=max(A1+B2) This formula displays the largest value contained within cells A1 and B2

Using The MIN (Minimum) Function

The MIN function within Calc allows you to extract the minimum value contained within multiple cells selected throughout a worksheet. You can also select a range of cells to allow the MIN function to extract the minimum value contained within the range.   The following are examples of formulas containing the MIN function:

=min(A1...A4) This formula displays the smallest value contained within cell range A1 through A4.

=min(A1+B2) This formula displays the smallest value contained within cells A1 and B2

Calculating Values Among Multiple Worksheets

Not only can you calculate values within an individual worksheet, but you can also calculate values contained within multiple worksheets as well. To calculate values within multiple worksheets, simply select the appropriate cell within another worksheet to present it within the formula you create.

Using The Function Wizard

The Calc spreadsheet application contains a comprehensive Function Wizard that can assist a user in creating a formula by using a graphic interface to point-and-click their way through the process. The Function Wizard displays over 300 functions that a user can select to perform a calculation. To start the Function Wizard, click on the Insert menu and choose Function from the menu options that appear. You may also hold down the CONTROL (CTRL) key and press F2 to start the Function Wizard, or press the Function button located within the Function Bar.

Section Nine: Saving a Document

Supported File Types for Saving

OpenOffice.org can open and save documents formatted in a wide array of file types. Although it might not be their primary office suite, many users have found OpenOffice.org to be a useful tool for opening and saving files not supported through their primary applications. Calc supports the following file formats:
* Data Interchange Format (*.dif)
* dBase (*.dbf)
* Hypertext Markup Language Documents (*.htm or *.html)
* OpenOffice.org 3.0 Native OpenDocument Spreadsheet (*.ods)
* OpenOffice.org 3.0 Native OpenDocument Spreadsheet Template (*.ots)
* OpenOffice.org 1.0 Spreadsheet Document (*.sxc)

- Microsoft Excel 5.0/95/97/2000/XP/2007 Documents (*.xls, *.xlsx)
- Microsoft Excel 2003 XML Documents (*.xml)
- Pocket Excel Documents (*.pxl)
- Portable Document Format Documents (*.pdf)
- StarCalc 3.0/4.0/5.0 Text Documents (*.sdc)
- StarCalc 3.0/4.0/5.0 Text Templates (*.vor)
- SYLK (*.slk)
- Text CSV (*.csv)

Saving a File as a Native Calc Document

To save a document in the native Calc 3.0 OpenDocument format, follow these steps:
1. Click on the File menu and choose Save As from the menu list.
2. A window will appear and prompt you to choose a location to save your document. Choose the location you want to save a document to in the Save In popup field.
3. In the field File Name, type the name you would like to save the file as.
4. In the Save As Type popup menu, select the OpenDocument Spreadsheet (.ods) file format.
5. Click the button SAVE to complete the operation.

Saving a File as a Microsoft Excel Document

To save a spreadsheet in the Microsoft Excel format, follow these steps:
1. Click on the File menu and choose Save As from the menu list.
2. A window will appear and prompt you to choose a location to save your document. Choose the location you want to save a document to in the Save In popup field.
3. In the field File Name, type the name you would like to save the file as.
4. In the Save As Type popup menu, select the appropriate Microsoft Excel (*.xls) file format.
5. Click the button SAVE to complete the operation.

Exporting a File as a Portable Document Format (PDF) Document

One of the many useful features OpenOffice.org has built-in to the office suite is the ability to export documents as a Portable Document Format (PDF) file. To save a spreadsheet as a read-only PDF file, follow these steps:
1. Click on the File menu and choose Export As PDF from the menu list.

2. A window will appear and prompt you to choose a location to save your document. Choose the location you want to save a document to in the Save In popup field.
3. In the field File Name, type the name you would like to save the file as.
4. In the File Format popup menu, make sure Portable Document Format (PDF) is selected.
5. Click the button SAVE to complete the operation.

(NOTE: OpenOffice.org documents saved as a PDF file is a convenient way to share read-only documents to other users that have a PDF reader application installed on their computer. However, OpenOffice.org cannot edit a document that has been saved as a PDF file. To save a document for editing at a later date, save the document in its Native OpenDocument file format.)

Exporting a File as a Web Page (HTML) Document

To save a document in the Hypertext Markup Language (HTML) format, follow these steps:
1. Click on the File menu and choose Save As from the menu list.
2. A window will appear and prompt you to choose a location to save your document. Choose the location you want to save a document to in the Save In popup field.
3. In the field File Name, type the name you would like to save the file as.
4. In the Save As Type popup menu, select the HTML (*.htm or *.html) file format.
5. Click the button SAVE to complete the operation.

Section Ten: Printing A Document

Using Cut, Copy and Paste

Using Cut, Copy and Paste is one of the most fundamental operations you will perform to correct document errors. You may also use these commands to transfer text or graphics from one document into another. If you are unfamiliar with using these operations, use these steps to assist in determining which to use when correcting document errors:
1. Select the text you want to cut or copy by clicking on the appropriate cell and selecting the text within the Formula Bar.

2. To eliminate text to reinsert in another location in the document, click the Edit menu and choose the Cut menu option.
3. To duplicate text in another part of the document, click the Edit menu and choose the Copy menu option.
4. Click on the cell you want the text to appear.
5. In the Edit menu, choose the Paste menu option.

Deleting Text

To permanently delete text from your Calc spreadsheet document, follow these steps:
1. Select the cell that contains the text you want to permanently delete.
2. Press the Delete key on your keyboard to permanently remove the text from the selected cell.

Using Undo

If you make the mistake of deleting something you didn't wish to do or make a formatting error, immediately go to the Edit menu and choose Undo from the menu list that appears to go back to the document's previous state before the error was made. You can continue to select the Undo menu command multiple times to continue to go back to each previous step.

Using Spellcheck

To use the OpenOffice.org spell check feature, follow these steps:
1. To spell check a specific word or sentence within a cell, select the text you wish to spell check by clicking on the appropriate cell and selecting the text within the Formula Bar.
2. Go to the Tools menu and select Spellcheck from the menu that appears. You may also press the F7 key on your keyboard to begin checking for spelling errors.
3. If any potential spelling errors appear, OpenOffice.org will indicate the potential error and give you a list of possible suggestions to correct the spelling.
4. If you see a spelling suggestion that would correct the error, select it from the Suggestions list and click the CHANGE button.
5. If you believe that the word in question is spelled correctly, you can click the IGNORE ONCE button to proceed to the next potential spelling error. If the word in question is spelled correctly and you use it often when creating

documents, you may click the ADD button to add it to the Spellcheck dictionary.

6. When you have completed checking for potential spelling errors, click the CLOSE button to exit and return to the document.

Using AutoCorrect

AutoCorrect is enabled by default. However, AutoCorrect can be enabled or disabled at any time. To enable or disable a specific AutoCorrect feature, go to the Tools menu and select AutoCorrect from the menu that appears. Once the AutoCorrect window appears, click on the tab related to the specific feature you wish to enable or disable and select the appropriate options.

Section Eleven: Beyond The Basics

Importing Calc Spreadsheets into Writer Documents

Importing a Calc spreadsheet as an OLE Object into a Writer document not only allows you to place the spreadsheet contents within a text document, but also allows you to edit the spreadsheet directly within the text document as well. To import a Calc spreadsheet as an OLE object, follow these steps:

1. Open both the Writer document you wish to import a spreadsheet into and the Calc spreadsheet you will be exporting data from.
2. Within the Calc spreadsheet, select the spreadsheet area to want to place within the Writer document.
3. Place your pointer within the selected area of the Calc Spreadsheet, hold down the left mouse button and drag the selected spreadsheet area into the Writer text document. Once the cursor appears at the location you wish to place the spreadsheet, release the mouse button. The spreadsheet in now inserted as an OLE object into the Writer document.
4. To edit the Calc spreadsheet directly within the Writer document, double-click the spreadsheet. If you need to have the menu commands available to edit the spreadsheet, right-click on the spreadsheet and choose Edit from the contextual menu that appears.

About Macros

In the latest version, Calc does provide some limited ability to run Microsoft Excel

Visual Basic scripts. In order to do so, you may need to enable this feature by clicking on the Tools | Options | Load/Save | VBA Properties menu.

Otherwise, in many cases, OpenOffice.org cannot execute the same macro code that Microsoft Office utilizes. This is because OpenOffice.org uses Basic code for its macros, while Microsoft Office uses Visual Basic for Applications (VBA) for its macros. While OpenOffice.org Basic and VBA share many similarities, objects and methods within each scripting language are different. In addition to Basic, OpenOffice.org also supports JavaScript and BeanShell for scripting macros.

To utilize the macros created in one application within another, you must edit the macros. OpenOffice.org can load macros that are contained within Microsoft Office documents. You can then view and edit the macro code within the OpenOffice.org Basic editor.

APPENDIX

 Quick Guide to Creating and Editing Impress Documents

Appendix C
Quick Guide to Creating and Editing
Impress Presentations

Section One: Overview of Impress

Starting Impress

To launch the Impress application within the Microsoft Windows operating system, follow these steps:

1. Beginning at the desktop, click on the Start button located in the lower-left corner of the screen, and select Programs or All Program from the menu list that appears.
2. Select the OpenOffice.org 3.0 application folder that appears, and select Impress from the applications options that appear.
3. Each time Impress is launched either from the Start Menu or from the New menu within OpenOffice.org, a Presentation Wizard will appear. Select the appropriate Presentation Type by clicking on the radio buttons provided. Follow the on-screen instruction that the wizard provides in creating a new presentation document.

To launch the Impress application within a Linux-based operating system, follow these steps:

1. Beginning at the desktop, click on the Start button located in the lower-left corner of the screen, and select Office Productivity from the menu list that appears.
2. Select the OpenOffice.org 3.0 Impress application icon from the list that appears, and the Impress application will launch.
3. Each time Impress is launched either from the Start Menu or from the File menu within OpenOffice.org, a Presentation Wizard will appear. Select the appropriate Presentation Type by clicking on the radio buttons provided. Follow the on-screen instruction that the wizard provides in creating a new presentation document.

Displaying Toolbars

Impress contains many toolbars to assist in formatting and editing your slide presentations. Sometimes you may need to view certain toolbars to assist you with creating your slides, while other toolbars may need to hidden from view to prevent from getting in your way and free up screen space for other tools. To view or hide a toolbar within Impress, follow these steps:

1. Click the View menu and select Toolbars from the menu list. A list of available toolbars will appear.
2. Select a toolbar to appear within Impress by simply clicking on the appropriate toolbar within the list. If a toolbar within the list has a checkmark beside it, this means that the toolbar is already visible within the Impress application.
3. If you wish to hide a toolbar from view within Impress, simply click on it from the list. Toolbars listed that do not have a checkmark beside them indicates that the toolbar is hidden from view within Impress.

Task Pane

The task pane within Impress allows you to perform a number of formatting options without accessing the standard application menus. Formatting options available through the task pane include Master Pages, Layouts, Custom Animation and Slide Transitions. If the Impress task pane is not visible when you open an Impress document, you may make it so by going to the View menu and select Task Pane from the menu that appears. A checkmark should appear next to the menu option when the task pane is visible. If you wish to hide the task pane from view within Impress, simply click on it from the list. When the menu option does not have a checkmark beside it, this indicates that the task pane is hidden from view within Impress.

Status Bar

If the Impress status bar, located at the bottom of the Impress application window, is not visible when you open an Impress document, you may make it so by going to the View menu and select Status Bar from the menu that appears. A checkmark should appear next to the menu option when the status bar is visible. If you wish to hide the status bar from view within Impress, simply click on it from the list. When the menu option does not have a checkmark beside it, this indicates that the status bar is hidden from view within Impress.

Adjusting Page View

To adjust the view of the document you are working in, click on the View menu and select Zoom from the menu list. You may also select to Zoom by clicking on the magnifying glass icon within the Standard toolbar located just beneath the main application menu.

Choosing a Slide Layout

To select a slide layout for an Impress slide presentation, follow these steps:
1. In the Slides pane located on the left side of the presentation editing window, select the slide that the layout will be applied to. If a new Impress presentation has been created, skip to Step #2.
2. Go to the View menu and select Task Pane from the menu that appears.
3. Click on the triangle located next to the Layouts selection within the task pane. A preview list of various slide layouts will appear.
4. Select the appropriate slide layout by clicking once on the slide preview option. When the dialog window appears asking whether to continue with the selection, click the YES button. The operation is now complete.

Creating a New Slide

To create a new slide within an Impress presentation document, click on the Insert menu and select Slide from the menu that appears. You may also create a new slide by using the Slide button located in the Standard toolbar within Impress.

Deleting a Slide

To delete a slide from an Impress presentation document, right-click on the slide within the Slide Pane that is to be removed from the presentation. Then select Delete Slide from the contextual menu that appears. If the Slide Pane, located on the left-hand side of the Impress application window, is not visible, you can make it so by clicking on the View menu at the top of the application window and select the Slide Pane menu option.

Using the Navigator

The Navigator allows a user to quickly view objects that are within a document. The Navigator displays "categories", or the various contents within the Navigator window. Within each category contains the objects that are present in the document.

To view and utilize the Navigator while creating and editing Impress documents, follow these steps:

1. To open the Navigator window, click on the Edit menu and select Navigator from the menu list. You may also view the Navigator window by pressing the F5 key at the top of your keyboard.
2. If you see a "+" icon located next to a category within the Navigator, that indicates that there is at least one object within the document related to that particular category. Click the "+" sign to expand the list to view the objects related to the category. To quickly jump to the location in your document where the object is placed, double-click on the object listed in the Navigator window.

Viewing and Editing the Styles and Formatting Organizer

The Styles and Formatting Organizer allows you to quickly select pre-defined formatting options to include in your documents simply by double-clicking on a style option listed within the Organizer. To view and edit the Openoffice.org Formatting Styles Organizer, follow these steps:

1. To view the organizer, click the Format menu and select Styles and Formatting or simply press the F11 key at the top of your keyboard. A palette will appear displaying by default the various paragraph styles available.
2. When the Organizer palette is open, you will notice a small toolbar within the window. You can view other formatting styles as well by clicking on the appropriate button. From left-to-right, the style options you may view include Graphics and Presentation styles. In the popup menu located at the bottom of the Styles Organizer window, be sure the menu has the option All Styles selected to view all of your available options for each style.
3. You can also create or modify formatting styles based upon existing styles by right-clicking on a style listed within the Organizer and select the appropriate command from the contextual menu that appears. You may also delete custom styles you created from the Organizer by right-clicking on it within the list.

How to Set OpenOffice.org to Automatically Open Microsoft Office Generated Files Using Windows

If you did not choose during the installation of OpenOffice.org to have the software automatically open Microsoft Office formatted documents, you may select to do so by following these steps:

1. Close all OpenOffice.org applications and return to your desktop.
2. Click on the Windows operating system Start button and select Control Panel from the list that appears. Then choose Add or Remove Programs from the submenu that appears, followed by the OpenOffice.org 3.0 list option, then click Install/Uninstall.
3. In the window that appears, click the NEXT button, select the Modify option and click NEXT until the wizard prompts you to select the file types you wish OpenOffice.org to automatically open for you.
4. Select or deselect the file types you wish OpenOffice.org to automatically open for you. Click NEXT until it prompts you to click Install to complete the setup. Clicking the Install button will make the necessary changes to automatically open the file types you selected. You should not need to have the installation CD inserted into your computer's CD-ROM to complete this process.

Section Two: Impress Basics

Inserting Text

To insert text into a slide, simply click within one of the pre-defined text boxes created within the selected layout. A cursor will appear to allow text to be entered.

Changing the Font Type

To change the font type of the text within your slide presentation, follow these steps:
1. Select the text you wish to change the font type.
2. Click on the Format menu and select Character from the menu list.
3. If it is not already selected, click the Font tab within the window that appears. Select the Font within the window list. Click the OK button to complete the selection.

You may also change the font type by using the Font Name popup menu located within the Formatting toolbar.

Changing the Font Size

To change the font size of the text within your slide presentation, follow these steps:

1. Select the text you wish to change the font size.
2. Click on the Format menu and select Character from the menu list.
3. If it is not already selected, click the Font tab within the window that appears. Select the font size within the window list. Click the OK button to complete the selection.

You may also change the font size by using the Font Size popup menu located within the Formatting toolbar.

Changing the Font Style (including Bold, Italicize, and Underline)

To change the font style of the text within your slide presentation, follow these steps:
1. Select the text you wish to change the font style.
2. Click on the Format menu and select Character from the menu list.
3. If it is not already selected, click the Font tab within the window that appears. Select the font style within the window list. Click the OK button to complete the selection.

You may also change the font style by using the appropriate Font Style buttons located within the Formatting toolbar.

Changing the Font Color

To change the font color of the text within your slide presentation, follow these steps:
1. Select the text you wish to change the font color.
2. Click on the Format menu and select Character from the menu list.
3. Click the Font Effects tab within the window that appears. Select the font color within the Font color popup menu. Click the OK button to complete the selection.

You may also change the font color by using the Font Color popup menu located within the Formatting toolbar.

Changing Text Alignment

To change the text alignment within your slide presentation, follow these steps:
1. Select the text or paragraph you wish to change the alignment.
2. Click on the Format menu and select Paragraph from the menu list.

3. Click on the Alignment tab in the window that appears. Select the alignment style (left, right, center or justified) by clicking on the radio button next to your desired selection.
4. Click the OK button to complete the selection.

You may also change the paragraph alignment by using the appropriate alignment buttons located within the Formatting toolbar.

Changing Slide Background Color and Pattern

To change the color or background pattern of an Impress slide presentation, follow these steps:
1. Click on the Format menu and select Page from the menu that appears.
2. When the Page Setup window appears, click on the Background tab located at the top of the window.
3. Impress provides several formats to change the color or pattern of a slide presentation, including applying a solid background color, applying a pre-defined gradient pattern, applying a hatching pattern in combination with a solid background color and applying a bitmap image as a background pattern. Select the appropriate color or pattern by utilizing the popup menus and/or radio buttons provided and defining the selection.
4. Click the OK button to complete the selection. A dialog box will appear asking whether the selection made should be applied to all slides within the Impress document or to apply to the current slide only. Make a selection and Impress will format the presentation accordingly.

Inserting Bullet and Numbering Lists

To insert bullet or numbered lists within your slide presentation, follow these steps:
1. Select the text box that will be formatted with a bulleted or numbered list.
2. Click on the Format menu and select Bullets and Numbering from the menu that appears.
3. Within the window that appears, you have numerous bullet and numbering format options available to you that are sorted within tabs that are presented along the top. Click on the tab that presents the bulleted or numbered format you wish to select to view your options.
4. Click on the bulleted or numbered list option within the Selection area to specify your desired format type.
5. Click the OK button to complete the selection.

You may also create a bulleted or numbered list by utilizing the Styles and Formatting Organizer. To view the Styles and Formatting Organizer, click on the Format menu and select Styles and Formatting from the menu list or simply press the F11 key on your keyboard. Then click on the Character Styles button (the second icon from the left at the top of the Organizer) to view your bulleted or numbered list format option.

Section Three: Inserting Clip Art, Graphics and Charts

Supported Graphic File Types

OpenOffice.org supports a wide array of file types for graphics files to be imported into Impress. If you have a graphic file you wish to import into your Impress document, chances are OpenOffice.org supports it. Supported graphic file types for importing into an Impress document include:

- Windows Bitmap (*.bmp)
- AutoCAD Interchange Format (*.dxf)
- Enhanced Metafile (*.emf)
- Encapsulated PostScript (*.eps)
- Graphics Interchange Format (*.gif)
- Joint Photographic Experts Group (*.jpg or *jpeg)
- OS/2 Metafile (*.met)
- Portable Bitmap (*.pbm)
- Kodak Photo CD (*.pcd)
- Macintosh Picture Format (*.pct or *.pict)
- Zsoft Paintbrush (*.pcx)
- Portable Graymap (*.pgm)
- Portable Network Graphic (*.png)
- Portable Pixelmap (*.ppm)
- Adobe Photoshop (*.psd)
- Sun Raster Image (*.ras)
- StarWriter Graphics Format (*.sgf)
- StarDraw 2.0 (*.sgv)
- StarView Metafile (*.svm)
- Truevision Targa (*.tga)
- Tagged Image File Format (*.tif or *.tiff)
- Windows Metafile (*.wmf)

- X Bitmap (*.xbm)
- X PixMap (*.xpm)

Inserting a Graphic or Clip Art

To insert a graphic or clip art image into your Impress slide presentation, follow these steps:
1. Click on the Insert menu and select the Picture menu option that appears.
2. When you select the Picture menu option, a submenu will appear allowing you to choose an image file or retrieve a picture from a scanner. Select the appropriate option.
3. If you selected to insert a picture from an image file, locate the file using Insert Picture window that appears. Click once on the file displayed to select the appropriate image to insert.
4. At the bottom of the Insert Picture window, OpenOffice.org gives you the option to link the file rather than embedding the image into the document. If you have an image that is being used in a number of places throughout the document, you can choose to link the image to reduce the file size of your document. If you ever move the image to another location, however, you will need to re-link the image for it to appear in the document. If you wish to link the image, click within the checkbox located next to the Link selection.
5. Click OK to complete your selection.

Adjusting a Graphic Image Location

If you wish to adjust the location of your graphic image, follow these steps:
1. Click once within the graphic image with your left mouse button. Small boxes will appear around the edge of the image when it has been properly selected.
2. Move your pointer within the graphic area. The pointer will transform into a black target icon. Holding down your left mouse button on the image, drag the image. Once you have the image in your desired location, release the mouse button.
3. If you wish to center the graphic within the page, select the image as detailed in Step #1. Then click the Center Horizontal tool within the Formatting toolbar located above your document's ruler. The image should then center itself within the page.

Resizing a Graphic Image

If you wish to resize an image or graphic within your slide presentation, follow these steps:
1. Click once within the graphic image with your left mouse button. Small boxes will appear around the edge of the image when it has been properly selected.
2. To proportionally resize the graphic, place your pointer on one of the small boxes located one the corner of the image. Your pointer will transform into a black bar with arrows on each end of it. Hold down the left mouse button and begin to drag either outward or inward to make your graphic larger or smaller, respectively. When you have resized it to the desired width and height, release the left mouse button.
3. If you know the exact width and height you wish your graphic to be, you may also resize an image by right-clicking on the image and select Graphics from the contextual menu that appears.

Inserting a Chart

If you wish to insert a chart into an Impress presentation, follow these steps:
1. Click on the Insert menu and select the Chart menu option that appears.
2. A pre-defined chart will appear within the slide presentation. To change the data to appear within the chart, click on the Edit menu and select the Chart Data menu option that appears. You may also change the data by clicking on the CHART DATA button located at the top of the chart editing window.
3. To change the type of chart, click on the Format menu and select the Chart Type menu option that appears. You may also change the chart type by clicking on the CHART TYPE button located at the top of the chart editing window.
4. To exit out of the chart editing window, click on the Window menu and select New from the menu option that appears.

Section Four: Saving and Printing a Presentation Document

Supported File Types for Saving

OpenOffice.org can open and save documents formatted in a wide array of file types. Although it might not be their primary office suite, many users have found

OpenOffice.org to be a useful tool for opening and saving files not supported through their primary applications. Writer supports the following file formats:
- Microsoft PowerPoint 97/2000/XP/2007 Presentation (*.ppt, *.pptx)
- Microsoft PowerPoint 97/2000/XP Presentation Templates (*.ppt)
- OpenOffice.org 3.0 Native OpenDocument Drawing (*.odg)
- OpenOffice.org 3.0 Native OpenDocument Presentation (*.odp)
- OpenOffice.org 3.0 Native OpenDocument Template (*.otp)
- OpenOffice.org 1.0 Native Presentation (*.sxi)
- OpenOffice.org 1.0 Native Presentation Template (*.sti)
- OpenOffice.org 1.0 Drawing
- StarDraw 5.0 Drawing (*.sda)
- StarDraw 3.0 Drawing (*.sdd)
- StarImpress 4.0/5.0 Presentation (*.sdd)
- StarImpress 4.0/5.0 Template (*.vor)

Saving a File as a Native Impress Presentation

To save a document in the native Impress 3.0 OpenDocument format, follow these steps:
1. Click on the File menu and choose Save As from the menu list.
2. A window will appear and prompt you to choose a location to save your document. Choose the location you want to save a document to in the Save In popup field.
3. In the field File Name, type the name you would like to save the file as.
4. In the Save As Type popup menu, select the OpenDocument Presentation (.odp) file format.
5. Click the button SAVE to complete the operation.

Saving a File as a Microsoft PowerPoint Document

To save a document in the Microsoft PowerPoint format, follow these steps:
1. Click on the File menu and choose Save As from the menu list.
2. A window will appear and prompt you to choose a location to save your document. Choose the location you want to save a document to in the Save In popup field.
3. In the field File Name, type the name you would like to save the file as.
4. In the Save As Type popup menu, select the appropriate Microsoft PowerPoint (*.ppt) file format.
5. Click the button SAVE to complete the operation.

Exporting a File as a Macromedia Flash Document

To save a document in the Macromedia Flash format, follow these steps:
1. Click on the File menu and choose Export from the menu list.
2. A window will appear and prompt you to choose a location to save your document. Choose the location you want to save a document to in the Save In popup field.
3. In the field File Name, type the name you would like to save the file as.
4. In the Save As Type popup menu, select the Macromedia Flash (*.swf) file format.
5. Click the button SAVE to complete the operation.

Exporting a File as a Portable Document Format (PDF) Document

One of the many useful features OpenOffice.org has built-in to the office suite is the ability to export documents as a Portable Document Format (PDF) file. To save a document as a read-only PDF file, follow these steps:
1. Click on the File menu and select Export As PDF from the menu list that appears.
2. A window will appear and prompt you to choose a location to save your document. Choose the location you want to save a document to in the Save In popup field.
3. In the field File Name, type the name you would like to save the file as.
4. In the File Format popup menu, make sure Portable Document Format (PDF) is selected.
5. Click the button SAVE to complete the operation.

(NOTE: OpenOffice.org documents saved as a PDF file is a convenient way to share read-only documents to other users that have a PDF reader application installed on their computer. However, OpenOffice.org cannot edit a document that has been saved as a PDF file. To save a document for editing at a later date, save the document in its Native OpenDocument file format.)

Exporting a File as a Web Page (HTML) Document

To save a document in the Hypertext Markup Language (HTML) format, follow these steps:
1. Click on the File menu and select Export from the menu list that appears.
2. A window will appear and prompt you to choose a location to save your document. Choose the location you want to save a document to in the

Save In popup field.
3. In the field File Name, type the name you would like to save the file as.
4. In the Save As Type popup menu, select the HTML (*.htm or *.html) file format.
5. Click the button SAVE to complete the operation.

Printing a Slide Presentation to Fit a Specific Page Size

To print an Impress slides to fit a specific page size, follow these steps:
1. If it isn't already, open the Impress presentation that is to be printed.
2. Click on the Format menu, select Page from the menu that appears and then select Page from the submenu that appears.
3. In the Layout Settings selection area, click the Fit Object To Paper Format checkbox.
4. In the Paper Format selection area, select one of the format options provided.
5. Click the OK button to complete the operation. Each slide selected is scaled to fit the printed page.

Printing a Slide Presentation for Handouts

To print Impress slides for use as handouts, follow these steps:
1. If it isn't already, open the Impress presentation that is to be printed.
2. Click on the View menu and select Handout Page from the menu list that appears.
3. Click on the Print button located within the Standard menu bar at the top of the Impress application window. You may also hold down the Control (CTRL) key and press P on the keyboard to prompt for the Print window, or click on the File menu and select Print from the menu that appears.

Section Five: Correcting Presentation Document Errors

Using Cut, Copy and Paste

Using Cut, Copy and Paste is one of the most fundamental operations you will perform to correct document errors. You may also use these commands to transfer text or graphics from one document into another. If you are unfamiliar with using these operations, use these steps to assist in determining which to use when correcting document errors:

1. Highlight the text you want to cut or copy.
2. To eliminate text to reinsert in another location in the document, click the Edit menu and choose the Cut menu option.
3. To duplicate text in another part of the document, click the Edit menu and choose the Copy menu option.
4. Place the cursor at the location you want the text to appear.
5. In the Edit menu, choose the Paste menu option.

Deleting Text

To permanently delete text from your presentation, follow these steps:

1. Highlight the text you want to permanently delete.
2. Press the Delete key on your keyboard to permanently remove the text from your document.

Using Undo

If you make the mistake of deleting something you didn't wish to do or make a formatting error, immediately go to the Edit menu and choose Undo from the menu list that appears to go back to the document's previous state before the error was made. You can continue to select the Undo menu command multiple times to continue to go back to each previous step.

Using Spellcheck

To use the OpenOffice.org spell check feature, follow these steps:

1. If you wish to spell check a specific word or sentence, select the text you wish to spell check. Otherwise, proceed to Step #2.
2. Go to the Tools menu and select Spellcheck from the menu that appears. You may also press the F7 key on your keyboard to begin checking for spelling errors.
3. If any potential spelling errors appear, OpenOffice.org will indicate the potential error and give you a list of possible suggestions to correct the spelling.
4. If you see a spelling suggestion that would correct the error, select it from the Suggestions list and click the CHANGE button.
5. If you believe that the word in question is spelled correctly, you can click

the IGNORE ONCE button to proceed to the next potential spelling error. If the word in question is spelled correctly and you use it often when creating documents, you may click the ADD button to add it to the Spellcheck dictionary.

6. When you have completed checking for potential spelling errors, click the CLOSE button to exit and return to the document.

Using AutoCorrect

AutoCorrect is enabled by default. However, AutoCorrect can be enabled or disabled at any time. To enable or disable a specific AutoCorrect feature, go to the Tools menu and select AutoCorrect from the menu that appears. Once the AutoCorrect window appears, click on the tab related to the specific feature you wish to enable or disable and select the appropriate options.

Using AutoFormat

Like AutoCorrect, the AutoFormat features are enabled by default. However, AutoFormat may also be enabled or disabled at any time. To enable or disable the AutoFormat feature, click on the Format menu, select AutoFormat from the menu that appears, and select While Typing from the submenu that appears. A checkmark will appear next to the submenu option when the feature is enabled.

Section Six: Viewing Impress Slide Presentations

Viewing Slide Show

To view a slide show within the Impress application, click on the Slide Show menu and select Slide Show from the menu options that appear or simply press the F5 key on the keyboard. To exit a slideshow, press the ESC key on the keyboard to return to the Impress editing window.

Configuring Slide Show Settings

To configure the Impress settings for viewing slide shows, follow these steps:
1. Click on the Slide Show menu and select Slide Show Settings from the menu options that appear.

2. When the Slide Show Settings window appears, select the appropriate configuration options.
3. When you have completed selecting the appropriate configuration options, click the OK button to complete the operation.

Adding Slide Transitions

To select slide transitions for an Impress presentation, follow these steps:
1. Click on the Slide Show menu and select Slide Transition from the menu options that appear.
2. The Slide Transition configuration options will appear in the Task Pane located within the Impress editing window. Configure the slide transitions by selecting from the appropriate options presented.
3. To apply the configuration to all slides within the presentation, click the APPLY TO ALL SLIDES button within the Task Pane. Otherwise, the slide transition configurations selected will apply only to the current slide being edited.

APPENDIX

D

Quick Guide to Creating and Editing

Base Databases

Appendix D
Quick Guide to Creating and Editing Base Databases

Section One: Overview of Base

Starting Base

To launch the Base application within the Microsoft Windows operating system, follow these steps:
1. Beginning at the desktop, click on the Start button located in the lower-left corner of the screen, and select Programs or All Program from the menu list that appears.
2. Select the OpenOffice.org 3.0 application folder that appears, and select Base from the applications options that appear.
3. Each time Base is launched either from the Start Menu or from the New menu within OpenOffice.org, a Database Wizard will appear. Select the appropriate Database Type by clicking on the radio buttons provided. Follow the on-screen instruction that the wizard provides in creating a new database or connecting to an existing network database.

To launch the Base application within a Linux-based operating system, follow these steps:
1. Beginning at the desktop, click on the Start button located in the lower-left corner of the screen, and select Office Productivity from the menu list that appears.
2. Select the OpenOffice.org 3.0 Base application icon from the list that appears, and the application will launch.
3. Each time Base is launched either from the Start Menu or from the File menu within OpenOffice.org, a Database Wizard will appear. Select the appropriate Database Type by clicking on the radio buttons provided. Follow the on-screen instruction that the wizard provides in creating a new database or connecting to an existing network database.

Displaying Toolbars

Base contains many toolbars to assist in formatting and editing your database. Sometimes you may need to view certain toolbars to assist you with creating your database, while other toolbars may need to hidden from view to prevent from getting in your way and free up screen space for other tools. To view or hide a toolbar within Base, follow these steps:

1. Click the View menu and select Toolbars from the menu list. A list of available toolbars will appear.
2. Select a toolbar to appear within Base by simply clicking on the appropriate toolbar within the list. If a toolbar within the list has a checkmark beside it, this means that the toolbar is already visible within the Impress application.
3. If you wish to hide a toolbar from view within Base, simply click on it from the list. Toolbars listed that do not have a checkmark beside them indicates that the toolbar is hidden from view within Base.

Status Bar

If the Impress status bar, located at the bottom of the Impress application window, is not visible when you open an Impress document, you may make it so by going to the View menu and select Status Bar from the menu that appears. A checkmark should appear next to the menu option when the status bar is visible. If you wish to hide the status bar from view within Impress, simply click on it from the list. When the menu option does not have a checkmark beside it, this indicates that the status bar is hidden from view within Impress.

Adjusting Page View

To adjust the view of the document you are working in, click on the View menu and select Zoom from the menu list. You may also select to Zoom by clicking on the magnifying glass icon within the Standard toolbar located just beneath the main application menu.

Using the Navigator

The Navigator allows a user to quickly view objects that are within a document. The Navigator displays "categories", or the various contents within the Navigator window. Within each category contains the objects that are present in the document.

To view and utilize the Navigator while creating and editing Impress documents, follow these steps:

1. To open the Navigator window, click on the Edit menu and select Navigator from the menu list. You may also view the Navigator window by pressing

the F5 key at the top of your keyboard.
2. If you see a "+" icon located next to a category within the Navigator, that indicates that there is at least one object within the document related to that particular category. Click the "+" sign to expand the list to view the objects related to the category. To quickly jump to the location in your document where the object is placed, double-click on the object listed in the Navigator window.

Viewing and Editing the Styles and Formatting Organizer

The Styles and Formatting Organizer allows you to quickly select pre-defined formatting options to include in your documents simply by double-clicking on a style option listed within the Organizer. To view and edit the Openoffice.org Formatting Styles Organizer, follow these steps:
1. To view the organizer, click the Format menu and select Styles and Formatting or simply press the F11 key at the top of your keyboard. A palette will appear displaying by default the various paragraph styles available.
2. When the Organizer palette is open, you will notice a small toolbar within the window. You can view other formatting styles as well by clicking on the appropriate button. From left-to-right, the style options you may view include Graphics and Presentation styles. In the popup menu located at the bottom of the Styles Organizer window, be sure the menu has the option All Styles selected to view all of your available options for each style.
3. You can also create or modify formatting styles based upon existing styles by right-clicking on a style listed within the Organizer and select the appropriate command from the contextual menu that appears. You may also delete custom styles you created from the Organizer by right-clicking on it within the list.

Registering a Database File

Before database records can be utilized with other applications within the OpenOffice.org office suite, the database document must be registered. If a database file is not registered within OpenOffice.org, then other applications within the suite will not be able to identify the correct database to extract the records from.

If a database is created using the Database Wizard, then the wizard can automatically register the database upon request during the creation process. However, Base databases can also be registered manually quickly and easily. To manually register a Base database file within OpenOffice.org, follow these steps:

1. With the database file already open, click on the Tools menu and select Options from the menu options that appear.
2. When the OpenOffice.org User Data window appears, click on the plus "+" icon located next to the OpenOffice.org Base option located on the left side. When doing so, a list of options will appear related to the Base application.
3. Select Databases from the OpenOffice.org Base options that appear by clicking on the label. When doing so, the list of databases that are already registered within OpenOffice.org will appear in the Registered Databases selection area on the right side of the window. To register the database document, click the NEW button, then click the BROWSE button in the Create Database Link dialogue window and locate the database file. After locating the file, select it and press the OPEN button. The Create Database Link dialogue window will reappear, where the OK button can be pressed to register the database.
4. To complete the registration, click the OK button within the OpenOffice.org User Data window.

Section Two: Working With Tables

Creating a New Database

To create a new Base database, follow these steps:

1. Start the Base application from the Start Menu. Or within OpenOffice.org, go to the File menu, select New from the menu options that appear and select Database from the submenu that appears.
2. When the Database Wizard window appears, select the Create A New Database radio button and click the NEXT button located at the bottom of the window.
3. In the next window, select to have the database registered by clicking on the Yes radio button. Within the same window, click both checkboxes available to have the software open the database for editing and have the table wizard assist with creating the necessary tables for the new database. Then click the FINISH button located at the bottom of the window.
4. When the Save As window appears, select the location where the database should be saved. Moreover, select the file type and file name for the

database. Then click the SAVE button.

5. After the application has saved the database, the Table Wizard window will appear. In the Category selection area, select whether the database will be used for business or personal purposes by clicking on one of the radio buttons provided. Depending on the category selected, the Sample Table popup menu will provide a list of possible databases to create. Select the type of database to be created from the Sample Table popup menu.

6. When a sample table has been selected, a list of available fields associated with the type of table will appear in lower half of the window. In the Available Fields selection area, click on a field to add to the table and click the RIGHT ARROW button. The field will then appear in the Selected Fields selection area. Repeat the process for each field to be added to the table. When all appropriate fields have been selected to appear in the table, use the UP and DOWN arrow buttons to change the order in which the fields will appear within the table. Then click the NEXT button located at the bottom of the window.

7. In the next window to appear in the Table Wizard, click on a field within the Selected Fields selection area. In the Field Information selection area, various formatting selections can be assigned to each field. Make the appropriate format options for the selected field. The repeat the process for each field available in the Selected Fields selection area. Then click the NEXT button.

8. In the next window to appear, select the checkbox available to have Base create a primary key for the table and select the Automatically Add A Primary Key radio button. Then click the NEXT button.

9. In the next window, type a name to identify the table being created using the text field provided. Moreover, select the Insert Data Immediately radio button. Then click the FINISH button to create the table for the database.

Creating a Table Using the Table Wizard

To create a new table within a database file, follow these steps:
1. In the Database pane located on the left side of the window, click on the Tables icon.
2. In the Tasks pane located at the top of the window, double-click Use Wizard To Create Table to launch the Table Wizard.
3. In the Category selection area, select whether the database will be used for business or personal purposes by clicking on one of the radio buttons provided. Depending on the category selected, the Sample Table popup menu will provide a list of possible databases to create. Select the type of

database to be created from the Sample Table popup menu.

4. When a sample table has been selected, a list of available fields associated with the type of table will appear in lower half of the window. In the Available Fields selection area, click on a field to add to the table and click the RIGHT ARROW button. The field will then appear in the Selected Fields selection area. Repeat the process for each field to be added to the table. When all appropriate fields have been selected to appear in the table, use the UP and DOWN arrow buttons to change the order in which the fields will appear within the table. Then click the NEXT button located at the bottom of the window.

5. In the next window to appear in the Table Wizard, click on a field within the Selected Fields selection area. In the Field Information selection area, various formatting selections can be assigned to each field. Make the appropriate format options for the selected field. The repeat the process for each field available in the Selected Fields selection area. Then click the NEXT button.

6. In the next window to appear, select the checkbox available to have Base create a primary key for the table and select the Automatically Add A Primary Key radio button. Then click the NEXT button.

7. In the next window, type a name to identify the table being created using the text field provided. Moreover, select the Insert Data Immediately radio button. Then click the FINISH button to create the table for the database.

Creating a Table Using the Table Design View

To create a new table within a database file using the Design View, follow these steps:

1. In the Database pane located on the left side of the window, click on the Tables icon.

2. In the Tasks pane located at the top of the window, single-click Create Table in Design View to launch the Design View window.

3. When the Table Design View window appears, click within the first available field underneath the Field Name column. Type a field name that best describes the information that will be entered into the field. When creating field names, be sure they do not contain any spaces. For example, a field name labeled Date Acquired should be typed as DateAquired. When completing the Field Name, press the Tab key on the keyboard to proceed to format the Field Type.

4. When tabbing to the Field Type column, a popup menu will appear to enable selection of the type of data the new field will contain. Select the

appropriate field type, and make any additional configurations needed associated with the field within the Field Properties selection area located at the bottom of the Table Design window. Then press the Tab key on the keyboard to proceed to the Description column.

5. In the Description column, type a description for the new field being created (optional).

6. Repeat steps 3 through 5 for each new field to be created. When completing the new field entries, click on the Window menu at the top of the Table Design window and select Close Window from the menu options that appear or simply press CTRL+W on the keyboard to return to the main Base application window. When closing the window, a prompt window may appear asking whether to save the changes being made to the table. Click the YES button to do so and the window will close.

Adding a New Field to a Table

To add a new field to an existing table, follow these steps:

1. In the Database pane located on the left side of the window, click on the Tables icon.

2. In the Tables pane located at the bottom-right of the window, select the Table to be edited by single-clicking on the icon.

3. Click on the Edit menu at the top of the application window and select Edit from the menu options that appear.

4. When the Table Design window appears, click within the first available field underneath the Field Name column. Type a field name that best describes the information that will be entered into the field. When creating field names, be sure they do not contain any spaces. For example, a field name labeled Date Acquired should be typed as DateAquired. When completing the Field Name, press the Tab key on the keyboard to proceed to format the Field Type.

5. When tabbing to the Field Type column, a popup menu will appear to enable selection of the type of data the new field will contain. Select the appropriate field type, and make any additional configurations needed associated with the field within the Field Properties selection area located at the bottom of the Table Design window. Then press the Tab key on the keyboard to proceed to the Description column.

6. In the Description column, type a description for the new field being created (optional).

7. Repeat steps 4 through 6 for each new field to be created. When completing the new field entries, click on the Window menu at the top of

the Table Design window and select Close Window from the menu options that appear or simply press CTRL+W on the keyboard to return to the main Base application window.

Changing the Length of a Field

To change the length of a field to add or reduce the number of characters that can be entered, follow these steps:
1. In the Database pane located on the left side of the window, click on the Tables icon.
2. In the Tables pane located at the bottom-right of the window, select the Table to be edited by single-clicking on the icon.
3. Click on the Edit menu at the top of the application window and select Edit from the menu options that appear.
4. When the Table Design window appears, click within the gray area to the left of the Field Name that is to be formatted to select the entire row.
5. In the Field Properties selection area located at the bottom of the Table Design window, select the data currently in the Length text field and enter the value for the new field length. If the data within the Length text field is grey, this symbolizes that the data length is pre-defined by the Field Type selected and cannot be changed without selecting another Field Type.
6. To exit the Table Design window, click on the Window menu at the top of the window and select Close Window from the menu options that appear or simply press CTRL+W on the keyboard to return to the main Base application window.

Saving a Table

To save additional changes made to a table within the Table Design window, click on the File menu and select Save from the menu options that appear. A table can also be saved by pressing CTRL+S on the keyboard or by clicking on the Save button located within the Table Design toolbar.

Adding Records to a Table

To add records to an existing table, follow these steps:
1. In the Database pane located on the left side of the window, click on the Tables icon.
2. In the Tables pane located at the bottom-right of the window, open the Table that records will be added to by double-clicking on the icon.

3. When the Table window appears, press the Tab key to automatically create a Record ID and begin entering a new record. Each time a new record is created, another record line is created to allow another record to be entered following the current one.

4. To exit the Table window, click on the Window menu at the top of the window and select Close Window from the menu options that appear or simply press CTRL+W on the keyboard to return to the main Base application window.

Editing Records Within a Table

To edit records within an existing table, follow these steps:

1. In the Database pane located on the left side of the window, click on the Tables icon.

2. In the Tables pane located at the bottom-right of the window, open the Table that records will be added to by double-clicking on the icon.

3. When the Table window appears, select the record field that is to be edited. Once the record field has been selected, editing can be performed.

4. To exit the Table window, click on the Window menu at the top of the window and select Close Window from the menu options that appear or simply press CTRL+W on the keyboard to return to the main Base application window.

Sorting Records

To sort records within a table, follow these steps:

1. Within an open database file, click on the Tables icon located on the left side of the document window within the Database pane.

2. In the Tables pane located on the bottom-right of the window, open the desired table for record sorting by double-clicking on its icon.

3. Using the left mouse button, click on the appropriate field label for the records to be sorted. When doing so, the entire column for the field will be selected.

4. To sort the records for the selected field, click either the SORT ASCENDING or SORT DESCENDING buttons located within the Table Data View toolbar at the top of the window. For example, if a user wishes to sort the records within the field labeled "LastName" in alphabetical order from A to Z, they would choose to sort in ascending order. If a user wishes to sort from Z to A, they would choose to sort in descending order. When doing so, the records are sorted accordingly.

Specifying Field Properties

After a table has been created, a user can specify that certain fields containing data have specific properties attributed to them. Examples include a specific field must contain an entry (the field cannot be left blank), that a field contain a default value in the event of many entries containing the same value, that a field should contain no more than a certain number of characters, that the data appearing within the field possess a specific format and more.

To specify field properties within a Base table, follow these steps:
1. In the Database pane located on the left side of the window, click on the Tables icon.
2. In the Tables pane located at the bottom-right of the window, select the Table to be edited by single-clicking on the icon.
3. Click on the Edit menu at the top of the application window and select Edit from the menu options that appear. A user can also select the edit command by right-clicking on the table icon and select Edit from the contextual menu that appears.
4. When the Table Design window appears, click within the gray area to the left of the Field Name that is to be formatted to select the entire row.
5. In the Field Properties selection area located at the bottom of the Table Design window, specify the appropriate field properties utilizing the options provided.
6. To exit the Table Design window, click on the Window menu at the top of the window and select Close Window from the menu options that appear or simply press CTRL+W on the keyboard to return to the main Base application window. When closing the window, a prompt window may appear asking whether to save the changes being made to the table. Click the YES button to do so and the window will close.

Deleting Records

To delete a record within a table, follow these steps:
1. In the Database pane located on the left side of the window, click on the Tables icon.
2. In the Tables pane located at the bottom-right of the window, open the Table that records will be added to by double-clicking on the icon.
3. When the Table window appears, right-click within the gray area to the left of the record and select Delete Rows from the contextual menu that

appears. The record will then be deleted from the table.

4. To exit the Table window, click on the Window menu at the top of the window and select Close Window from the menu options that appear or simply press CTRL+W on the keyboard to return to the main Base application window.

Section Three: Working With Queries

Creating a Query Using The Query Wizard

To create a new query within a database file, follow these steps:

1. In the Database pane located on the left side of the window, click on the Queries icon.
2. In the Tasks pane located at the top of the window, double-click Use Wizard To Create Query to launch the Query Wizard.
3. When the Query Wizard window appears, the first step will be to select the fields from an existing table to include in the query. In the Tables popup menu, select a table and then select the appropriate fields. Then click the NEXT button.
4. In the second step of the Query Wizard, select which fields the query is to sort using the Sorting Order selection areas provided. Then click the NEXT button.
5. In the third step of the Query Wizard, select the search conditions for the query using the Search Conditions selection area provided. Then click the NEXT button.
6. In the fourth step of the Query Wizard, a summary will be presented based upon the search conditions selected in the previous step (optional). If the summary does not reflect the search conditions that are desired, click the BACK button to return to the Search Conditions selection screen. Otherwise, click the NEXT button to proceed to Step #5 of the Query Wizard.
7. In the fifth step of the Query Wizard, specify the groupings for the query using the Grouping selection area provided (optional). Then click the NEXT button.
8. In the sixth step of the Query Wizard, select the grouping conditions for the query using the Grouping Conditions selection area provided (optional). Then click the NEXT button.
9. In the seventh step of the Query Wizard, assign an alias to the fields selected for the query using the alias textbox provided (optional). Then click the NEXT button.

10. In the eighth and final step of the Query Wizard, an overview of the query specifications is given. A name can be given for the query by utilizing the Query Name textbox provided. Moreover, select how to proceed with the creation of the query by selecting the radio buttons provided. To complete the creation of the query, click the FINISH button.

Creating a Query Using the Query Design View

To create a new query within a database file using the Design View, follow these steps:

1. In the Database pane located on the left side of the window, click on the Queries icon.
2. In the Tasks pane located at the top of the window, single-click Create Query in Design View to launch the Design View window.
3. When the Query Design View window appears, the Add Table or Query window will also appear. Using the radio buttons available within the window, tables or queries that have been created within the database file are listed for availability to perform a query. To select a table or query, single-click among those listed and click the ADD button. If a query may be performed among multiple tables or queries, repeat the selection procedure. Once all desired tables or queries have been selected, click the CLOSE button within the Add Table or Query window. The Query Design View window will be available, and the tables or queries previously selected will be available within the upper pane.
4. In the fourth step of the creating a query, select which fields to utilize to run the query by using the first Field popup menu provided within the lower pane of the window. A popup menu can be made available within any field in the lower pane by simply by using the mouse pointer to click within the desired field.
5. In the fifth step of creating a query, select the table that is associated with the field from Step #4 by using the Table popup menu provided within the same column.
6. In the sixth step, select the sort criteria for the query using the Sort popup menu provided within the same column (optional).
7. If statistical calculations are desired for the query, the seventh step of creating a query is to select the function for the calculation desired by using the Function popup menu provided within the same column (optional). Functions supported within Base include Average, Count, Maximum, Minimum, Sum and Group. Depending upon the function selected, criterion may also need to be selected by entering the appropriate values within

the Criterion field provided within the same column. For example, if the desired value to query from the records are all of those within the table fields selected with a value of 5 or greater, then select **Minimum** from the Function popup menu and enter **5** within the Criterion filed provided.

8. If multiple fields are desired for selection to perform a query, repeat steps #4 through #7 above using the additional columns provided within the lower pane of the Design View window. If the additional fields should appear when the query is created, select the appropriate fields by using the computer's mouse and clicking within the appropriate Visible checkboxes.

9. To complete the creation of the query, run the query by clicking on the Edit menu and selecting Run Query from the menu options that appear. Queries can also be ran by clicking on the Run Query button located within the Query Design toolbar at the top of the application window. If the toolbar is not visible, it can be made to appear by clicking on the View menu, select Toolbars from the menu options and selecting Query Design from the submenu options that appear.

10. To save the query performed, click the File menu and select Save As from the menu options that appear. When doing so, a window will appear prompting a Query Name to be entered. Enter an appropriate query name and click the OK button. When returning to the main database file window, click on the Queries icon located on the left side of the window within the Database pane. When doing so, the query that was saved should appear within the Queries pane in the lower portion of the window.

Using the Query Design View Window

An alternative to using the Query Wizard to create a query is to utilize the Query Design View window. While both methods of creating a query can provide the same results, the use of the Query design view can provide more flexibility during the query creation process. To use the Query Design View window to create a query, see the instructions for "Creating a Query Using the Query Design View" available in this appendix.

Selecting Fields for a Query

In order to create a query using the Query Design View, one must first select one or more tables so that fields are available for querying. When creating a new query using the Query Design View, the application will automatically ask for tables or queries to be selected for use in creating a new query. However, before a query has been saved or cleared, fields within other tables can be selected to perform a new query.

To select fields for creating a query using the query design view, follow these steps:
1. Within the Query Design View window, click the Insert menu and select Add Table or Query from the menu options that appear.
2. When the Add Table or Query window appears, click the radio buttons available within the window to view a list of tables or queries that have been created within the database file that are available for performing a query.
3. To select a table or query, single-click among those listed and click the ADD button. If a query may be performed among multiple tables or queries, repeat the selection procedure.
4. Once all desired tables or queries have been selected, click the CLOSE button within the Add Table or Query window. The Query Design View window will be available, and the tables or queries previously selected will be available within the upper pane.

Running a Query

Once criteria have been selected to perform a query, the RUN command must be executed to produce its results. To run a new query within a database file, follow these steps:
1. Using the Query Design View, enter the desired criteria for the query. This includes selecting desired fields, sort criteria, functions and more.
2. Once the desired criteria for a query has been selected, run the query by clicking on the Edit menu and selecting Run Query from the menu options that appear. Queries can also be ran by clicking on the Run Query button located within the Query Design toolbar at the top of the application window. If the toolbar is not visible, it can be made to appear by clicking on the View menu, select Toolbars from the menu options and selecting Query Design from the submenu options that appear.

Saving a Query

Once a query has been ran, a query can be saved so that the results can be

accessed later. To save a new query within a database file, follow these steps:
1. To save the query performed, click the File menu and select Save As from the menu options that appear.
2. When selecting the Save As menu option, a window will appear prompting a Query Name to be entered. Enter an appropriate query name and click the OK button. The query has now been saved.
3. When returning to the main database file window, click on the Queries icon located on the left side of the window within the Database pane. When doing so, the query that was saved should appear within the Queries pane in the lower portion of the window. The query can be viewed by double-clicking its icon within the window.

Printing the Results of a Query

At the time of the printing of this book, queries cannot be printed using Base. If a situation arises where records from a database needs to be available in print form, consider creating a report. While reports cannot perform statistical calculations or detailed criteria selected for querying, data selected for the creation of a report can be sorted and grouped. For more information regarding the creation of a report within Base, see the instructions for "Creating a Report Using the Report Wizard" available in this appendix.

Closing a Query

To close a query that has been created, follow these steps:
1. Within the query window, click the File menu and select Close from the menu options that appear.
2. If the query has not been saved, the Base application may display a prompt window asking whether to save the changes made to the query. If the query is to be saved so that its results can be viewed later, click the YES button to proceed in naming the query and saving it before it is closed. If the query should not be saved, click the NO button and the query is closed.

Clearing the Query Design

If a user wishes to make corrections or changes to criteria selected prior to or after running a query, they can clear the Query Design View window as opposed to closing it and restarting. To clear the Query Design View window, click the

Edit menu and select Clear Query from the menu options that appear. The Query Design View window can also be cleared by clicking on the Clear Query button located within the Query Design toolbar at the top of the application window. If the toolbar is not visible, it can be made to appear by clicking on the View menu, select Toolbars from the menu options and selecting Query Design from the submenu options that appear.

Deleting a Query

Once a query has been created and saved, it can be deleted from the list of queries appearing in the main database file window. To delete a saved query from a database file, follow these steps:

1. Within the main database file window (the window that appears when first opening the file), click on the Queries icon located on the left side of the window within the Database pane. When doing so, the query that was saved should appear within the Queries pane in the lower portion of the window.
2. Select the query that is to be deleted by single-clicking it within the Queries pane.
3. To delete the selected query, click the Edit menu and select Delete from the menu options that appear. Deleting a query can also be accomplished by right-clicking on the query and selecting Delete from the contextual menu that appears.

Including All Fields in a Query

When creating a query where all fields need to be included, a user could individually select each field using the multiple Field popup menus provided within the lower pane of the Query Design View window. However, a user could choose to include all fields within a query by simply selecting the field name containing the asterisk from the first available Field popup menu.

To include all fields in a query, follow these steps:

1. Begin the process of creating a new query by selecting fields for the query. (See the instructions "Selecting Fields for a Query" within this appendix for details regarding this process, if needed.)
2. Once a list of fields are available for querying, use the first Field popup menu provided within the lower pane of the window to select the field name

that contains an asterisk (*) in its name. This selection is usually the first to appear in within the popup menu. A popup menu can be made available within any field in the lower pane by simply by using the mouse pointer to click within the desired field.

3. Complete the query by selecting the desired criteria. When completed, run the query. All the fields available for selection should be included in the query results.

Entering Criteria

When a user creates a query, they are usually doing so to view records that fulfill certain criteria. Criteria can be included in a query by entering text or numerical values within the Criterion field located under the field name to which it applies. When entering numerical values, be sure to type the numbers without any additional characters included. For example, if the criterion to query includes **$2,000**, then the numerical value should be typed as **2000** within the Criterion field.

Using Comparison Operators Within Queries

A number of comparison operators are supported within the Base database application. Supported comparison operators include > (greater than), < (less than), >= (greater than or equal to), <= (less than or equal to) and NOT (not equal to).

To utilize these comparison operators within a query, simply type the appropriate comparison operator within a Criterion field in addition to the desired text or numerical value for the criterion. For example, if the desired criterion for a field is to be all records that is greater than three, type **>3** within the appropriate Criterion field.

Using Compound Criteria Within Queries

Base, as with many database applications, support the use of compound criteria within queries. Compound criterion typically involves two types: AND criterion and OR criterion. With AND criterion, each criterion selected for their respected fields must be true for the results to appear within the completed compound criteria query. With OR criterion, any true result for each individual criterion will appear within the completed compound criteria query.

To enter compound criteria within queries using AND criterion, follow these steps:
1. Begin the process of creating a new query by selecting at least two fields for the query. (See the instructions "Selecting Fields for a Query" within this appendix for details regarding this process, if needed.)
2. For each field selected for a query, enter the desired criterion within the appropriate Criterion field. Each criterion may include text, numerical values or comparison operators.
3. When completing the selection of desired criteria, run the query. The query should only include results that are true for each criterion selected.

To enter compound criteria within queries using OR criterion, follow these steps:
1. Begin the process of creating a new query by selecting at least two fields for the query. (See the instructions "Selecting Fields for a Query" within this appendix for details regarding this process, if needed.)
2. For the first field selected for a query, enter the desired criterion within the appropriate Criterion field. The criterion may include text, numerical values or comparison operators.
3. For any of the additional fields selected for a query, enter the desired criterion within the OR field located under the same column as its associated field.
4. When completing the selection of desired criteria, run the query. The query should include all results that are true for any of the criterion selected.

Using Wildcards for Queries

When entering a criterion for a query, regular expressions can be used. However, Base also supports the use of wildcards when entering criteria as well. Wildcards are characters that are used in substitute of regular characters to either broaden or narrow query results. Two wildcard expressions are supported within Base: "?" and "*".

The "?" wildcard is used to substitute for exactly one arbitrary character. For example, typing "Ho?se" would return House and Horse. The "*" wildcard is used to substitute zero or more characters. For example, typing "B*t" will return all record entries starting with a "B" and ending in a "t", such as Bat or Boot.

Selecting Criteria for a Field to Not Appear in the Query Result

Occasionally, a query may need to be created where the criteria selected for a particular field should not appear in the results. If selected criteria should not appear in the results when a query is ran, a user may specify this output by utilizing the Visible checkboxes within the lower pane of the Query Design View window. To make a criterion visible or invisible within the results of a query, use the mouse pointer to click within the appropriate checkbox. If a checkbox is empty, this indicates that the criterion for the selected field will not appear in the results when a query is run.

Sorting Data in a Query

When creating queries, one of the options a user has is to select whether to sort the results of a query in ascending or descending order. For example, if a user wishes to sort the query results of last names in alphabetical order from A to Z, they would choose to sort in ascending order. If a user wishes to sort a query from Z to A, they would choose to sort in descending order.

To select the sort criteria for a query, use the Sort popup menu provided within the lower pane of the Query Design View window. More than one field can be selected for sorting, depending upon the query results the user wishes to create. If multiple fields are selected for sorting, fields located nearest to the left side of the window are sorted first. Therefore, users should select the fields of most importance for querying beginning on the left side of the Query Design View window.

Omitting Duplicates Using the Distinct Values Command

Depending upon the number of fields and the criteria selected when creating a query, duplicate entries may appear within the query results. If duplicate results occur and the user wishes to omit all duplicates from the query results, the user may do so by executing the Distinct Values command.

To execute the Distinct Values command within Base, follow these steps:

1. Begin the process of creating a new query, if have not already done so.

(See the instructions "Selecting Fields for a Query" within this appendix for details regarding this process, if needed.)

2. Click the Edit menu and select Distinct Values from the menu options that appear. Users can also execute the Distinct Values command by right-clicking within the row label area of the Query Design View window (the gray area on the left side of the lower window pane that contains the name of each query selection option) and select Distinct Values from the contextual menu that appears.

3. Once the desired criteria for a query has been selected and the Distinct Values command has been executed, run the query by clicking on the Edit menu and selecting Run Query from the menu options that appear. Queries can also be ran by clicking on the Run Query button located within the Query Design toolbar at the top of the application window. If the toolbar is not visible, it can be made to appear by clicking on the View menu, select Toolbars from the menu options and selecting Query Design from the submenu options that appear.

Section Four: Working With Reports and Forms

Creating a Report Using the Report Wizard

To create a new report using the Report Wizard, follow these steps:

1. In the Database pane located on the left side of the window, click on the Reports icon.

2. In the Tasks pane located at the top of the window, single-click Use Wizard To Create Report to launch the Report Wizard.

3. When the Report Wizard window appears, the first step will be to select the fields from an existing table to include in the report. In the Tables or Queries popup menu, select the table or query data will be selected from and then select the appropriate fields. Then click the NEXT button.

4. In the next step of the Report Wizard, customize the field labels by entering the labels into the text fields provided (optional). Then click the NEXT button.

5. In the third step of the Report Wizard, customize the group levels using the selection area provided (optional). Records are grouped based upon the values in the selected fields. Up to four fields can be grouped in a report. Once fields have been selected for grouping, click the NEXT button.

6. In the fourth step of the Report Wizard, customize the sort order of the fields using the selection area provided. Then click the NEXT button.

7. In the fifth step of the Report Wizard, select the layout in which the report

data will be presented (optional). Make sure Default is selected for the header and footer layout, as well as the data layout, if the report should not possess a custom layout. Make the appropriate layout selection and click the NEXT button.

8. In the final step of the Report Wizard, select a title to save a report as by entering a title into the text field provided. Also, select to create a static report or a dynamic report by clicking the appropriate radio button provided. A static report is where the data in the report will not change, and a dynamic report is where the data in the report may change periodically based upon the data entered into the corresponding table. Then click the FINISH button to complete the process of creating a report.

Printing a Report

To print a report that has already been created, follow these steps:
1. Within the report window, click on the File menu and select Print from the menu options that appear. Or press CTRL+P on the keyboard to prompt the Print window to appear.
2. To print one copy of the entire report, simply press the OK button and the report will begin to print. Otherwise, use the Page Range and Copies selection area to customize the print configuration before clicking the OK button.

Creating a Form Using The Form Wizard

To create a form using the Form Wizard, follow these steps:
1. In the Database pane located on the left side of the window, click on the Forms icon.
2. In the Tasks pane located at the top of the window, single-click Use Wizard To Create Form to launch the Form Wizard.
3. When the Form Wizard window appears, the first step will be to select the fields from an existing table to include in the form. In the Tables or Queries popup menu, select the table or query data will be selected from and then select the appropriate fields. Then click the NEXT button.
4. In the next step of the Form Wizard, select whether to add a subform or to continue with the primary form creation. Then click the NEXT button.
5. If the creation of a subform was not selected in the step above, skip to Step #7 below. If the creation of a subform was selected in the step above, the third step of the Form Wizard is to select the fields from another existing table to include in the form. In the Tables or Queries popup menu, select

the table or query data will be selected from and then select the appropriate fields. Then click the NEXT button.

6. In the fourth step of the Form Wizard, select the appropriate fields to join between the subform field and the main subform field using the popup menus presented. Then click the NEXT button.

7. In the fifth step of the Form Wizard, customize the arrangement of the forms using the Label Placement and Arrangement selection areas provided (optional). Then click the NEXT button.

8. In the sixth step of the Form Wizard, select the data entry mode using the selection area provided. Then click the NEXT button.

9. In the seventh step of the Form Wizard, select the appropriate styles to be applied to the form utilizing the selection areas provided. Then click the NEXT button.

10. In the final step of the Form Wizard, select a name to save the form as by entering a form name into the text field provided. Then, using the radio buttons provided, select how to proceed after the form has been created. Click the FINISH button to complete the process of creating a form.

Printing a Form

To print a form that has already been created, follow these steps:

1. Within the form window, click on the File menu and select Print from the menu options that appear. Or press CTRL+P on the keyboard to prompt the Print window to appear.

2. To print one copy of the entire form, simply press the OK button and the report will begin to print. Otherwise, use the Page Range and Copies selection area to customize the print configuration before clicking the OK button.

Section Five: Saving a Database File

Saving a File as a Native Base Database Document

Currently, the only file type supported for saving a Base database file is the native OpenDocument format. To save a document in the native Base 3.0 OpenDocument format, follow these steps:

1. Click on the File menu and choose Save As from the menu list.

2. A window will appear and prompt you to choose a location to save your document. Choose the location you want to save a document to in the

Save In popup field.
3. In the field File Name, type the name you would like to save the file as.
4. In the Save As Type popup menu, select the OpenDocument Database (.odb) file format.
5. Click the button SAVE to complete the operation.

Section Six: Correcting Database Document Errors

Using Cut, Copy and Paste

Using Cut, Copy and Paste is one of the most fundamental operations you will perform to correct document errors. You may also use these commands to transfer text or graphics from one document into another. If you are unfamiliar with using these operations, use these steps to assist in determining which to use when correcting document errors:
1. Highlight the text you want to cut or copy.
2. To eliminate text to reinsert in another location in the document, click the Edit menu and choose the Cut menu option.
3. To duplicate text in another part of the document, click the Edit menu and choose the Copy menu option.
4. Place the cursor at the location you want the text to appear.
5. In the Edit menu, choose the Paste menu option.

Deleting Text

To permanently delete text from your database, follow these steps:
1. Highlight the text you want to permanently delete.
2. Press the Delete key on your keyboard to permanently remove the text from your document.

Using Undo

If you make the mistake of deleting something you didn't wish to do or make a formatting error, immediately go to the Edit menu and choose Undo from the menu list that appears to go back to the document's previous state before the error was made. You can continue to select the Undo menu command multiple times to continue to go back to each previous step.

Section Seven: Importing Into and Exporting From Base

Unlike many database applications, Base (as of version 3.0) does not have Import or Export commands that allow you to easily exchange records between other database applications such as Access or FileMaker Pro. However, database records from other applications can be imported into and exported from Base using a workaround technique. In either situation, a spreadsheet file will be utilized to exchange data between Base and another database application.

Importing Records Into Base

To import records from another database application into Base, follow these steps:

1. Using the database application that currently contains the database tables and records to be imported into Base, use the application's Export command to export the records into a spreadsheet file. Fore example, if the records to be imported into Base are currently stored in a Microsoft Access file, use Access' Export command to export the records from a selected table as a Excel spreadsheet file.

2. Next, a new Base database file needs to be created. Start the Base application from the Start Menu. Or within OpenOffice.org, go to the File menu, select New from the menu options that appear and select Database from the submenu that appears.

3. When the Database Wizard window appears, select the Create A New Database radio button and click the NEXT button located at the bottom of the window.

4. In the next window, select to have the database registered by clicking on the Yes radio button. Within the same window, click the checkbox available to have the software open the database for editing. Then click the FINISH button located at the bottom of the window.

5. When the Save As window appears, select the location where the database should be saved. Moreover, select the file type and file name for the database. Then click the SAVE button.

6. Next, open the spreadsheet file created in Step #1 that contains the records to be imported into Base. When the spreadsheet file opens, select the cells that contain the data to be imported. The Select All command should not be used when performing this task.

7. With the spreadsheet cells selected that contain the records to be imported

into Base, click the Edit menu and select Copy from the menu options that appear.

8. Now switch over to the database document created at the end of Step #5. With the database file open, single-click on the Tables icon located on the left side of the window in the Database pane.

9. Within the Tables pane located in the lower portion of the database window file, click the right mouse button and select Paste from the contextual menu that appears. When doing so, the Copy Table window will appear.

10. Within the Copy Table window, type a name for the new table using the text field provided. Under the Options area of the window, leave the Definition and Data radio button selected. Also, click the checkbox provided to have Base create a primary key for the field name ID. Then click the CREATE button.

11. Open the new table created by double-clicking its icon with the left mouse button. When the table opens, the records selected from the spreadsheet file should appear.

Exporting Records From Base

To export records from Base for usage within another database application, follow these steps:

1. Make sure the database file in which records will be exported from is registered within OpenOffice.org. (See the instructions "Registering a Database File" within this appendix for details regarding this process, if needed.)

2. Create a new Calc spreadsheet document by clicking the File menu, select New from the menu options that appear and select Spreadsheet from the submenu options that appear.

3. When the new Calc spreadsheet document appears, click the View menu and select Data Sources from the menu options that appear. Data Sources can also be viewed by pressing the F4 key on the computer keyboard.

4. Just above the Calc worksheet area on the left is a window that will appear listing all registered databases. Next to the database in which records will be exported from, click the "+" icon next to it. Then click the "+" icon next to the Tables icon to view all tables contained within the database file selected. Select the table in which records will be exported from by single-clicking its icon with the left mouse button.

5. Once a database table has been selected, the records contained within that table will appear to the right of the registered database list. The records are now available for copying to the worksheet. The easiest way

to do so is by clicking on the empty record label box located to the upper-left corner of the record area. Then, holding the left mouse button down, drag the pointer down to cell A1 within the worksheet area. The pointer when placed above cell A1 will transform itself to include a "+" icon below the end of itself. This indicates that the data can now be placed within the worksheet. To do so, simply release the left mouse button and the records will now copy into the Calc worksheet.

6. With the records copied into the spreadsheet document, go to the File menu and select Save As from the menu options that appear.

7. A window will appear asking to choose a location to save the document. Choose the location to save a document to in the Save In popup field.

8. In the field File Name, type the name to save the file as.

9. In the Save As Type popup menu, select the file format to save the document in a format that is supported by the database application in which the records will be copied into. For example, if the records are to be imported into a Microsoft Access database file, select the Microsoft Excel (.xls) file format.

10. Click the button SAVE to complete in saving the spreadsheet file.

11. Once the records are saved within a spreadsheet file, most database applications support importing those records by selecting the file using the Import command. For example, the records saved within a file formatted as a Microsoft Excel (.xls) document can be imported into Microsoft Access by using its Import Wizard. Use the application's Help menu to view documentation regarding importing data from a spreadsheet file.

APPENDIX

E
Answers to Review Questions for Each Lesson

Appendix E
Answers to Review Questions for Each Lesson

Lesson One

1. Q: What is the maximum number of columns Calc supports in the newest version of OpenOffice.org?

   A: 1024

2. Q: What are the enhanced features available in the version of Notes within OpenOffice.org 3.0?

   A: The new version of Notes in OpenOffice.org 3.0 provides additional formatting, spell checking and accessibility features while displaying notes within the margins.

3. Q:What is the purpose of the Start Center in OpenOffice.org?

   A: The Start Center allows the selection of an application within the office productivity suite without having to click the File | New menu.

4. Q: (True or False) Detailed information regarding accessibility features available within OpenOffice.org can be found by selecting the Help menu and use the search term *accessibility*.

   A: True.

5. Q: (True or False) OpenOffice.org has the capability to automatically open Microsoft Office generated files.

   A: True.

Lesson Two

1. Q: Which key would you press on your keyboard to allow you to select text

within different areas of a document as the same time?

A: Control (Ctrl) key.

2. Q: Which primary menu item would you select within OpenOffice.org to change font styles and types, as well as to insert bulleted and numbered lists?

    A: Format menu.

3. Q: Approximately how many file formats does OpenOffice.org support for opening and saving word processing documents?

    A: OpenOffice.org supports over 20 file formats for opening and saving word processing documents.

4. Q: (True or False) Text can be formatted in bold type by either selecting the Format | Character menu option or by pressing the Bold format button located in the Formatting toolbar.

    A: True.

5. Q: (True or False) Documents exported in the Portable Document Format (PDF) file type can be edited later with OpenOffice.org.

    A: False.

Lesson Three

1. Q: Which primary menu item would you select within OpenOffice.org to make nonprinting characters visible when editing a document?

    A: View menu.

2. Q: What is the name of the separate text area at the top of each page that is often used to insert page number fields within a research paper?

    A: Header.

3. Q: What type of document formatting option allows you to embed explanatory notes within a research paper, where the notes are placed at the bottom of the page?

    A: Footnotes.

4. Q: (True or False) A page break is represented with a blue line running across the document editing area.

    A: True.

5. Q: (True or False) Paragraphs can be sorted into alphabetical order without having to use the cut-and-paste method.

    A: True.

Lesson Four

1. Q: Which page orientation would you normally select to create a brochure?

    A: Landscape.

2. Q: What is the name of the format feature that makes pages easier to read by preventing gray shadows from appearing between the lines of text?

    A: Register-True.

3. Q: What menu would you select to create columns within a Writer document?

    A: Format.

4. Q: (True or False) The PDF file format is one of the preferred formats among graphic artists and commercial printers.

    A: True.

5. Q: (True or False) You can utilize the arrow keys located in the center of the keyboard to move the cursor within a word processing document.

A: True.

Lesson Five

1. Q: By default, how many worksheets does a Calc spreadsheet document contain when you create a new document?

    A: Three (3).

2. Q: Columns are labeled _____ while rows are labeled _____ within the layout of a spreadsheet document.

    A: Columns are labeled alphabetically while rows are labeled numerically.

3. Q: What do the pound signs (###) within a cell indicate?

    A: This is an indication that the width of the cell isn't wide enough to display all of the characters of the value that is currently there.

4. Q: (True or False) Because spreadsheets can be very long in width, often you will need to customize the orientation and scaling print configuration options before sending the document to the printer.

    A: True.

5. Q: (True or False) The SUM function can be used to add, subtract, multiply and divide values within a selected cell range.

    A: False.

Lesson Six

1. Q: What menu would you select to add a new worksheet within a Calc spreadsheet document?

    A: Insert.

2. Q: When subtracting values among cells, does the SUM function need to be utilized? Why?

   A: No, because the SUM functioned is utilized only for adding values among cells.

3. Q: What type of image compression would need to be selected to export a PDF file in the highest quality possible?

   A: Lossless Compression.

4. Q: (True or False) Cells can be resized by utilizing either the mouse pointer within the column and row label area or by selecting the View menu.

   A: False.

5. Q: (True or False) Like the Writer word processing application bundled with OpenOffice.org, Calc has the ability to export spreadsheet documents as a Portable Document Format (PDF) file.

   A: True.

Lesson Seven

1. Q: Font styles can be applied to text within a Calc spreadsheet document by utilizing the _____ toolbar or the _____ menu.

   A: Formatting, Format.

2. Q: How would the value 25% be represented within a Calc spreadsheet document?

   A: 0.25

3. Q: What symbol represents multiplication within a spreadsheet formula?

   A: The asterisk "*" symbol.

4. Q: (True or False) Toolbars can be made visible or hidden by utilizing the

View menu.

A: True.

5. Q: (True or False) Many of the menu and toolbar options that are available for formatting text within Writer are the same within Calc as well.

A: True.

Lesson Eight

1. Q: What are two methods in which you can format text within an Impress presentation document?

   A: By either selecting the Character menu option from the Format menu or by utilizing the Standard toolbar located above the editing area.

2. Q: What menu option would you select to change the color or background of a slide?

   A: Click the Format menu and select the Page menu option.

3. Q: What would you need to do to view an Impress document as a slide show?

   A: Either select the Slide Show option within the Slide Show menu or press the F5 key while the Impress document is open.

4. Q: (True or False) Spellcheck is a feature that is not available within the Impress application.

   A: False.

5. Q: (True or False) Bulleted lists can be converted to numbered lists within a slide, if desired.

   A: True.

Lesson Nine

1. Q: For changes to tables and records to remain permanent within Base, what do you need to do prior to closing the document or application?

   A: Click the File menu and select Save, or click the SAVE button within the toolbar.

2. Q: What is a database record?

   A: A record is simply data that is entered and saved within a table.

3. Q: What does a computer user have to do before they can utilize the data contained within a Base database document for use in a Writer document?

   A: The Base database document must be registered within the OpenOffice.org office productivity suite.

4. Q: (True or False) Unlike Microsoft Access, OpenOffice.org Base doesn't have a Form Wizard for creating mailing labels.

   A: True.

5. Q: (True or False) Users cannot add and delete fields after the table creation process has taken place.

   A: False.

Lesson Ten

1. Q: What are two methods to change the format of data presented within query results?

   A: Change the format within the Query Design View window and specifying field properties within the corresponding table.

2. Q: Within Base, which command should a computer user execute prior to running a query to eliminate duplicate entries?

A: Distinct Values command.

3. Q: What is a query?

    A: A query can be thought of as simply a subset, or filtered set, of records from a table that was created by specifying certain criteria to obtain a desired result.

4. Q: (True or False) If a user wishes to make corrections or changes to criteria selected prior to or after running a query, they must close the Query Design View window it and start over by creating a new query.

    A: False.

5. Q: (True or False) Within Base, a user can create a report either using the Report Wizard or by utilizing the Report Design View window.

    A: False.

Index

LaVergne, TN USA
09 November 2009

163553LV00004B/61/P